Praise for *Practical Virtues*

"A powerful collection."

—*Miami Herald*

"Well written . . . rings with sincerity. . . . Families will find this book helpful."

—*Cleveland Plain Dealer*

"Thoughtful. . . . This collection . . . will inspire."

—*Library Journal*

"Motivational and spiritual."

—*Black Issues Book Review*

"A treasure trove of African-American spirituality."

—*Publishers Weekly*

D0752776

THE REVEREND FLOYD H. FLAKE is the senor pastor of the Greater Allen A.M.E. Cathedral of New York in Jamaica, Queens, and is the president of Wilberforce University in Ohio. He is also the founder of the Allen Christian School, which he established with his wife, THE REVEREND M. ELAINE MCCOLLINS FLAKE. She is the co-pastor of the Greater Allen A.M.E. Cathedral. They live in Old Westbury, New York, with their four children.

Practical Virtues

Readings, Sermons, Prayers, *and* Hymns
for the African American Family

REVERENDS FLOYD H. FLAKE
AND
M. ELAINE McCOLLINS FLAKE

Amistad
AN IMPRINT OF *HARPERCOLLINS*PUBLISHERS

A hardcover edition of this book was published in 2003 by Amistad, an imprint of HarperCollins Publishers, as *Practical Virtues: Everyday Values and Devotions for African American Families.*

PRACTICAL VIRTUES. Copyright © 2003 by Floyd and Elaine Flake. All rights reserved. Printed in the United States of America. No part of this book may be used or reproduced in any manner whatsoever without written permission except in the case of brief quotations embodied in critical articles and reviews. For information, address HarperCollins Publishers Inc., 10 East 53rd Street, New York, NY 10022.

HarperCollins books may be purchased for educational, business, or sales promotional use. For information, please write: Special Markets Department, HarperCollins Publishers Inc., 10 East 53rd Street, New York, NY 10022.

Scripture quotations are from the King James Version of the Bible.

FIRST AMISTAD PAPERBACK EDITION 2004

Designed by Deborah Kerner / Dancing Bears Design

Printed on acid-free paper

The Library of Congress has catalogued the hardcover edition as follows:
Flake, Floyd.
Practical virtues : everyday values and devotions for African American families / Floyd Flake and M. Elaine McCollins Flake.—1st ed.
p.   cm.
Includes bibliographical references.
ISBN 0-06-009060-X
1. American literature—African American authors—Study and teaching.
2. Didactic literature, American—Study and teaching.   3. American literature—African American authors.   4. African Americans—Literary collections.   5. Conduct of life—Literary collections.   6. African Americans—Books and reading.   7. African Americans—Conduct of life.
8. African American families.   I. Flake, M. Elaine McCollins.   II. Title.
PS153.N5F55   2003
810.9'896073'071—dc21   2003044439

ISBN 0-06-009061-8 (pbk.)

04 05 06 07 08 WBC/RRD 10 9 8 7 6 5 4 3 2 1

For ALIYA MARIAMA,

NAILAH LORICE,

ROBERT RASHEED,

HAROLD HASAN,

and NIA RENEE

CONTENTS

Honesty   *169*

Love   *207*

Loyalty   *245*

Prudence   *281*

INTRODUCTION

In the sermons we preach every Sunday we try to answer one essential question: *How are we to live?*

How are we to live in peace with one another when violence assaults us on the street corners? How are we to raise our children to value more than what the mass market offers them? How are we to find satisfaction in ordinary work when we witness daily the fabulous lifestyles of millionaire athletes and entertainers who are our most visible role models? How are we to rise above the drug culture, and the poverty of both body and soul? How are we to feel free when we too often are treated like second-class citizens? How are we to find the joy within life's disappointments and setbacks, heartaches and blues?

How are we, as African Americans in the twenty-first century, to live?

We need only look back to our own heritage for the answers. The way to live is with the kind of moral character our forebears defined, with the diligence and loyalty and responsibility they exemplified, as men did all they could to support families and to keep them together, and women taught their children to love and respect all people. The courage, faith, and compassion our ancestors displayed were phenomenal. We know they exemplified these traits because of the stories, songs, letters, and poems they left behind. Our literary and oral traditions have made it clear that whatever good we've misplaced in the throes of becoming Americans with black skin, we surely did once have.

The time has come to discover our moral strength, to reclaim those attitudes and beliefs we seem to have lost along the way as our own again.

How are we to live? Not by whining and complaining. Not by falling into complacency. Not by lowering our standards or wavering in our morals. Not by reactive rather than proactive approaches to problems.

We are to live according to our virtues.

What Are Virtues?

Many thoughtful persons, great and small, have tried to come up with definitions and a definitive list of virtues over the centuries. Countless words have been written and spoken on whether virtues are a means or an end, whether they are absolute or relative, whether they are the cause or result of *behaving* virtuously. Aristotle said, "To act virtuously is not to act against inclination; it is to act from inclination formed by the cultivation of the virtues." We are not really concerned in this book with this kind of abstract discussion. We want to talk about virtues as most people perceive them, and how they work in our day-to-day lives.

From the Greeks and Romans to the early Christians to Jane Austen, Benjamin Franklin, and Marian Wright Edelman, the concept of virtues has evolved. There have been ethical virtues for citizens:

temperance, justice, courage, and wisdom. There have been academic virtues for philosophers: integrity and utilitarianism. There have been theological virtues for congregants: faith, hope, and charity. In this book, we offer practical, living virtues for every day: not merely words but principles to breathe into being. Virtues with soul.

Let us explain what we mean by practical virtues. Virtues reflect our core values, but they go beyond abstract thought to demand action. They are *habits* of the mind, the heart, and the soul. By definition, practical virtues are hands-on, useful, and applicable to daily life. They are moral yardsticks against which to measure our behavior. Virtue begins with character: integrity, commitment, keeping promises, what we represent and how we represent those things that define the quality of our life. We don't merely read about and ponder practical virtues; they must be *practiced* and exercised, like flexing a spiritual muscle.

For us as African American ministers, for our congregants, and for most of the African American community, virtues are part of our relationship to God, and therefore sacrosanct. So, yes, our virtues are Bible-based. They are the fruit of the spirit. In fact, when first we began to discuss this book project with our friends and colleagues, more than once upon our mentioning the title did we hear, "Practical Virtues for African Americans? Well, that would have to be the Bible." We consider *Practical Virtues* a devotional book, and our hope is that it will become your path to a uniquely African American spiritual literacy.

The following list of virtues is drawn from our own ministry and teaching. They are the subjects we most often return to in sermons. Many are biblical, but they also appear in most of the world's religious traditions. They are the most basic and strongest of virtues:

- COURAGE
- DILIGENCE
- FAITH
- FORBEARANCE

- ◆ FORGIVENESS
- ◆ HONESTY
- ◆ LOVE
- ◆ LOYALTY
- ◆ PRUDENCE
- ◆ RESPONSIBILITY
- ◆ SERVICE
- ◆ TRUSTWORTHINESS

We are born with what we call these foundational virtues, but we have to grow into our full capacity for living virtues. Virtues are not a *part* of life but a *way* of life. While our attending temple, mosque, or church regularly may teach us virtue, it is our responsibility to carry those teachings with us at all times and to conduct our lives based on what we learn. Virtue cannot stop at the door of our place of worship. We must not only hear but also listen to the teachings of our ancestors and our modern-day leaders, if virtue is to survive. When carefully studied and regularly contemplated, virtue thrives.

When we don't develop our virtues, we flounder and fail as human beings. Our lives feel lacking, although we might not know why. As Maya Angelou has said of virtue, "We need to examine what the absence of those qualities has done to our communal spirit, and we must learn how to retrieve them from the dust heap of non-use and return them to a vigorous role in our lives."

Some virtues will come easier for you than for me; others will come easier for me than for you. Some of us are naturally more responsible than others; some are more honest. But we all have virtues to cultivate, virtues we need to be mindful to exercise. While I'm over here working on one virtue, you're working on another. We're all trying to reach the same place—a happy, successful, meaningful life—and we have to allow for our differences, for bends and detours in the road, while on the journey. Paul Laurence Dunbar, the nineteenth-century poet, perfectly summarized this idea in his poem "Accountability," which begins:

> "We is all constructed diff'rent,
> d'aint't no two of us de same. . . ."

Developing moral character is a lifelong process affected by factors over which we may not have control as well as situations we encounter along the way. The challenge is to maintain our virtues no matter what the circumstances, no matter how tempted we are to compromise for the sake of convenience.

The Color of Virtues

Olaudah Equiano, author of *The Interesting Narrative of the Life of Olaudah Equiano*, wrote in 1789 of a free school erected "for every denomination of black people, whose minds are cultivated here, and forwarded to virtue. . . ."

How apt that phrase, "forwarded to virtue" is for us today, when we live amidst constant societal pressures that push us out of our comfort zones. At this moment in time, the role models young black people aspire to most are athletes or entertainers. What respect consists of and who receives respect is often based on money and fame instead of virtue. The age where those heroes our children looked up to felt a responsibility to model their moral sense is long gone. Look at NBA superstars and the adulation they receive. Then read in *Sports Illustrated* about the player who has eight different children by eight different wives. Or the famous rap singers and their infamous trials.

We have a crying need to shape thought among a hip-hop generation, to teach the members of that generation how to move from resistance and reaction to a proactive approach to life. We need to show them that you can "have it all" and still have nothing if you have no character. We need to say, "What you define as success is very temporary. It is your virtue that you can have for a lifetime." We need to remind them of the words of the Prophet Isaiah: "The grass withers and the flowers fade, but the Word of God stands forever."

Americans have allowed the media and culture to define morality. There has to be a redefinition of what's right and wrong, a new moral education. The rap culture, for example, is a reflection of America in general, but how it's played out in black culture has been particularly detrimental. The lax language and sloppy clothes are undermining family by devaluing obedience and glamorizing disrespect. This book can remind a generation of black children to be more discerning, more spiritually and morally literate.

While virtues *are* colorless, our life experience is different because we are black. Therefore, how we interpret and express virtues must be within the framework of our black heritage, our present and our past. The interpretation of the virtues is similar to how we interpret the Bible within the context of black culture. We develop a theology or a philosophy based on the perspective through which we view the world and on our image of God formed through our historical experiences.

For example, as people of color, we have our own take when we read in the Bible (Mark 5:25–34) about the woman with the issue of blood. Her story—being ostracized, having to live on the outskirts of town, never being able to find acceptance because of a physical reality she had no control over—we can relate to that! And we relate to her in a much more visceral, powerful way than most white people might.

Nearly 150 years ago, the intellectual and minister Alexander Crummell wrote, "The race problem is a moral one.... Its solution will come especially from the domain of principles. Like all the other great battles of humanity it is to be fought out with the weapons of truth."

Today there is still the sense of rebellion against injustice in the land. We seem to be asking a collective question, growing louder ever since the civil rights movement of the 1960s brought us another degree of freedom: *Am I free now to just do what I feel?* The answer is no. Our interdependence means we have responsibility and obligations to other people—now more than ever. How do we position ourselves for the future when by census definition, we're moving to a society that will be almost raceless and colorless in its homogenous blending of ethnic groups? You cannot bring the baggage of resentment, of amorality, of irresponsibility into that new society and hope to survive. Ultimately, we survive based on our ability to embrace virtues that teach us to get beyond acts and behaviors that contribute to a criminal justice system that grows on our backs and redefines us in terms of a new kind of slavery. Again Alexander Crummell expressed this eloquently, when he wrote in 1861:

For near three centuries the Negro race in exile and servitude has been groveling in lowly places, in deep degradation. Circumstance and position alike have divorced us from the pursuits which give nobleness and grandeur to life. In our time of trial we have shown, it is true, a matchless patience, and a quenchless hope; the one prophetic of victory, and the other the germ of a high Christian character, now developing. These better qualities, however, have been disproportioned, and the life of the race in general has been alien from ennobling and aspiring effort.

But the days of passivity should now come to an end. The active, creative, and saving powers of the race should begin to show themselves. The power of the Negro, if he has such power, to tell upon human interest, and to help shape human destinies, should at an early day make full demonstration of itself. We owe it to ourselves, to our race, to show that we are capable of "receiving the seed of present history in a kindly yet a vigorous soil, and [that we can] reproduce it, the same, and yet new, for a future period" in all the homes of this traduced, yet vital and progressive race.

The passage speaks to another reason for us to practice virtue. In our post–September 11 world, character, community, and civility have emerged as our best hope for moving beyond the horror. A strong foundation of virtues is the prerequisite to building character, forging community, and encouraging civility.

About the Book

We've organized the book according to the twelve virtues listed previously. We introduce each virtue with a brief description of what it means to us, as individuals with our own histories and as members of a racial group with an even longer history. Occasionally, we enlarge upon our beliefs by quoting famous people on a particular virtue.

Following the definition of and introduction to each virtue is a selection of entries relating in some way to that virtue. Every entry was hand-selected to get us thinking about virtue through the African American lens. Some might be obvious examples of the virtue in action; others might be fables about the pitfalls of *not* living the virtue. Still others might be more subtle in how they illuminate or deepen our understanding of a virtue. In those cases, we've provided our interpretation of the piece. Other entries include short factual or historical notes.

We do not mean to be a comprehensive anthology, nor are we making a literary, scholarly, or historical statement. Still, we hope readers will pick up on some literary, historical, and yes, even scholarly debates emerging in the African American canon just by dipping into the material in this way.

In order to become an entry in the book, a contribution had to meet several criteria. Drawing on a vast amount of material, we searched for selections that were personally relevant and subjectively appealing to us. Some entries are well known. Frederick Douglass,

Maya Angelou, or Sojourner Truth are included in *Practical Virtues* by dint of their reputations and their eloquence. If we found a piece written by a little-known or unknown person, it had to demonstrate quite clearly a virtuous moment or experience or else articulate something about a virtue in a unique way or voice. Entries by Anne Moody or Lorene Cary, Philippe Wamba or Felicia R. Lee are included because of their singular illumination of a virtue.

We decided at the outset not to exclude an entry on the basis of race. If a piece addressed a virtue that fit and spoke to a particular need, we didn't think it mattered whether the author was black or white. John Newton, not only a white man but a former slave owner, wrote the beautiful song "Amazing Grace." We often preach about him and how he redeemed himself, and naturally the hymn is represented here. Again, it comes back to our belief that virtues themselves are without color.

John Newton was not the only one of the authors we include who had a checkered history. You may be surprised at the travails of others such as Nella Larsen, who was accused of plagiarism, or Claude McKay, who was imprisoned. Our logic was that if, for example, a reader comes away from Nella Larsen's "Sanctuary" pondering what it means to be trustworthy—why it's important, why we should seek it—that's reason enough to include her.

On the other hand, there were certain stories we deliberately left out because of their distasteful treatment of race. Even if a moral lesson could be extracted from, for example, the Uncle Remus or Stackalee stories, the price we'd pay in painful reading would not be worth it.

You may notice that some African American writers whose work is clearly of crucial significance to African American literature may *not* be found here. It's important to understand that this is *not* an anthology of black writers but rather a handbook of virtues. We evaluated each entry according to its ability to spark lively examination of a virtue. Some authors, therefore, have more than one entry: Nella Larsen, Frances E. W. Harper, Booker T. Washington, and Oseola McCarty.

In the "Exercise Virtue" section after each entry, we've included ideas for discussion, journaling, and further thinking about each virtue, to help readers gain an even greater moral fluency. We deliberately gave these exercises a devotional flavor so that they are equally suitable for Sunday school classes or daily meditations. Instead of simply reading a selection and feeling as if you've "gotten" it, we ask that you take another step and use our questions as a springboard for change. It might be a change in a behavior or perhaps in an attitude, but we invite you to pick up this book not merely as a passive experience but as a partner in an act of virtue.

Some of the exercises ask you to internalize virtues—for example, by reflecting on the meaning of nonviolence during the civil rights movement and how it relates to courage. But the greater goal is to have a more outward virtuous existence, a personal virtue practice for all the world to see. So after reading "How the Slaves Helped Each Other," we suggest you exercise the virtue of love by thinking of five unexpected things you can do in the next five days to show someone you love them.

We deliberately chose twelve virtues for this volume because we wanted to encourage families to pick one virtue each month for study, reading aloud, and discussion. Too often we lament the deterioration of the black family without seeking solutions within ourselves and within the teachings of our own history. *Practical Virtues* provides such solutions. It doesn't matter which virtue you choose in a given month, nor do you need to stick to this suggestion. But there is a large, wide-ranging amount of material included, and focusing on a single virtue for a whole month gives your family an easy, built-in approach. It also is enough time to really delve into a particular virtue, to explore the various expressions of it both in the readings and in your own lives. Within a virtue, feel free to read the selections in any order you wish. We arranged them more for a sense of rhythm and flow than according to chronology or reading level.

By the time your family finishes a month's worth of poems and stories and Bible passages and essays and songs, you might want to work on a family definition of that virtue. This could be a marvelous opportunity to collaborate, or you could each formulate one and then share them. It's also a fine way to exchange memories and family stories, to create your own version of a compendium of family virtues.

You will undoubtedly discover your own way of incorporating the book into your daily life. Some of you may find sharing the shorter stories at the dinner table enjoyable. Some might want to tape-record longer entries to listen to and talk about while driving. Others might choose a special day of the week to hold a family gathering and read—or sing, in the case of spirituals—aloud from the book.

With our busy schedules, we haven't always found time to sit down to dinner with our children. So long ago we began a habit of letter-writing when we had something important to communicate. Perhaps you'll take a page from our own family's book and start writing letters to one another on how you're trying to practice virtue or how you notice it playing out in others.

Whether it's a daily, weekly, or monthly practice, make using this book part of the texture of your life. Let it combat the disrespect inherent in the hip-hop culture gone awry. Let it inform how we respond to a relative struggling with substance abuse. Let it assist you in your child-rearing. Let it become the antidote to the trap of materialism, so that we no longer need to reward a good report card, for example, with money.

Because virtue is its own reward.

The Virtuous Life

We live virtuously by incorporating moral insights into the small moments that add up to our days. We all face disappointments, attacks, crises that challenge our integrity and faith. As a husband, father, and man, as a wife, mother, and woman, we each face the same challenges as anyone else. As pastors of a large church, we've had our share of times when we had to struggle to maintain our virtues. Our followers are faithful to the mission because they have trust in us, belief that we're going to do things properly and with accountability.

When we preach, standing as a solitary messenger before an expectant congregation, we take on a responsibility to enthusiastically proclaim the truths of the Gospel, which for us are essentially the virtues. As they have gathered for worship, those who have come to us have brought with them their various problems, concerns, and expectations. Fears need to be calmed, minds need to be strengthened, and hearts need to be gladdened. As their ministers, we must provide a word or a message that transforms and makes a difference in the lives of all who hear.

Our hope is that this book encourages the same transformation in the lives of its readers. The carefully chosen entries that follow contain sermons that are as powerful as you'll ever hear. Read them aloud, read them once more, and then ponder this:

How are we to live? By being honest, prudent, responsible, and diligent in our daily duties. Offering trust, service, forbearance, and forgiveness whenever called upon to do so—and even when not called upon. With courage, faith, love, and loyalty, we will live not only for ourselves but for our children and grandchildren. We will create legacies of virtue. We will end the vicious cycle of self-destructive spirit and the breakdown of morality perpetuated for too long by each succeeding generation. We will start a *virtuous* cycle.

We know in the deepest part of our hearts that we can do it. . . . We have soul on our side.

Practical
Virtues

Courage

A firmness of spirit and strength of the soul, COURAGE is the state of mind that enables you to face difficulty or danger with confidence in spite of fear.

Every day we live, we exercise courage. From the moment we wake in the morning to the minute we lie down to sleep at night, we must be courageous. Courage is a spirit within that compels us to face dangerous and difficult situations rather than withdrawing into ourselves. It is knowing that we are capable of achieving successes in spite of the odds against us. Courage is not the absence of fear; rather, it is acting or speaking *despite* our fear.

On Sunday mornings, when I stand before my congregation, it can be daunting to think that thousands of men, women, and children are listening to what I have to say. I know the power of words and I know that it is my responsibility to speak with integrity and conviction, so I must maintain confidence and composure when I deliver my sermons. It is not always easy to take controversial or nontraditional positions with sermon content, but I cannot allow fear to rule me. To the contrary, I must rule fear.

Our history as African Americans is marked by the necessity and determination to maintain courage in the midst of abuse and mistreatment, oppression and persecution. The words of Claude McKay echo in our souls: "If we must die, let it not be like hogs / Hunted and penned in an inglorious spot." Countless black men and women have demonstrated remarkable courage in the face of considerable obstacles.

From Harriet Tubman to Martin Luther King, Jr., our ancestors have stood in the face of injustice and boldly challenged the world to acknowledge its inadequacies and remedy its wrongs. We will never forget the courage of our past, for it is what shapes the prosperity of our present and offers hope for the future.

Of course, there is much more yet to be done, and there are many more obstacles to overcome. As a people, we have come far, but we have much farther to go. Courage is the legacy of our history. It is not a remnant of our past but a heritage that has been handed down to us. The bravery of our ancestors must inspire us to live courageously.

Although we cannot all be Harriet Tubmans or Martin Luther Kings in terms of notoriety or public acclaim, we can appropriate their dauntless spirits. The desire to make a difference in this world and to have a positive impact on the lives of others should motivate us to dream big dreams. And our faith in God should give us the courage to turn our dreams into realities, for often our own fear is the only thing preventing us from attaining greatness and success.

In times of fear or vacillation, I often recall the words God spoke to Joshua, commanding him to deliver the Israelites from the wilderness: "Be strong and of a good courage; be not afraid, neither be thou dismayed: for the Lord thy God is with thee whithersoever thou goest" (Joshua 1:9).

Like the Israelites, we live beneath God's watchful protection. We need never fear when we know that God is with us. Our faith gives us courage. As we are guided by God, we are further bolstered by the love of our friends and family members. We must not be ashamed to embrace the support of others.

Finally, we must release the power within us—the power that fuels courage. Courage is a strength of the heart. As African Americans, we know too well that things are not always fair or just, but we cannot forever blame the world for our misfortunes. Success is not granted but earned; it is gained through taking positive action and not waiting for someone else to do for us what we can do for ourselves. We all have the ability to find happiness, but we must start the search with courage.

Frances E. W. Harper

The Book of Esther relates incidents in the lives of two queens, Esther and Vashti, both of whom are courageous in the face of oppression, but in strikingly different ways. While Esther's story is reported in more detail in the scriptures, I am especially drawn to the story of the Persian queen, Vashti, the lesser-sung heroine in the Book of Esther. As interpreted by Frances E. W. Harper in "Vashti," a poem published in 1857 in Poems on Miscellaneous Subjects, *the queen is a model of both moral integrity and courage.*

Vashti

She leaned her head upon her hand
And heard the King's decree—
"My lords are feasting in my halls;
Bid Vashti come to me.

"I've shown the treasures of my house,
My costly jewels rare,

But with the glory of her eyes
No rubies can compare.

"Adorn'd and crown'd I'd have her come,
With all her queenly grace,
And, 'mid my lords and mighty men,
Unveil her lovely face.

"Each gem that sparkles in my crown,
Or glitters on my throne,
Grows poor and pale when she appears,
My beautiful, my own!"

All waiting stood the chamberlains
To hear the Queen's reply.
They saw her cheek grow deathly pale,
But light flash'd to her eye:

"Go, tell the King," she proudly said,
"That I am Persia's Queen,
And by his crowds of merry men
I never will be seen.

"I'll take the crown from off my head
And tread it 'neath my feet,
Before their rude and careless gaze
My shrinking eyes shall meet.

"A queen unveil'd before the crowd!—
Upon each lip my name!—
Why, Persia's women all would blush
And weep for Vashti's shame!

"Go back!" she cried, and waved her hand,
And grief was in her eye:
"Go, tell the King," she sadly said,
"That I would rather die."

They brought her message to the King;
Dark flash'd his angry eye;
'Twas as the lightning ere the storm
Hath swept in fury by.

Then bitterly outspoke the King,
Through purple lips of wrath—
"What shall be done to her who dares
To cross your monarch's path?"

Then spake his wily counsellors—
"O King of this fair land!
From distant Ind to Ethiop,
All bow to thy command.

"But if, before thy servants' eyes,
This thing they plainly see,
That Vashti doth not heed thy will
Nor yield herself to thee,

"The women, restive 'neath our rule,
Would learn to scorn our name,
And from her deed to us would come
Reproach and burning shame.

"Then, gracious King, sign with thy hand
This stern but just decree,

That Vashti lay aside her crown,
Thy Queen no more to be."

She heard again the King's command,
And left her high estate;
Strong in her earnest womanhood,
She calmly met her fate,

And left the palace of the King,
Proud of her spotless name—
A woman who could bend to grief,
But would not bow to shame.

Exercise Courage:

- The queen in Harper's poem refuses to parade herself before a bunch of "merry" men out of self-respect. This reasoning suggests that Harper believes there are times when defiance of authority is acceptable and necessary—a kind of courage we have in abundance in our history as African Americans. (Harper herself was a fugitive for defying a Maryland law—punishable by enslavement—that barred a free black person from entering the state.) Do you display the courage of your own convictions as Vashti did?

- Vashti's refusal to come before the king threatens everything the king and his men believe in. The queen's defiance renders them fearful that all of the women in Persia will follow Vashti's lead and not obey their husbands. As a result, Vashti is deposed and, as the scriptures (Esther 2:1–18) tell us, replaced by the beautiful Esther. Why do you think Harper ends the poem on such a triumphant note for Vashti? Does the more courageous deed always lead to a happy ending?

- Oppression, prejudice, and liberation are themes that appear throughout the Book of Esther. Read the scriptures and compare the courage of the two heroines, Vashti and Esther. Ask your family, "Who's the bigger hero?"

- Frances E. W. Harper often wrote about the need for self-sacrifice and good Christian living. How does Vashti's action in the poem point to a broader, deeper, and more courageous way of living? Is this the way you choose to live?

- Aretha Franklin's 1960s demand for "Respect" echoes the cry of so many women and men who live in this country today. Whether it means walking off the job, joining a different church, or standing up to someone you love, confronting abusive and inhumane situations is difficult but necessary when you realize how valuable you are. The legacies of Vashti, the woman who would not be shamed, and Esther, the woman who demanded to be heard, inspire us to reject compromise and fear as we pray for the courage to become our best selves. Repeat this prayer for inspiration when you need to build up your courage in the face of life's many challenges:

> Prayer for courage: Dear Lord, Thank you for making me in your image. Thank you for showing me every day that I am a unique and valuable individual. Give me the wisdom to recognize that which robs me of human dignity, and the courage to demand change or walk away. Help me to remember that there are blessings that come with obeying *your* voice and not the voice of those who would tell me to compromise my personhood. My hope is in you, not in any person, position, or place, and I will not allow fear of loss or rebuke keep me from saying "No" to shame and humiliation. Give me the spirit of Vashti so that I might not be held hostage to comfort and ease. Give me the spirit of Esther so that I might let my voice be heard when silence would be the more popular response to life's injustices. In the name of Jesus, I pray this prayer. Amen.

Arthur Ashe

A rthur Ashe was a hero both on and off the tennis court, leaving behind a legacy of sportsmanship, activism, and philanthropy. Raised in Richmond during segregation, Ashe learned to play tennis on the local public courts. He attended UCLA on a tennis scholarship and in 1963 became the first African American selected to represent the United States in the Davis Cup. In 1969, he applied to play in the South African Open, fully aware that he would be denied because of the color of his skin. The denial of his application helped spark American activism against apartheid. Ashe went on to win Wimbledon in 1975 at the age of thirty-one, and was ranked number one in the sport that year. He retired from tennis in 1980, a year after his first heart surgery; in 1983 he underwent a second surgery. After his retirement, he became a tennis commentator and was heavily involved in philanthropic work. In 1988, Ashe's life changed forever. He was diagnosed with AIDS, contracted from blood transfusions he had received during his heart surgeries. In 1992 he announced that he was HIV-positive. This announcement, as well as his work to educate people about the AIDS epidemic, greatly moved the American public. Ashe succumbed to this debilitating disease in 1993. In the following excerpt from his autobiography, Days of Grace, written with Arnold Rampersad, Ashe recalls the day that he received the devastating news that he was HIV-positive.

from Days of Grace

T he news that I had AIDS hit me hard but did not knock me down. I had read of people committing suicide because of despair caused by infection with HIV. Indeed, in the preceding year, 1987, men suffering from AIDS were 10.5 times more likely to commit suicide than non-HIV-infected people who were otherwise similar to them.

In 1988, the AIDS suicide rate fell, but only to 7.4 times the expected rate. In 1990, it was 6 times the expected rate. The drop continued, but the far greater likelihood of suicide among AIDS patients persists, according to a 1992 issue of the *Journal of the American Medical Association.* (Incidentally, most of the HIV-infected men who kill themselves use prescription drugs to do so, instead of the guns that most male suicides use.) The main reason for the decline in this suicide rate, according to the report, was the general improvement in treatment, including the development of drugs that gave AIDS patients more hope. By 1992, however, the suicide rate was starting to rise again, as many of the therapies for AIDS, including those I was dependent on, began to show their limitations.

For me, suicide is out of the question. Despair is a state of mind to which I refuse to surrender. I resist moods of despondency because I know how they feed upon themselves and upon the despondent. I fight vigorously at the first sign of depression. I know that some depression can be physically induced, generated by the body rather than the mind. Such depression is obviously hard to contain. But depression caused by brooding on circumstances, especially circumstances one cannot avoid or over which one has no control, is another matter. I refuse to surrender myself to such a depression and have never suffered from it in my life.

Here is an area in which there are very close parallels between ordinary life and world-class athletic competition. The most important factor determining success in athletic competition is often the ability to control mood swings that result from unfavorable changes in the score. A close look at any athletic competition, and especially at facial expressions and body language, reveals that many individuals or even entire teams go into momentary lapses of confidence that often prove disastrous within a game or match. The ever-threatening danger, which I know well from experience, is that a momentary lapse will begin to deepen almost of its own accord. Once it is set in motion, it seems to gather enough momentum on its own to run its course. A few falling pebbles build into an avalanche. The initiative goes to one's opponent, who seems to be impossibly "hot" or "on a roll"; soon, victory is utterly out of one's reach. I've seen it happen to others on the tennis court; it has sometimes happened to me. In life-threatening situations, such as the one in which I now found myself, I knew that I had to do everything possible to keep this avalanche of deadly emotion from starting. One simply must not despair, even for a moment.

I cannot say that even the news that I have AIDS devastated me, or drove me into bitter reflection and depression even for a short time. I do not remember any night, from that first moment until now, when the thought of my AIDS condition and its fatality kept me from sleeping soundly. The physical discomfort may keep me up now and then, but not the psychological or philosophical discomfort.

I have been able to stay calm in part because my heart condition is a sufficient source of danger, were I to be terrified by illness. My first heart attack, in 1979, could have ended my life in a few chest-ravaging seconds. Both of my heart operations were major surgeries, with the risks attendant on all major surgery. And surely no brain operation is routine. Mainly because I have been through these battles with death, I have lost much of my fear of it.

I was not always that way. I had been a sickly child, but for most of the first thirty-six years of my life, until 1979, I nurtured a sense of myself as indestructible, if not actually immortal. This feeling persisted even after my heel surgery in 1977. For nine years since my first heart attack, however, I had been living with a powerful sense of my own mortality. And I have had many other signs, in the deaths of others, that have led me to think of my own end as something that could be imminent. So AIDS did not devastate me. AIDS was little more than something new to deal with, something new to understand and respond to, something to accept as a challenge, as if I might defeat it.

One can ready oneself for death. I see death as more of a dynamic than a static event. The actual physical manifestation of the absence of life is simply the ultimate step of a process that leads inevitably to that stage. In the interim, before the absolute end, one can do much to make life as meaningful as possible.

What would have devastated me was to discover that I had infected my wife, Jeanne, and my daughter, Camera. I do not think it would make any difference, on this score, whether I had contracted AIDS "innocently" from a blood transfusion or in one of the ways that most of society disapproves of, such as homosexual contacts or drug addiction. The overwhelming sense of guilt and shame would be the same in either case, if I had infected another human being.

A friend of mine has ventured the opinion that as much as I love Jeanne, I am truly crazy about Camera. Well, Jeanne loves me, but I think she, too, is truly crazy about Camera. The thought that this beautiful child, not yet two years old, who has brought more pure joy into our lives than we had ever known before we laid eyes on her, could be infected with this horrible disease, because of me, was almost too much even to think about.

Both Jeanne and Camera were quickly tested. Both, thank God, were found to be free of any trace of HIV. Their testing has continued, and they remain free of infection.

Exercise Courage:

- Arthur Ashe's courage in the face of illness and death reminds me of Psalm 91, and particularly verses 5 and 6: "Thou shalt not be afraid for the terror by night; nor for the arrow that flieth by day; Nor for the pestilence that walketh in darkness; nor for the destruction that wasteth at noonday." Are there other Bible passages you look toward for examples of valiance and courage?

- Ashe writes, "One can ready oneself for death. I see death as more of a dynamic than a static event . . . Before the absolute end, one can do much to make life as meaningful as possible." Ashe's courage in the face of death is remarkable, but not unexpected, given the many trials he faced—and conquered—during his lifetime. He was a man with a purpose so strong that his only concern was to leave a legacy of commitment to the things he most believed in and cherished. African Americans have a history of commitment to a higher cause, even in the face of death. Which African American leaders, male and female, have displayed great courage in this regard?

- In Philippians I:12–14, Paul writes: "But I would ye should understand, brethren, that the things which happened unto me have fallen out rather unto the furtherance of the gospel; So that my bonds in Christ are manifest in all the palace, and in all other places; And many of the brethren of the Lord, waxing confident by my bonds, are much more bold to speak the word without fear." The word of God is one of love and compassion and acceptance; think about the ways in which Arthur Ashe's AIDS diagnosis opened up a dialogue around AIDS and enabled people to speak about the disease, to accept those who had AIDS or were HIV-positive, and saved the lives of millions of people who had suffered in silence. Read Philippians I with your family and discuss the parallels between Paul's commitment to spreading the word of God, no matter what the cost, and Arthur Ashe's commitment to opening up the sport of tennis to minorities and speaking out about South African apartheid and AIDS.

- Think of the thing you're most afraid of doing and visualize yourself doing it.

- Anyone facing illness or even death can take heart in what Ashe writes about doing "much to make life as meaningful as possible." A friend who was losing her mother to cancer told me about the bittersweet last days of her mother's life. The siblings carried their mother out to her favorite spot on the sundeck on days when she had the strength, and placed a bird feeder outside her window for times when she really wasn't able to leave her bed. Even the smallest acts of love fill life with meaning and can help other people find their courage. How might you help someone find courage?

Ellen and William Craft

AS TOLD BY JOSEPHINE BROWN

Ellen and William Craft were a married couple but could not live together because they belonged to different slave owners. Their escape from slavery in 1848 is legendary. Ellen Craft—who was her master's daughter and had been given to her half sister as a slave in childhood—posed as a white man, taking advantage of her light complexion. With William acting as her slave, the couple made the dangerous journey to Philadelphia. The Crafts are remembered not only for their escape to freedom but also for their courageous acts throughout their lifetime on behalf of other people. They were active in the Boston abolitionist movement, and William was appointed vice president of the League of Freedom, a group formed in opposition to the Fugitive Slave Law of 1850. When their masters began to pursue them, the couple sought safety in England, where they remained through the Civil War. The Crafts started a farm and a school for former slaves on a Georgia plantation following the war. The Ku Klux Klan eventually burned the farm, and white opponents of the school forced the Crafts to close its doors to Ellen's seventy-five students. Their continued courage in the face of such antagonism is still an inspiration nearly a century and a half later. The Crafts certainly embody the teachings of Joshua 1:9: "Be strong and of a good courage." A free black woman named Josephine Brown documented their tale of escape in her book Biography of an American Bondman, by His Daughter, published in 1856.

from Biography of an American Bondman, by His Daughter

Now, William," said Ellen, "listen to me, and take my advice, and we shall be free in less than a month."

"Let me hear your plans, then," said William.

"Take part of your money and purchase me a good suit of gentlemen's apparel, and when the white people give us our holiday, let us go off to the North. I am white enough to go as the master, and you can pass as my servant."

"But you are not tall enough for a man," said the husband.

"Get me a pair of very high-heeled boots, and they will bring me up more than an inch, and get me a very high hat, then I'll do," rejoined the wife.

"But then, my dear, you would make a very boyish-looking man, with no whiskers or moustache," remarked William.

"I could bind up my face in a handkerchief," said Ellen, "as if I was suffering dreadfully from the toothache, and then no one would discover the want of beard."

"What if you were called upon to write your name in the books at the hotel?"

"I would also bind up my right hand and put it in a sling, and that would be an excuse for not writing."

"I fear you could not carry out the deception for so long a time, for it must be several hundred miles to the free States," said William.

"Come, William," entreated his wife, "don't be a coward! Get me the clothes, and I promise you we shall both be free in a few days. You have money enough to fit me out and to pay our passage to the North, and then we shall be free and happy." This appeal was too much for William to withstand, and he resolved to make the attempt, whatever might be the consequences.

Permission having been obtained from their master, William and Ellen went to spend their Christmas on Dr. Collins's farm, twelve miles from Macon. It was understood that the slaves were to start on their journey on the 24th of December, 1848, and to return to their employer on the day after Christmas. At the appointed time, instead of going to the farm, the husband and wife went to the railway depot, and took the six o'clock train for Philadelphia. Dressed in her new suit, with her hat of the latest fashion, and high-heeled boots, with a pair of spectacles, she had rather a collegiate appearance. Under the assumed name of William Johnson, she took her seat in a first-class

car, while William, with his servant's ticket, entered the *Jim Crow car*. At
Savannah, the fugitives took a steamboat for Charleston, and from
thence, by railway and steamboat, they arrived at Philadelphia in four
days. Many thrilling incidents occurred during their journey. At
Charleston, *Mr. Johnson* stopped at the best hotel, and was not a little
surprised to find himself seated near the Hon. John C. Calhoun at the
dinner table. Both at Richmond and Washington, the fugitives came
very near being detected. But the most amusing incident that happened during this novel journey was *Mr. Johnson's* making the acquaintance of a white family, who were also coming North. On the second
day of the journey, a well-dressed old gentleman, accompanied by his
two daughters, both unmarried, but marriageable, entered the car in
which *Mr. Johnson* was, and took seats a short distance from him. The
old gentleman, being rather communicative, soon entered into conversation with the young *man* in spectacles. "You appear to be an invalid,"
said the gray-haired gentleman, as he looked earnestly into the face of
Mr. Johnson.

"Yes," replied the other, "I have long been afflicted with inflamma-
tory rheumatism."

"Ah! I know what that is, and can heartily sympathize with you,"
returned the old man. From the time of this conversation, both father
and daughters appeared to take great interest in the young invalid. At
every depot where they took refreshment, William acted his part as
servant admirably. He waited on the old gentleman and his daughters,
as well as on his own master, and by his politeness and attention
attracted the notice of all.

"That is a valuable servant of yours," said the old gentleman to *Mr.
Johnson*, as William passed through the cabin of the steamer, while on
the way from Savannah to Charleston.

"Yes, sir, he is a boy that I am very much attached to," returned the
young man.

"Good negroes are valuable appendages," said the old man, yawn-
ingly, as he pulled his gold watch from his pocket to see the time. As

the train approached Richmond, the old gentleman expressed great regret that they were to lose the company of their new acquaintance.

"I am also sorry that we are to part," remarked *Mr. Johnson.* It was then discovered that Miss Henrietta, the oldest of the young ladies, seemed to have more interest in the young man than one would entertain for a mere acquaintance. "We are very much fatigued with this long journey," said the old gentleman, "and I am sure you must be tired; why won't you stop with us and rest yourself for a few days? My wife, knowing that you have been our traveling companion, will be glad to welcome you, and my daughter Henrietta here will be delighted." Miss Henrietta, feeling that this gave her an opportunity to speak, said, "Do, *Mr. Johnson,* stop and regain your strength. We have some pretty walks about Richmond, and I shall be so pleased to show them to you." The young invalid found that this was carrying the joke too far, and began to regret his intimate acquaintance with the young lady. However, he gave, as an excuse for declining the invitation, that urgent business demanded his immediate presence in Philadelphia, and promised them he would pay them a visit on his return to Georgia.

William and Ellen Craft, on their arrival in Philadelphia, committed themselves to the care of Mr. Brown, who was on a lecturing tour through Pennsylvania, and he brought them on to Boston. The Fugitive Slave Law drove them to England, where they again joined their old friend. Through Mr. Brown's influence, an interest was created for William and Ellen in England, and they were placed in a school, where they remained two years.

Exercise Courage:

- Ellen and William Craft were aware that if identified as a married slave couple, they would have been severely punished. But Ellen's desire to raise a child without worrying that he or she could be sold into slavery was far more important to her than any risks the couple might face in their escape to the North. The couple's courage, based in love for each other and their unborn children, made them fearless. Parents can relate to the risks that the Crafts took to ensure the future of their family, especially since many of our own parents and grandparents left the Jim Crow South, angering whites who relied upon our cheap labor, in order to raise us in an environment free of lynchings, segregated schools, and limited job opportunities. Ask a relative about how your own ancestors overcame obstacles during slavery, Jim Crow, or the Depression.

- Slave narratives remind us that we are a brave and courageous people. Be sure to tell these stories to the young people in your life. Involve your family in creating a scrapbook commemorating those family members who displayed courage in the face of great adversity. Include mementos of heroic figures whose lives have taught you about courage.

- A firm belief in the rightness of what they were doing gave the Crafts courage to set out on their journey. How do you prepare yourself for a difficult journey? Who encourages you most in your own life?

Eloise Greenfield

*H*arriet Tubman freed more than 300 slaves on the Underground Railroad. This *poem by award-winning children's book author Eloise Greenfield is a concise and simple depiction of Tubman's amazing story and a reminder of her great courage.*

Harriet Tubman

Harriet Tubman didn't take no stuff
Wasn't scared of nothing neither
Didn't come in this world to be no slave
And wasn't going to stay one either

"Farewell!" she sang to her friends one night
She was mighty sad to leave 'em
But she ran away that dark, hot night
Ran looking for her freedom

She ran to the woods and she ran through the woods
With the slave catchers right behind her
And she kept on going till she got to the North
Where those mean men couldn't find her

Nineteen times she went back South
To get three hundred others
She ran for her freedom nineteen times
To save black sisters and brothers
Harriet Tubman didn't take no stuff
Wasn't scared of nothing either
Didn't come in this world to be no slave
And didn't stay one either

And didn't stay one either

Exercise Courage:

- In sermons, I have often stressed the abject circumstances from which Harriet Tubman arose to become a woman of awesome courage. From the horrors of slavery and in spite of maltreatment and abuse, one of history's greatest freedom fighters and abolitionists emerged. Courage to do big things may seem out of reach for us—there can be only so many Harriet Tubmans, after all—but it is possible to summon up courage for daily living if we acknowledge a higher plan in our lives. Many people do not fulfill their divine purpose because they are discouraged and distracted by adversity and setbacks. Trouble, missed opportunity, or cruel injustices cause many of us to vacate the paths that would lead to fulfillment of purpose. We must always remember that mistakes, heartbreaks, and inequities do not negate or change our purpose. Marrying the wrong person, having a baby that you did not plan, or getting wrongly fired from the job that you love may alter your plans, but not your purpose. Your purpose stands in spite of life's disappointments and assault. You were born to be who you were born to be, regardless. What might the higher purpose for your life be? Do you have the courage to find out?

- Legacies of courage can inspire us to more courageous living. Make a list of historical figures who inspire you with their courage. Then make a list of people you know personally who are courageous. Do you see any common denominators?

Melba Patillo Beals

In the landmark decision of Brown v. Board of Education, *handed down on May 17, 1954, the Supreme Court ruled that segregation in public schools was unconstitutional. Educators, activists, politicians, and parents who had protested the segregated school system—in which black students received second-rate educations—applauded the ruling. Many whites, however, did not welcome integration, which Melba Patillo Beals learned firsthand. As one of the first students to integrate Central High School in Little Rock, Arkansas, in 1957, she and her family experienced racial harassment and hostility so intense that it captured national attention. In a bittersweet chapter from her autobiography,* Warriors Don't Cry, *Beals, who went on to become a successful broadcast journalist and writer, recalls the graduation day of her friend Ernie Green, the first African American to graduate from Central High.*

from Warriors Don't Cry

Central High School Negroes Pass: One on Honor Roll
Principal Matthews Says He Will Not Reveal Grades
But Confirms Green Will Graduate.
—Arkansas Gazette, *May 23, 1958*

"Let's keep the nigger from graduating." That was the rallying cry in the halls of Central High that unleashed unimaginable terror upon us. Pressure was exerted on all eight of us; the goal was to get us out by any means possible. In case that plan failed, our antagonists worked at convincing us that even if Ernie had the grades to graduate, he should not march with the other seniors to receive his Central High diploma.

"We ain't gonna let no nigger wear our cap and gown," one boy shouted at me as I walked the hallway to English class. I pushed my way past him, flashed a smile and a pleasant "Thank you."

At first, some of my late-night telephone callers pleaded with me in a civil tone to ask Ernie to receive his diploma by mail. "We don't want his picture taken with us. My daddy says you-all ain't getting back in our school next year, no how. So this is the only time we'll have that ink spot in the middle of all those pictures the news people take."

Another gruff-voiced man became angrier with each rude call. "We're gonna hang us a nigger at the same time your nigger takes our diploma," he said. On and on those calls came, keeping our phone ringing almost as much as it had at the beginning of the school year. At the same time, I received threatening notes sneaked into my books and in my locker.

I could see more evidence that the principal, vice principals, and teachers had lost any hopes of corraling belligerent students. Even as school officials observed them, clusters of students threw rocks as we entered or exited the building. The hallways were like a three-ring circus, with hooligans completely ignoring commands to cease their outrageous behavior.

Because the situation was growing more explosive, Mrs. Huckaby called us into her office to double-check on our scheduled exams. While inside school, we were once again closely followed by bodyguards.

I was much more frightened than I had been in recent months because there were no longer islands of sanity within the insanity of that school. Just outside the principal's office, people threw rotten eggs and walked on my heels, whereas before that area had been a comparatively safe place to walk.

During those last days, time seemed to drag on and on as though some divine force were slowing the hands on the clock. I had no choice but to perform one of the most hazardous duties of the day—opening my locker. That meant standing still for several minutes, with my eyes and attention focused inside while my back was exposed to passersby.

I had developed a habit of reaching my hand into my locker to find hidden objects before I poked my face in. On Tuesday afternoon, I was searching my locker for my eyeglass case when I reached my hand down deep inside to see whether or not it had fallen. Suddenly there was the sound of popping guns and the smell of smoke just behind me. I quickly turned to see a flaming object flying toward my face. I put my hand up to deflect it. That's when I felt the pain on my first three fingers. I had shielded my eyes from several sparking hot firecrackers linked together by a wire. My hand hurt, but I could only be grateful it wasn't my eyes that had been burned.

As I was issued bandages from the office to dress the wound, I consoled myself by thinking of the calendar on the kitchen wall. I had marked off almost all the days of the month of May. Ernie would attend baccalaureate services the following Sunday evening, and graduation would be the following Tuesday, one week from this day. I would be an unwelcome Central High student in that building only a few more days.

"What are you staring at, nigger?" I was indeed staring, transfixed and elated at seeing what the boy was carrying. It was the sight I had been waiting for, praying for.

"The graduation gown Ernie's gonna wear," I said loud and clear. I couldn't help responding to his snide remark as I glared back at the boy wearing the flattop haircut and black shirt. In his right hand he was carrying his gown on a hanger, and his left hand was holding his cap. He was attempting to block my way, but he had no free hands. I simply made a wide circle around him. Nothing, not even his foul mouth spewing ugly words, could make me unhappy at that moment. The sight of that gown meant summer and freedom were right around the corner.

At home the phone calls were coming fast and vicious. "We got a way of gettin' you darkies now, for certain. We're offering ten thousand dollars for your head on a platter." I gulped as I replaced the receiver in its cradle. I couldn't help thinking about how that was an awful lot of money. Poor folks might take a notion to collect. They'd get ten thousand dollars for my head. Did that mean they'd have to cut it off to collect? I told Grandma India of my fears.

"Surely you've got something better to do besides speculating about white folks' silliness," she said.

"I can't help worrying about Ernie. One of those students could be an impostor—anybody could wear a robe."

"Impostor?" Grandma looked up from her needlework with a question.

"You know, someone from the KKK who wants to collect that reward money could pretend to be a graduate."

"I don't think Ernie is in any real danger during graduation because he'll be there among six hundred and one white graduates. Besides, God's watching after Ernie just like he's watching over you."

"But . . ." I tried to continue being in my pity pot. She motioned me to shush my mouth and hold my hands out so she could circle the embroidery thread around them to straighten it out. After a long moment she said, "You're fretting a mighty lot this evening. Hard work is always the cure for worry. So busy yourself doing those dishes and getting ready for your final exams."

I had always imagined that my last day of the term at Central High School would be marked by a grand ceremony, with a massive choir singing hallelujah, or perhaps some wonderful award from my community—a parade maybe. I imagined the roar of helicopters overhead towing flying banners of congratulations—something—anything. But it was just the same as any other day. Four of us, Thelma, Elizabeth, Jeff, and I, rode home together early that afternoon. We wouldn't be going back to Central High for at least three months. Long spaces of silence punctuated our talk about how we thought we did on our exams.

"It's over," Conrad said, greeting me as I climbed the steps to our front door. "You don't have to integrate anymore."

"Well, praise the Lord," Grandma India said, her arms wide open to receive me. "You see, you made it." She squeezed me and kissed my cheek.

"Well, well, young lady, welcome to summer." Mother Lois handed me a large box that I rushed to open. "You're very special to have come through all this. I thought you deserved a special summer outfit."

Early on Wednesday morning, I built a fire in the metal trash barrel in the backyard, fueled by my school papers. Grandma had said it would be healing to write and destroy all the names of people I disliked at Central High: teachers, students, anyone who I thought had wronged me. It was against the law to burn anything at that time of the year, but she said a ceremony was important in order to have the official opportunity to give that year to God. Grandma India stood silent by my side as I fed the flame and spoke their names and forgave them.

After a long moment she walked over to water her flower bed. The four-o'clocks were blooming purple and red. We stood together for what must have been half an hour, with only the sound of the crackling fire and the garden hose. Finally she said, "Later, you'll be grateful for the courage it built inside you and for the blessing it will bring."

Grateful, I thought. Never. How could I be grateful for being at Central High? But I knew she was always right. Still I wondered just how long I would have to wait for that feeling of gratitude to come to me.

COVERAGE CURBED TO ASSURE DIGNITY
OF CENTRAL HIGH SCHOOL GRADUATION
Each Graduating Senior to Receive
8 Admission Tickets;
Press Admitted Only by Ticket
—Arkansas Gazette, *May 27, 1958*

Even though I had made it through the school year, Ernie still had to survive that one final brave act. I counted on being with him, on applauding for him from our isolated though well-guarded section of the audience.

"None of you will be allowed to attend either the graduation commencement or the baccalaureate service," Mother Lois announced over dinner. "The authorities believe it would not only risk your lives, but also make it more difficult for them to protect Ernie and his family should they have to do so. They've also forbidden any nonwhite reporters or photographers to attend."

"But, Mom!"

"But nothing. This is no time to satisfy a whim and unravel everything you've accomplished. There'll be enough of a circus, what with the soldiers, FBI, city police, and who knows all."

"The paper says every policeman not on vacation will be on duty from six o'clock on," Grandma said. "They wouldn't go to all that trouble and expense unless they expected something to happen."

"Besides," Mother Lois continued, "their best efforts should be directed to protecting Ernie."

She's right, I thought to myself. It was selfish of me to want to go, I suppose. But what I knew to be practical advice didn't lessen my disappointment at not being able to watch Ernie march triumphantly to the stage to receive that diploma. That night I wrote in my diary:

Dear God,
Please walk with Ernie in the graduation line at Central. Let him be safe.

Quigley Stadium was where the 101st troops set up their headquarters. It was there, on Tuesday evening, May 27, with 4,500 people looking on, that Ernie received his diploma. I held my breath as I listened to the radio broadcast news of the graduation ceremonies. At 8:48 P.M., Ernie became the first of our people to graduate from Central High School in all its forty-nine years. Chills danced up my spine as I sat in the big green living room chair with Mama and Grandma nearby. "It really happened," I whispered. "We made it."

The audience had been applauding those who previously marched, but when Ernie appeared they fell silent.

"What the heck," Mother Lois said. "Lots of people in the rest of the world are applauding for Ernie and for all of you who made it through this year."

"Who cares if they applaud—they didn't shoot him. There was no violence. Everybody is alive and well." Grandma stood and applauded.

Ernie was escorted from the stadium by police to a waiting taxi in which he, his family, and their guests departed. The newspapers said Ernie's diploma cost taxpayers half a million dollars. Of course, we knew it cost all of us much, much more than that. It cost us our innocence and a precious year of our teenage lives.

Exercise Courage:

- After encouraging her granddaughter to perform a forgiveness ritual "in order to have the official opportunity to give that year to God,"

Grandma India tells Beals: "Later, you'll be grateful for the courage it built inside you and for the blessing it will bring." Grandma India's words echoes those of Romans 8:18: "For I reckon that the sufferings of this present time are not worthy to be compared with the glory which shall be revealed in us." Read Romans 8 with your family and discuss the ways in which Grandma India transmits its messages to her granddaughter in this chapter.

- This passage is as much about Beals' courage standing up for her friend as it is about Ernie's courage facing the tormentors at school. Why is it hard to stand up for someone who is facing a challenging situation, even when we feel in our heart it is the right thing to do? Are you ever embarrassed to ally yourself with someone who is on an uphill climb? Do you fear other kinds of repercussions? Summon the courage to stand up for one another.

- Beals faced death threats and violence from students, faculty, and white community members alike. Today, many of our students are shipped to schools where their very lives are endangered on a daily basis or where they are the lone black student at a school in which their race and cultural backgrounds are sometimes belittled. Our children are courageous, but their courage is rarely acknowledged in popular culture. Who acts as a Grandma India in your children's lives? Is it you?

Rosa Parks

On December 1, 1955, Rosa Parks, an NAACP secretary from Montgomery, Alabama, was ordered to give up her seat on the bus to a white man. When she refused, Parks was arrested and fined fourteen dollars. Her arrest inspired a citywide boycott of the Montgomery bus system and the support of a young minister named Martin Luther King, Jr. The boycott lasted 382 days, during which time the Supreme Court ruled that segregation on city buses was unconstitutional. In Rosa Parks:

My Story, *written with Jim Haskins, Parks explains why she refused to give up her seat—and it wasn't because she was tired.*

from Rosa Parks: My Story

MONTGOMERY, ALABAMA, 1955

When I got off from work that evening of December 1, I went to Court Square as usual to catch the Cleveland Avenue bus home, I didn't look to see who was driving when I got on, and by the time I recognized him, I had already paid my fare. It was the same driver who had put me off the bus back in 1943, twelve years earlier. He was still tall and heavy, with red, rough-looking skin. And he was still mean-looking. I didn't know if he had been on that route before—they switched the drivers around sometimes. I do know that most of the time if I saw him on a bus, I wouldn't get on it.

I saw a vacant seat in the middle section of the bus and took it. I didn't even question why there was a vacant seat even though there were quite a few people standing in the back. If I had thought about it at all, I would probably have figured maybe someone saw me get on and did not take the seat but left it vacant for me. There was a [black] man sitting next to the window and two [black] women across the aisle.

The next stop was the Empire Theater, and some whites got on. They filled up the white seats, and one man was left standing. The driver looked back and noticed the man standing. Then he looked back at us. He said, "Let me have those front seats," because they were the front seats of the black section. Didn't anybody move. We just sat right where we were, the four of us. Then he spoke a second time: "Y'all better make it light on yourselves and let me have those seats."

The man in the window seat next to me stood up, and I moved to let him pass by me, and then I looked across the aisle and saw that the two women were also standing. I moved over to the window seat. I could not see how standing up was going to "make it light" for me. The more we gave in and complied, the worse they treated us.

I thought back to the time when I used to sit up all night and didn't sleep, and my grandfather would have his gun right by the fireplace, or if he had his one-horse wagon going anywhere, he always had his gun in the back of the wagon. People always say that I didn't give up my seat because I was tired, but that isn't true. I was not tired physically, or no more tired than I usually was at the end of a working day. I was not old, although some people have an image of me as being old then. I was forty-two. No, the only tired I was, was tired of giving in.

The driver of the bus saw me still sitting there, and he asked was I going to stand up. I said, "No." He said, "Well, I'm going to have you arrested." Then I said, "You may do that." These were the only words we said to each other. I didn't even know his name, which was James Blake, until we were in court together. He got out of the bus and stayed outside for a few minutes, waiting for the police.

As I sat there, I tried not to think about what might happen. I knew that anything was possible. I could be manhandled or beaten. I could be arrested. People have asked me if it occurred to me then that I could be the test case the NAACP had been looking for. I did not think about that at all. In fact if I had let myself think too deeply about what might happen to me, I might have gotten off the bus. But I chose to remain.

Exercise Courage:

- "I thought back to the time when I used to sit up all night and didn't sleep, and my grandfather would have his gun right by the fireplace. . . ." Memories of the racial violence she experienced as a child gave Parks the courage to remain in her seat despite the threat of arrest or possible physical harm at the hands of the police. Her action was not politically motivated or preplanned in any way—she just knew at that moment that if she didn't take a stand, things would never change. What are some of the emotions that can inspire courage? Can anger? Sadness? Love? From what place in her heart do you think Parks was able to summon her courage?

- In 2 Corinthians 12:10, Paul writes, "Therefore I take pleasure in infirmities, in reproaches, in necessities, in persecutions, in distresses for Christ's sake: for when I am weak, then am I strong." The African American community in Montgomery experienced extraordinary racial persecution in the 1950s and 1960s, in a city where segregation was strictly enforced. And yet the bus boycott, led by these African American citizens, became one of the biggest sparks in the civil rights movement. Discuss with your family the ways in which the "weakness" of the African American community in Montgomery made its members strong. How were they able to galvanize support for the civil rights movement?

- Think about the amount of courage it took for Rosa Parks to remain seated. Then read Matthew 5:5—"Blessed are the meek: for they shall inherit the earth"—while keeping in mind a picture of Parks in her bus seat. Would you describe Parks as "meek"? How might the Beatitudes be a meditation on courage? Try your own meditation on courage.

Claude McKay

Born in 1889 in Jamaica, Claude McKay was a major poet of the Harlem Renaissance. The youngest of eleven children, McKay was brought up with a suspicion of whites that he inherited from his father, whose own father had been enslaved. This suspicion shaped McKay's writings, as did the communal closeness he observed among Jamaican farmers. After a short-lived trade apprenticeship and brief stint as a police constable in Kingston, McKay returned to his village, where Walter Jekyll, a British collector of Jamaican folklore, helped him publish his first book, Songs of

Jamaica, *in 1912. He immigrated to the United States the following year, where he attended Tuskegee Institute in Alabama and Kansas State College. McKay then moved to Harlem, where he kept writing and supported himself through hotel and railroad work. His poetry was published in* The Liberator, *the avant-garde magazine* The Seven Arts, *and various leftist magazines. The following poem was written in 1919 in response to the "Red Summer," a period of intense violence against blacks in Chicago and dozens of other American cities. This poem would become an anthem of resistance and was later quoted by Winston Churchill during World War II.*

If We Must Die

If we must die, let it not be like hogs
Hunted and penned in an inglorious spot,
While round us bark the mad and hungry dogs,
Making their mock at our accursed lot.
If we must die, O let us nobly die,
So that our precious blood may not be shed
In vain; then even the monsters we defy
Shall be constrained to honor us through dead!
O kinsmen! We must meet the common foe!
Though far outnumbered let us show us brave,
And for their thousand blows deal one deathblow!
What though before us lies the open grave?
Like men we'll face the murderous, cowardly pack,
Pressed to the wall, dying, but fighting back!

Exercise Courage:

• In the context of the racial violence at the time the poem was written, McKay believes that if we must die at the hands of injustice, we must die nobly and with honor: "We must meet the common foe! Though far outnumbered, let us show us brave." Read Psalm 1:6: "For the Lord knoweth the way of the righteous: but the way of the ungodly shall perish." Think about how its message mirrors that of "If We Must Die."

- Celebrate the courage of the African American families who were faced with unspeakable terror in 1919. Consider the courage of African Americans facing lynch mobs and attacks on their property and families. Read about the "Red Summer" of 1919 with your family and then reread McKay's poem. See the Municipal Reference Collection on the Chicago Public Library website for more information, or read *Race Riot: Chicago in the Red Summer of 1919* by William M. Tuttle, Jr.

- Have each family member try writing a short poem of his or her own based on reading about the "Red Summer" and thinking about courage.

- What are your reflections about violence and nonviolent approaches to civil obedience? Do you have the courage to find the right response? How does the poem fall on our ears today in the face of violence?

Sojourner Truth

This version of Sojourner Truth's famous speech before the Women's Rights Convention in Akron was published in the Anti-Slavery Bugle on June 21, 1851. Other versions have been published and the actual language of her speech appears differently in some historical accounts and literary anthologies, but the sureness of her courage in the face of sexual and racial stereotypes has never been in dispute.

Ar'n't I a Woman? Speech to the Women's Rights Convention in Akron, 1851

I want to say a few words about this matter. I am a woman's rights. I have as much muscle as any man, and can do as much work as any man. I have plowed and reaped and husked and chopped and mowed, and can any man do more than that? I have heard much about the sexes being equal. I can carry as much as any man, and can eat as much too, if I can get it. I am as strong as any man that is now. As for intellect, all I can say is, if woman have a pint, and man a quart—why can't she have her little pint full? You need not be afraid to give us our rights for fear we will take too much—for we can't take more than our pint'll hold. The poor men seem to be all in confusion, and don't know what to do. Why, children, if you have woman's rights, give it to her and you will feel better. You will have your own rights, and they won't be so much trouble. I can't read, but I can hear. I have heard the Bible and have learned that Eve caused man to sin. Well, if woman upset the world, do give her a chance to set it right side up again. The Lady has spoken about Jesus, how he never spurned woman from him, and she was right. When Lazarus died, Mary and Martha came to him with faith and love and besought him to raise their brother. And Jesus wept and Lazarus came forth. And how came Jesus into the world? Through God who created him and a woman who bore him. Man, where is your part? But the women are coming up blessed be God and a few of the men are coming up with them. But man is in a tight place, the poor slave is on him, woman is coming on him, he is surely between a hawk and a buzzard.

Exercise Courage:

- Even young children can appreciate the sentiments of Sojourner Truth's message. Ask family members to discuss a time when each of them might have felt like they were not given an opportunity they were due—a chance to go to school or be promoted, for example. Reflect on the feelings that result in even the most seemingly innocuous circumstances and discuss ways for coping courageously with these setbacks. Then make a list of three acts of courage you could perform in the near future.

• Think about the last time you voiced an opinion that was unpopular. How were you received? Start a dialogue with your family about the idea of speaking up courageously—at school, at work, in your own home. Talk about how speaking up for your position is an act of courage.

• It helps to verbalize your intent to act with courage. If you find it hard to act courageously in specific circumstances, try telling someone ahead of time what you would like to do, so that he or she can encourage you if you falter.

• Sojourner Truth never learned to read and write. Many children today are in the same predicament. Become a literacy volunteer or reading partner in your local school or community center. Read to an elderly neighbor, or a hospital or nursing home patient. Encourage your children of middle and high school age to read to younger siblings and to sign up for reading volunteer programs in local nursery or elementary schools. Organize a literacy volunteer project for a Sunday school class, Girl or Boy Scout troop, or other organizations in which young people participate.

Felicia R. Lee

Felicia R. Lee, *a journalist at the* New York Times, *wrote this letter to her young son following the September 11 terrorist attacks. Published in the paper on Sunday, October 21, 2001, the letter eloquently addresses the courage our nation displayed on that horrifying day and must continue to foster in the years ahead.*

Coping: A Letter to a Child in a Difficult Time

My Dear Son:

You are only three years old, and have only a vague sense of the tumult and sadness in the city since September 11. I imagine that the passage of a decade will let you read this with maturity and perspective. What I cannot predict are the circumstances of our family or our city on that day. But during a week in which the threat of bioterrorism grew, a week in which a seven-month-old boy in the city was sickened by anthrax, I offer you the thoughts I have already shared with your twelve-year-old brother.

In the streets, at your school, or sitting at our kitchen table, I have talked to many other parents who share my apprehension. For many of us, the anthrax-infected baby has been an emotional tipping point, scary in a different way from massive burning towers crashing to earth.

Every normal parent instinctively wants to protect his or her child. Some of your friends' parents have told me that they have thought, if only fleetingly, of moving to the suburbs or to a small city. Or they have flirted with the idea of buying gas masks or guns or stockpiling antibiotics. Or they just wonder whether to take their children on the subway.

For now, your father, your brother, and I have decided we want to stay in the city. The only way we know how to help heal New York's bruised spirit is to turn inward, to take the long view. This is not just a battle against terrorism or even a test of bravery. It is about life's fragility and uncertainty suddenly writ large.

So here we are, trying to balance self-preservation and the desire to continue the life we came to New York to create.

Unlike me and your father, you are a native New Yorker. This has been your only home. By the time you were two, you knew how to hail a taxi. When the doorbell rings, you ask if dinner is being delivered, the food made with recipes that come from places like Japan, Mexico, and India. Everybody and everything is here in this city, which has a spirit of adventure, defiance, and eccentricity unlike anywhere else.

In our own little universe, the characters include the dancing man with the feather in his hat who makes you laugh when he sweeps our Manhattan block, and the micro-scopic dogs at which you bark as they are escorted down the street by their sweet old ladies.

This is a wonderful city, son, because there are enough people here who try to get along, who try to understand one another. In our family, in which your father and I have different skin colors and different religions and your older brother was born of your father's former marriage, difference is more than a notion. We have friends who are gay, who have fled war, whose parents were in concentration camps. In this city, with its critical mass of outsiders, survivors, and strivers, many of us find a measure of comfort that is lacking in most places.

Your maternal grandparents are refugees from the Deep South. They fled the back of the bus, inferior schools, physical brutality. They settled in Chicago, but your mother was determined to conquer New York. None of your grandfather's five brothers learned to read and write because of educational apartheid, but here I sit off Times Square, a staff writer for one of the best newspapers in the world.

Your father spoke only serviceable English when he came here from Italy twenty years ago, lured by everything from J. D. Salinger's books to the myth of the melting pot. But this city allowed him to thrive as a psychotherapist.

Our triumphs are not simply self-congratulation. Rather, they reflect a collective tri-umph of New York's brand of American reinvention. Reinvention of law, custom, self.

If we flee the city, family by family, who will be left? And will we be targets some-where else? New York is more than where we live. It represents our guts, our idealism, our loathing for cookie-cutter living. As your brother says, the men who flew into the Twin Towers that Tuesday morning as you sat at home watching cartoons will win if we retreat. We will only leave if there is a strong chance that our lives are at stake.

Despite what happens, and despite where we make our home by the time you read this letter, son, remember that we are New Yorkers.

Love Always,
Mommy

Exercise Courage:

- Lee's letter illustrates courage in a number of ways: courage in the face of adversity, certainly, but also courage in diversity, and courage in our beliefs. Talk to your own children about courage as it relates to standing up for your beliefs. Or write them a letter so they have a permanent document of your courage.

- As Americans we embrace diversity, and yet this is one of the reasons we found ourselves the targets of hatred on September 11. Many African Americans surely feel, as Lee does, that "difference is more than a notion." How are you teaching your own children to celebrate and nurture diversity?

- As we continue to process and remember the events of September 11, I hope parents everywhere will tell their children stories of the many courageous individuals whose heroic relief and rescue efforts came to light in the weeks and months following that most tragic of events. Remember the courage of others and you may just find more of it in yourself.

- I like to think that what Lee says about New York—that it "represents our guts, our idealism, our loathing for cookie-cutter living"—can just as readily be said about American courage in general, post–September 11. As a family, make a list of all the things you love about our country. Does the list inspire courage in you?

Diligence

A conscientious devotion to accomplishing what you set out to do,
DILIGENCE is an earnest determination that guides you toward the
fulfillment of your duties and the realization of your goals.

When I left Texas to attend Wilberforce University in Ohio, I got off the Greyhound with less than ten dollars in my pocket. But my determination to be the first in my family to earn a college degree prompted me to ask the president for a job on my very first day on campus. He obliged with an opportunity to work in the school cafeteria.

From the time I entered college until I left seminary seven years later, the cafeteria was my primary source of funds with which to pay my college tuition. I helped cook breakfast, served the lunch line and washed pots and dishes, and cleaned up in the evenings, sometimes working more than fifty hours a week. Although my work schedule competed with a rigorous study schedule, I was diligent in pursuit of my dream. My hard work paid off when I finished my coursework in December of 1967 and marched with the class of May 1968 to receive my diploma.

I am tired of seeing people of color despair. I am tired of hearing the words "I can't." I tell you right now, you can, you can, you can. Life will not always be perfect. In fact, things can and will be perfectly miserable. But please do not ever quit. Quitting is far too easy.

Some of you don't even realize that you have quit. If you have decided that prosperity and happiness are for others, you have quit. If you don't expect things to get better in your life, you have quit. If you are telling yourself that you are substandard or undeserving because you are black, or poor, or uneducated, or fat, or unattractive, then you have definitely quit. Diligence is having the self-pride to keep going when you feel like giving up.

We who have lived in America know what it means to have to contend with the fury and brokenness that grow out of prejudice, alienation, and hatred. We know how difficult it is to move outside our assigned places of mediocrity and inferiority. A close friend of mine was pursuing a Ph.D. in biology at the University of Tennessee in Memphis. After completing her coursework, she took her qualifying exams. Three of the four members of the committee passed her without hesitation, but the fourth member, a Caucasian male, refused, claiming that she was not "ready." He suggested that she settle for another master's degree and forget the Ph.D. She knew he had the power to rob her of her degree, but this diligent woman refused to allow this man to rob her of her dream. She kept focused on her goal while raising a family and finally earned her BA, MA, and Ph.D. in nursing from the same school, where she is a member of the faculty today. If we search for this diligence within ourselves, our goals will never be out of reach. Do not settle. Do not allow yourself to be trapped by mediocrity. Refuse to be content with the status quo. If you find opportunities, take them, and if you find no opportunities, make them.

Too many people spend too many days complaining about too much work. Even if our jobs seem boring or our tasks seem menial, our work is something we need to take pride in. Booker T. Washington delivered an important message when he discussed the dignity of labor. As Washington pointed out, doing work that the world needs allows us greater independence and instills us with greater self-worth.

Work, we must always remember, is not just something we do from 9 to 5. When you get home, you may be exhausted, but you must not allow yourself to collapse. One thing I cannot stand is the phrase "must-see TV." There is no such thing as must-see TV. What we all *must* do is invest our time in improving our lives rather than spend every spare moment watching television or being entertained. As the Bible teaches us, "The soul of the sluggard desireth, and hath nothing: but the soul of the diligent shall be made fat" (Proverbs 13:4).

In chapter 6, verse 7 of Galatians, Paul explains that we reap what we sow. Now, to sow is to plant, to sow is to work the land and to carry out responsibilities. When a woman sows, she tills the soil. She digs up the dirt and casts seeds into the ground. When the sowing is over, she has to wait. Sowing does not deliver instant gratification. The rewards of sowing will never be immediate.

But as Arna Bontemps illustrates in his poem "A Black Man Talks of Reaping," (see p. 50) even if we never enjoy the bounty of our labor, at some point our hard work will pay off, though the reward may be bittersweet. Diligence is sowing proudly and devotedly. Diligence is having the patience to wait for the harvest.

Remember that the Lord has confidence in you. Perseverance and tenacity must not be passé for the woman or the man of God. "For God," we are reminded, "is not unrighteous to forget your work and labor of love, which ye have shewed toward his name, in that ye have ministered to the saints, and do minister" (Hebrews 6:10).

So do not despair, though the road may be rough. Do not falter because the labor is long and hard. Sadness may endure for a night, but joy comes in the morning. Your sowing will not go unnoticed or unrewarded. Frustration and disappointment are inevitable, but we must remain diligent, remembering that nothing we do is done in vain.

Booker T. Washington

One of the most difficult feats to master in life is pressing ahead when we encounter difficulty or transition. Hardship makes most of us want to give up or give in to self-pity or anger. Booker T. Washington's Up from Slavery *is an inspiring example of diligence in the face of hardship. We glimpse Washington's constant and earnest effort to accomplish his education, but we also see his innate understanding of the value of work itself.*

from Up from Slavery

At one time it looked as if I would have to give up the idea of returning to Hampton [Institute, in Virginia], but my heart was so set on returning that I determined not to give up going back without a struggle. I was very anxious to secure some clothes for the winter, but in this I was disappointed, except for a few garments which my brother John secured for me. Notwithstanding my need of money and clothing, I was very happy in the fact that I had secured enough money to pay my traveling expenses back to Hampton. Once there, I knew that I could make myself so useful as a janitor that I could in some way get through the school year.

Three weeks before the time for the opening of the term at Hampton, I was pleasantly surprised to receive a letter from my good friend Miss Mary F. Mackie, the lady principal, asking me to return to Hampton two weeks before the opening of the school, in order that I might assist her in cleaning the buildings and getting things in order for the new school year. This was just the opportunity I wanted. It gave me a chance to secure a credit in the treasurer's office. I started for Hampton at once.

During these two weeks I was taught a lesson which I shall never forget. Miss Mackie was a member of one of the oldest and most cultured families of the North, and yet for two weeks she worked by my side cleaning windows, dusting rooms, putting beds in order, and what not. She felt that things would not be in condition for the opening of school unless every window-pane was perfectly clean, and she took the greatest satisfaction in helping to clean them herself. The work which I have described she did every year that I was at Hampton.

It was hard for me at this time to understand how a woman of her education and social standing could take such delight in performing such service, in order to assist in the elevation of an unfortunate race. Ever since then I have had no patience with any school for my race in the South which did not teach its students the dignity of labor.

During my last year at Hampton every minute of my time that was not occupied with my duties as a janitor was devoted to hard study. I was determined, if possible, to make such a record in my class as would cause me to be placed on the "honor roll" of commencement speakers. This I was successful in doing. It was June of 1875 when I finished the regular course of study at Hampton. The greatest benefits that I got out of my life at the Hampton Institute, perhaps, may be classified under two heads:

First was contact with a great man, General S. C. Armstrong, who, I repeat, was in my opinion the rarest, strongest, and most beautiful character that it has ever been my privilege to meet.

Second, at Hampton, for the first time, I learned what education was expected to do for an individual. Before going there I had a good deal of the then rather prevalent idea among our people that to secure an education meant to have a good, easy time, free from all necessity for manual labor. At Hampton I not only learned that it was not a disgrace to labor, but learned to love labor, not alone for its financial value, but for labor's own sake and for the independence and self-reliance which the ability to do something which the world wants done brings.

Exercise Diligence:

- What do you suppose is meant by "the dignity of labor"? Try to express the dignity of labor the next time you find yourself having to work for the things you desire in life.
- Sometimes we are convinced by the situations we find ourselves in that the tables will never turn. Keep in mind the example of optimism and hard work in Washington's story as you go about your own work from day to day. Don't lose heart. Be diligent in the pursuit of your goals.
- Have you ever given up on something that was important to you? A relationship? Losing weight? A better job? Going back to school? Let this story inspire you to keep steadfast in the things that matter to you. It is always too soon to quit.

Paul Laurence Dunbar

Paul Laurence Dunbar, the son of ex-slaves, is considered the first African American to be recognized as a poet. He wrote poems in both African American dialect and standard English. "The Seedling" is an enduring example of one of his classically inspired poems and an apt metaphor for diligence.

The Seedling

As a quiet little seedling
Lay within its darksome bed,
To itself it fell a-talking,
And this is what it said:

"I am not so very robust,
But I'll do the best I can";
And the seedling from that moment
Its work of life began.

So it pushed a little leaflet
Up into the light of day,
To examine the surroundings
And show the rest the way.

The leaflet liked the prospect,
So it called its brother, Stem;
Then two other leaflets heard it,
And quickly followed them.

To be sure, the haste and hurry
Made the seedling sweat and pant;
But almost before it knew it
It found itself a plant.

The sunshine poured upon it,
And the clouds they gave a shower;
And the little plant kept growing
Till it found itself a flower.

Little folks, be like the seedling,
Always do the best you can;
Every child must share life's labor
Just as well as every man.

And the sun and shower will help you
Through the lonesome, struggling hours,
Till you raise to light and beauty
Virtue's fair, unfading flowers.

Exercise Diligence:

- Read this poem aloud to a child. Then take a walk together outdoors to find seedlings.
- A seedling might suggest fragility, but Dunbar's poem lets us see that diligence and doing the "best you can" yields a certain power. Apply yourself diligently to at least one task that is ordinarily something you feel you are not strong enough or focused enough or attentive enough to do. Repair an appliance, plant a garden, or bake a pie from scratch.
- Think about your own "work of life"—what are some ways you might begin to grow in your work?

Langston Hughes

L *angston Hughes gives voice to how hard it is to grow up black in America. We see in much of his writing an acute understanding of the many obstacles to African-American accomplishment—poverty, racist policies and attitudes, disparities in educational opportunities. But as we see poignantly and most assuredly in the way this mother instructs her son, Hughes also encourages us to press ahead, to move forward, and to not give up.*

Mother to Son

Well, son, I'll tell you:
Life for me ain't been no crystal stair.
It's had tacks in it,
And splinters,
And boards torn up,
And places with no carpet on the floor—
Bare.
But all the time I'se been a climbin' on,
And reachin' landin's,
And turnin' corners,
And sometimes goin' in the dark
Where there ain't been no light.
So boy, don't you turn back.
Don't you set down on the steps
'Cause you finds it's kinder hard.
Don't you fall now—
For I'se still goin', honey,
I'se still climbin',
And life for me ain't been no crystal stair.

Exercise Diligence:

- In spite of hardships, the mother in this poem feels good about how she has led her life and wants her son to feel the same way about his own life. Do you feel good about the way you are climbing the stairs of your own life?
- I don't think we can underestimate the importance of a family context when we think about modeling virtues or family values for our children. Remind your children, not only in words, but in deeds,

where you came from, what you've accomplished, what your values are. If they know from whence they came, they'll better understand themselves.

- Write your own "Mother to Son," or "Father to Son," or "Father to Daughter" letter or poem.

- What splinters, hard, bare floors, or dark corners are you facing now in your own life? Can you summon up the kind of personal pride evidenced by the mother in this poem to work through and, with diligence, get past them?

Constance Garcia-Barrio

This ant story, originating in Ghana and told here by Constance Garcia-Barrio, an associate professor of Spanish at West Chester University in Philadelphia, is a bit of a twist on the story of the hardworking ant we remember from Aesop.

The Ant Story

One day an ant had a great stroke of luck. He found a huge crumb that even had a dab of grape jelly on it. He laughed out loud, knowing how happy everyone at the anthill would be with a taste of that crumb.

But when he started dragging the crumb toward the anthill, he realized he had a tough task ahead of him. His antennae quivered, his legs strained, and his jaw ached as he slowly dragged that crumb. "This is too much for me," he moaned. "I can't do it alone. I can't. I can't!"

When the bee came along, the ant yelled, "Stop and help me with this crumb!"

"Buzz," said the bee. "Sorry. I have all this pollen to carry back to my hive." And the bee flew off.

Soon the beetle, a practical joker, wandered by. When the ant asked him to help, the beetle said, "Sure!" and he took a big bite out of the crumb.

"I made it lighter for you, didn't I?" he hooted, walking away. The ant stood there fussing and fuming.

A spider had been watching the whole thing from her web up in a tree. She'd heard enough of the ant's "I can't! I can't!" She spun a thread down to where the ant was.

"I'm going to solve your problem," she said. "I'm going to wrap this crumb up and take it home to my children," she said, starting toward the crumb.

"You can't do that, not with my crumb," the ant yelled. Furious, the ant grabbed the crumb, pushed, pulled, shoved, and hauled. Before he knew it, he stood at the opening of the anthill, with the crumb beside him.

When the spider saw him there, she winked at him and said, "See? I knew it. You can do a lot more than you think you can."

"And you know what?" says the storyteller, pointing at the audience. "I bet you can, too!"

Exercise Diligence:

- The ant surprises himself in this story. Have you ever been surprised by your own ability and accomplished something you never dreamed you could do? What was it? Tell a child that story about yourself.
- Life is hard. There are always difficult tasks. The key to living abundantly is knowing that we cannot give up every time we get wounded or feel discouraged. Pray for stamina in daunting situations.

Patrice Gaines

A ward-winning journalist and author Patrice Gaines continues to write even after her retirement from the Washington Post, where she was a reporter for *sixteen years. But Gaines' successes did not come easily: Before she found her passion in journalism, she was a victim of rape and domestic abuse and had served a prison sentence for heroin possession. In this excerpt from* Laughing in the Dark: From Colored Girl to Woman of Color—a Journey from Prison to Power, *Gaines discusses her escape from a self-imposed hell and how her one-day-at-a-time diligence got her life back on track.*

from Laughing in the Dark

I would, in fact, sometimes forget my goal because I was so busy just trying to put one foot in front of the other, trying to live through one day—then another. Working in low-paying jobs as a clerk-typist and teletype operator; making it through periods of unemployment; working late nights with a catering group serving at white country clubs. Budgeting carefully, never able to save; searching for the right day-care center for my daughter, Andrea; trying to turn an ugly, cheap apartment into a cheerful home that a child would love to live in. And always, desperately searching for that man who would make me feel better. All of this made me forget sometimes that what I was really trying to do was to change my life.

But I did it—with perseverance. Before I could see the relationship between one part of my life and another, I worked on different sections of it, separately. I went to a community college to study English and took business courses to learn shorthand so I could get better secretarial jobs. I read self-help books, pop psychology that introduced me to the notion that there was untapped power within me. New friends entered my life, old ones fled. Throughout everything, I wrote. It seemed a natural progression: The child who read books to escape grew into a young woman who wrote to relieve herself of pain. Writing always consoled me, had always been my way of talking to God—and to myself.

Now, in my job as a reporter at the *Washington Post*, I run into young girls who remind me of my old self. I see them in courtrooms where they sit by loyally as their boyfriends are sentenced for selling crack, or, much too often, for murder. I see them standing in line during visiting hours at the D.C. jail, many of them toting babies on their hips. I have talked to them, told them my story even as I listened to theirs. But, like me at their age, they are largely silent victims. The media always cover their boyfriends, generally overlooking them. This oversight, I know, probably reinforces their own sense of powerlessness.

So this is my ode to those young sisters, those children with womanish ways, who give it up before there is really anything to give; those tender black girls whom I did not have enough time to talk to because I was on deadline.

I want them to know that no matter how low they fall, they can get back up; no matter how many times they stumble, they can still walk tall. That neither racism nor sexism can stop a determined mind, or a heart beating with love for the very body that carries it. It is a lesson for all people, regardless of race or sex; for anyone who has had to overcome a challenge.

Exercise Diligence:

- Putting one foot in front of the other is what diligence is all about. And while it's true that just getting through the obstacles of a day can make you lose sight of your goal, your persistence will take you where you want to go. Working overtime on a report may bring you closer to promotion. Extra hours in the library will help you on the chemistry test. An afternoon weeding the garden will keep the flowers blooming. Make a list of the steps you need to take this week to accomplish at least three goals.

- We should all be "on deadline" to give this advice to a young person in our life: "No matter how low [you] fall, [you] can get back up; no matter how many times [you] stumble, [you] can still walk tall. . . . Neither racism nor sexism can stop a determined mind, or a heart beating with love for the very body that carries it." What other ways might you help a young person to discover her or his "untapped" power?

- After experiencing years of abuse, much of it self-imposed, Patrice Gaines decided that she had to change her life. But she realized that change required more than the quick-fix solutions she had turned to in the past. "I would learn that change doesn't happen overnight; that sometimes it takes years, particularly trying to remake yourself from the roots." Gaines learned that change requires day-to-day work, planning, and patience. Make a plan to fix something in your life—whether it's a broken relationship or a loose handle on your kitchen cabinet. Figure out what it takes to fix it, then work at it diligently until it's done.

- Proverbs 21:5 teaches that "The thoughts of the diligent tend only to plenteousness, but of every one that is hasty only to want." How is this sentiment illustrated in Patrice Gaines' story? Discuss the meaning of this proverb with your family; give examples and talk about some ways haste leads to poverty.

Arna Bontemps

P oet and novelist Arna Bontemps was a devout Seventh-Day Adventist whose writings were often more spiritual in theme than other works of the Harlem Renaissance period. "A Black Man Talks of Reaping," first published in 1926, shows the frustration of a man whose diligence goes unrewarded.

A Black Man Talks of Reaping

I have sown beside all waters in my day.
I have planted deep, within my heart the fear
That wind or fowl would take the grain away.
I planted safe against this stark, lean year.

I scattered seed enough to plant the land
In rows from Canada to Mexico
But for my reaping only what the hand
Can hold at once is all that I can show

Yet what I sowed and what the orchard yields
My brother's sons are gathering stalk and root,
Small wonder then my children glean in fields
They have not sown, and feed on bitter fruit.

Exercise Diligence:

- "A Black Man Talks of Reaping" is an allusion to Galatians 6:7: "Be not deceived; God is not mocked: for whatsoever a man soweth, that shall he also reap." Unfortunately, as Bontemps' poem illustrates so solemnly, this has not been the reality for African Americans and other oppressed groups. We have not always been able to reap what we've sown. Still, we include the poem as a meditation on diligence, because the difficulties we face, the sometimes bitter fruit of our experience, should not keep us from diligence.

- With your children, look up the definitions for "reap" and "glean" in a dictionary. Talk about the difference in the meanings, and discuss them in the context of diligence.

- In the context of our experience as African Americans, diligence is sometimes itself a bitter pill. I like to think that Psalms 126, verses

5 and 6, undoes some of the pain of our ancestors' gleaning rather than reaping. "They that sow in tears shall reap in joy. He that goeth forth and weepeth, bearing precious seed, shall doubtless come again with rejoicing, bringing his sheaves with him." Might not the sheer artistry of this poem be one way we can come to terms with the idea of "sowing in tears" and "reaping in joy"?

W. E. B. DuBois

W. E. B. DuBois, born in Massachusetts in 1868, became one of the greatest black leaders of the twentieth century. After receiving a BA from Fisk University, he went on to attend Harvard and became the first African American to receive a Ph.D. One of the founders of the NAACP, DuBois authored many books on African American history and founded the influential magazine The Crisis. *He expatriated to Ghana and died there, at the age of ninety-five, in 1963. In the following narrative, "My Evolving Program for Negro Freedom," DuBois recalls his early years in Great Barrington and the ways in which the community passed on the value of hard work, sacrifice, and diligence in pursuing one's goals.*

from What the Negro Wants

MY MIDNIGHT CLASSMATE

Once upon a time, I found myself at midnight on one of the swaggering streetcars that used to roll out from Boston on its way to Cambridge. It must have been in the spring of 1890, and quite accidentally I was sitting by a classmate who would graduate with me in June. As I dimly remember, he was a nice-looking young man, almost dapper; well-dressed, charming in manner. Probably he was rich or at least well-to-do, and doubtless belonged to an exclusive fraternity, although that I do not know. Indeed I have even forgotten his name. But one thing I shall never forget and that was his rather regretful admission (that slipped out as we gossiped) that he had no idea as to what his lifework would be, because, as he added, "There's nothing which I am particularly interested in!"

I was more than astonished—I was almost outraged to meet any human being of the mature age of twenty-two who did not have his life all planned before him, at least in general outline; and who was not supremely, if not desperately, interested in what he planned to do.

Since then, my wonder has left my classmate, and been turned in and backward upon myself: How long had I been sure of my lifework and how had I come so confidently to survey and plan it? I now realize that most college seniors are by no means certain of what they want to do or can do with life; but stand rather upon a hesitating threshold, awaiting will, chance, or opportunity. Because I had not mingled intimately or understandingly with my Harvard classmates, I did not at the time realize this, but thought my rather unusual attitude was general. How had this attitude come to seem normal to me?

MY EARLY YOUTH

The small western New England town where I was born, and several generations of my fathers before me, was a middle-class community of Americans of English and Dutch descent, with an Irish laboring class and a few remnants of Negro working folk of past centuries. Farmers and small merchants predominated, with a fringe of decadent Americans; with mill-hands, railroad laborers, and domestics. A few manufacturers formed a small aristocracy of wealth. In the public schools of this town, I was trained from the age of six to sixteen, and in its schools, churches, and general social life I gained my patterns of living. I had almost no experience of segregation or color discrimination. My schoolmates were invariably white; I joined quite naturally all games, excursions, church festivals; recreations like coasting, skating, and ball-games. I was in and out of the homes of nearly all my mates, and ate and played with them. I was a boy unconscious of color discrimination in any obvious and specific way.

I knew nevertheless that I was exceptional in appearance and that this riveted attention upon me. Less clearly, I early realized that most of the colored persons I saw, including my own folk, were poorer than the well-to-do whites; lived in humbler houses, and did not own stores; this was not universally true: My cousins, the Crispels, in West Stockbridge, had one of the most beautiful homes in the village. Other cousins, in Lenox, were well-to-do. On the other hand, none of the colored folk I knew were so poor, drunken, and sloven as some of the lower Americans and Irish. I did not then associate poverty or ignorance with color, but rather with lack of opportunity; or more often with lack of thrift, which was in strict accord with the philosophy of New England and of the nineteenth century.

On the other hand, much of my philosophy of the color line must have come from my family group and their friends' experience. My father dying early, my immediate family consisted of my mother and her brother and my older half brother most of the time. Near to us in space and intimacy were two married aunts with older children, and a number of cousins, in various degrees removed, living scattered through the county and state. Most of these had been small farmers, artisans, laborers, and servants. With few exceptions all could read and write, but few had training beyond this. These talked of their work and experience, of hindrances which colored people encountered, of better chances in other towns and cities. In this way I must have gotten indirectly a pretty clear outline of color bars which I myself did not experience. Moreover, it was easy enough for me to rationalize my own case, because I found it easy to excel most of my schoolmates in studies if not in games. The secret of life and the loosing of the color bar, then, lay in excellence, in accomplishment; if others of my family, of my colored kin, had stayed in school, instead of quitting early for small jobs, they could have risen to equal whites. On this my mother quietly insisted. There was no real discrimination on account of color—it was all a matter of ability and hard work.

This philosophy was saved from conceit and vainglory by rigorous self-testing, which doubtless cloaked some half-conscious misgivings on my part. If visitors to school saw and remarked my brown face, I waited in quiet confidence. When my turn came, I recited glibly and usually correctly because I studied hard. Some of my mates did not care, some were stupid; but at any rate I gave the best a hard run, and then sat back complacently. Of course, I was too honest with myself not to see things which desert and even hard work did not explain or solve: I recognized ingrained difference in gift; Art Gresham could draw caricatures for the *High School Howler*, published occasionally in manuscript, better than I; but I could express meanings in words better than he; Mike McCarthy was a perfect marble player, but dumb in Latin. I came to see and admit all this, but I hugged my own gifts and put them to test.

When preparation for college came up, the problem of poverty began to appear. Without conscious decision on my part, and probably because of continuous quiet suggestion from my high school principal, Frank Hosmer, I found myself planning to go to college; how or where, seemed an unimportant detail. A wife of one of the cotton mill owners, whose only son was a pal of mine, offered to see that I got lexicons and texts to take up the study of Greek in high school, without which college doors in that day would not open. I accepted the offer as something normal and right; only after many years did I realize how critical this gift was for my career. I am not yet sure how she came to do it; perhaps my wise principal suggested it. Comparatively few of my white classmates planned or cared to plan for college—perhaps two or three in a class of twelve.

I collected catalogues of colleges and over the claims of Williams and Amherst, nearest my home, I blithely picked Harvard, because it was oldest and largest, and most widely known. My mother died a few months after my graduation, just as though, tired of the long worry and pull, she was leaving me alone at the post, with a certain characteristic faith that I would not give up.

I was, then, an orphan, without a cent of property, and with no relative who could for a moment think of undertaking the burden of my further education. But the family could and did help out and the town in its quiet and unemotional way was satisfied with my record and silently began to plan. First, I must go to work at least for a season and get ready for college in clothes and maturity, as I was only sixteen. Then there was the question of where I could go and how the expenses could be met.

The working out of these problems by friends and relatives brought me face-to-face, for the first time, with matters of income and wealth. A place was secured for me as timekeeper, during the building of a mansion by a local millionaire, in whose family an ancestor of mine had once worked. My job brought me for the first time in close contact with organized work and wage. I followed the building and its planning: I watched the mechanics at their work; I knew what they earned, I gave them their weekly wage and carried the news of their dismissal. I saw the modern world at work, mostly with the hands, and with few machines.

Meantime in other quarters a way was being made for me to go to college. The father of one of my schoolmates, the Reverend C. C. Painter, was once in the Indian Bureau. There and elsewhere he saw the problem of the reconstructed South, and conceived the idea that there was the place for me to be educated, and there lay my future field of work. My family and colored friends rather resented the idea. Their Northern Free Negro prejudice naturally revolted at the idea of sending me to the former land of slavery, either for education or for living. I am rather proud of myself that I did not agree with them. That I should always live and work in the South, I did not then stop to decide; that I would give up the idea of graduating from Harvard, did not occur to me. But I wanted to go to Fisk, not simply because it was at least a beginning of my dream of college, but also, I suspect, because I was beginning to feel lonesome in New England; because, unconsciously, I realized that as I grew older, the close social intermingling with my white fellows would grow more restricted. There were meetings, parties, clubs to which I was not invited. Especially in the case of strangers, visitors, newcomers to the town was my presence and friendship a matter of explanation or even embarrassment to my schoolmates. Similar discriminations and separations met the Irish youth, and the cleft between rich and poor widened.

On the other hand, the inner social group of my own relatives and colored friends always had furnished me as a boy most interesting and satisfying company; and now as I grew, it was augmented by visitors from other places. I remember a lovely little plump and brown girl who appeared out of nowhere, and smiled at me demurely; I went to the East to visit my father's father in New Bedford, and on that trip saw well-to-do, well-mannered colored people; and once, at Rocky Point, Rhode Island, I viewed with astonishment ten thousand Negroes of every hue and bearing. I was transported with amazement and dreams; I apparently noted nothing of poverty or degradation, but only extraordinary beauty of skin-color and utter equality of men, with absence so far as I could see of even the shadow of the line of race. Gladly and armed with a scholarship, I set out for Fisk.

Exercise Diligence:

- The blacks and whites who settled in DuBois's hometown were thrifty, valued education, and promoted the values of hard work. Walk through the business district of your own community with a neighborhood child or one of your young relatives. Introduce the child to one of the many hardworking people you encounter. Ask a butcher, grocer, electrician, or accountant to describe the work that they do.

- As a child, DuBois's talents were encouraged by his schoolteachers and by community members who wanted him to succeed. I Timothy

4:14–16 says, "Neglect not the gift that is in thee, which was given thee by prophecy, with the laying on of the hands of the presbytery. Meditate upon these things; give thyself wholly to them; that thy profiting may appear to all. Take heed unto theyself, and unto the doctrine; continue in them: for in doing this thou shalt both save thyself, and them that hear thee." In what ways did DuBois's life-work mirror this passage? Let your friends and family know you care about their progress. Support each other in your work.

Georgia Douglas Johnson

Georgia Douglas Johnson was one of the most prominent writers of the Harlem Renaissance. She applied for numerous writing fellowships throughout her lifetime, but never received any grants. Yet Johnson continued to write amidst rejection from publishers and fellowship committees, demonstrating remarkable diligence in pursuit of her goal to write. The perseverance of the speaker in her poem "The Black Runner," originally published in Opportunity Journal in September 1925, reveals the same strength in the face of opposition that Johnson herself exercised throughout her life.

The Black Runner

I'm awake, I'm away!
I have jewels in trust,
They are rights of the soul
That are holy and just;
There are deeds to be done,
There are goals to be won,
I am stripped for the race
In the glare of the sun;
I am throbbing with faith
I can! And I must!

My forehead to God—
My feet in the dust.

Exercise Diligence:

- The runner is a bright, shining symbol of our strength and perseverance. Read this poem aloud to your children at bedtime or include it in a Sunday school lesson as an example of diligence.
- Repeat the mantra "I can and I must" when you are next facing a challenging task.
- I love the idea that I can keep my "forehead to God." What does this phrase mean to you? That you are always face front and chin up with God? That you look ahead with God as your guide? Instill in your children the idea that their diligence will be rewarded if they endeavor to be "forehead to God" in life.

Oseola McCarty

When Oseola McCarty was twelve years old, she quit school to care for an aunt who was ill. She began taking in laundry to make ends meet, working diligently for more than seventy-five years until she retired in 1994 at the age of eighty-six. McCarty has said she did not believe in retirement: "Work is a blessing. As long as I am living, I want to be working at something. Just because I am old doesn't mean I can't work." We get a taste of Miss McCarty's work ethic in this excerpt from an interview with her conducted by Phil Hearn of the Center for Oral History and Cultural Heritage at the University of Southern Mississippi. McCarty's story is one of the most inspiring examples of a life lived simply and well that we know.

from An Oral History with Miss Oseola McCarty

Interviewer: Tell me what a typical day would have been like for you when you were doing that: what time you got up in the morning and what you did during the day and how you juggled washing clothes with taking care of your aunt. Just tell me what a day was like.

McCarty: Uh-huh. Now, I get up early every morning. I go to bed about ten or eleven o'clock. I be ironing. You know, that's to keep work and trying to make a living, to help make a living. Because, I mean, my grandmother would wash and iron. And then when my mother would, she'd come and visit her, she'd get her a job and go to work. She worked out for Mr. S. J. Garroway. And him and his wife lived up on Fourth Street and she worked up there for them.

Interviewer: Okay. Were y'all making enough money to pay your bills and get by and do okay?

McCarty: Yes sir, yes sir. We loved to work. My whole family was workers, just like I worked when I was able to. I worked all the time, night and day. Anything I wanted, I'd see it, I'd go at it and get the money to pay it. And when I turned my business over to Mr. Lofton, I didn't owe nobody nothing. Nobody.

Interviewer: Well, now tell me how you handled your business. How did that work?

McCarty: Well, I just worked and saved my money and put it in the bank. Every month I'd put so much in the bank.

Interviewer: How would you get business? How would people hear about you and how would they—

McCarty: They loved my work. See, I do my work good and I didn't have no trouble. I'd get more work than I could do. Somebody always, "Ola," or calling me, "Ola, come will you do such-and-such a thing for me?" If they wanted a party, they'd want you to fix some table linens for them. I'd do that. Or curtains, I'd do that.

Just whatever they want me to do, I'll do it, but I'd be doing it at home.

Interviewer: Right. So they would bring—

McCarty: They'd bring them to me and I'd wash and iron them and tell them a day to come back and get them and they'd come back.

Interviewer: Well, how, what would be a typical day? How many people would, how many customers would you have, could handle, in, say, one day's time? What time did you start in the morning and what time did you get through at night?

McCarty: I started along about seven, seven-thirty and then I worked until about ten or eleven o'clock at night. Then I'd get put off and go to bed.

Interviewer: Now during that time, you would wash. Tell me how you did that? Tell me how you washed it.

McCarty: We washed so many days a week. We'd wash Monday, Tuesday, Wednesday, and Thursday. We cut off along about twelve o'clock and then from then on we ironed. And we ironed every night, every night. We'd wash in the daytime and iron at night. That's the way we did it.

Interviewer: How did you actually wash the clothes?

McCarty: We washed them with a rub board like that, in a zinc tub and a wash pot, boil them, boil them clothes and then—

Interviewer: Was this in your backyard?

McCarty: In the backyard. We had a washhouse. My uncle built us a washhouse.

Interviewer: Then how would you dry them?

McCarty: We'd put them out on the line. And they'd dry before you— and we had a handwringer. You ever seen a handwringer?

Interviewer: Yes, ma'am.

McCarty: Well, we turned it and when you go to the line, all the water near about squeezed out of them and they'd dry as fast as the sunshine. Dry as fast as you could hang them upon the line, they'd dry.

Interviewer: That's kind of hard work, though, wasn't it?

McCarty: No sir, it wasn't hard. I liked that, I really liked it. I love washing and ironing now. And if my hand was just well, I'd be washing and ironing to the day.

Exercise Diligence:

- McCarty's diligence and stamina are remarkable, but perhaps even more inspiring is her outright love of her work. Is it the ironing and washing she really loves or is it the productivity, the usefulness, the earning of a living wage that she loves? Or is it both?

- If we teach our children that the only reason we work is to have money, we end up with people doing harmful things. Tell McCarty's story to your children. Talk about work as something that can make you proud, as McCarty's did her.

- To be able to do work that you love is a wonderful blessing, and I'm grateful that I'm able to stand before a congregation every Sunday doing something that I love to do. But even if the work you do is not your joy in life, there is value in work that lets you sustain yourself and your family. If we are diligent in our work, we become mindful of its value and it frees us, no matter how discouraged we may feel at the end of a hard day. Practice mindfulness in your work. Be mindful of the outcome of your diligence. Look for work you can love.

- Hang fresh laundry on a line in the sun. Or choose another task that you normally do with the help of a machine and do it by hand as an exercise in good old-fashioned diligence.

- Make a point to thank the service station attendant, checkout clerk, construction workers, or other working people you encounter in a day. Like Oseola McCarty, these people deserve our appreciation for working diligently to make our world a better place.

Mary Church Terrell

Mary Church Terrell was a principal figure in the national black women's club movement in the late nineteenth and early twentieth centuries. She was asked by the sisters of Delta Sigma Theta of Howard University to write a creed for the sorority, which we include here as an example of a great leader's rules for living right and making your way in the world with diligence.

from A Colored Woman in a White World

I will strive to reach the highest educational, moral, and spiritual efficiency which I can possibly attain.

I will never lower my aims for any temporary benefit which might be gained.

I will endeavor to preserve my health, for however great one's mental and moral strength may be, physical weakness prevents the accomplishment of much that might otherwise be done.

I will close my ears and seal my lips to slanderous gossip.

I will labor to ennoble the ideals and purify the atmosphere of the home.

I will always protest against the double standard of morals.

I will take an active interest in the welfare of my country, using my influence toward the enactment of laws for the protection of the unfortunate and weak and for the repeal of those depriving human beings of their privileges and rights.

I will never belittle my race, but encourage all to hold it in honor and esteem.

I will not shrink from undertaking what seems wise and good, because I labor under the double handicap of race and sex; but, striving to preserve a calm mind with a courageous, cheerful spirit, barring bitterness from my heart, I will struggle all the more earnestly to reach the goal.

Exercise Diligence:

- Post a copy of Mary Church Terrell's creed on your refrigerator door. The rules are also a great message to enclose in a graduation or birthday card for a young woman in your family, church, or neighborhood.
- If we let go of bitterness, anger, or the weight of being disadvantaged because of our sex or race in order to reach a goal, we "struggle all the more earnestly to reach the goal." This is the very essence of diligence. Are there things you can let go of now, so that your own struggle will be more earnest?

Faith

*A confident belief in God and a trusting acceptance
of God's will, FAITH gives you the hope to live beyond
the mundane and to see beneath the superficial.*

Climbing a mountain is hard. Climbing a mountain without
believing you can do it is impossible. Although we are not all
mountain climbers, we can all be believers. In order to succeed,
we must believe that we can succeed; in order to accomplish our
goals, we must believe we have the power to accomplish our
goals. There is no life without faith.

Imagine trying to ride a bike not believing that you have the
potential and ability to ride. Try going on a job interview without believing that you can get the job. There is no point. Without faith, your dreams will never come true. Without faith, you
have no dreams.

In the Bible, Job shows us the need for faith. In this well-
known story, Job, a man described as "perfect and upright,"
demonstrates the resilience of true faith in God. As the story
goes, God gives Satan permission to test Job's faith by first

destroying his property, then murdering his children, and finally devastating his health. These plagues are designed to test whether Job's faith can withstand sufferings that he cannot explain or understand.

As African Americans, we can identify with Job. Although we have been subjected to centuries of hatred and prejudice, we cannot allow misfortunes to weaken our faith. We all know that this is no easy task. My own experiences have shown me how quickly our faith can wane in times of trouble.

After my husband [Floyd] was elected to Congress in 1987, our family was exposed to the nasty side of vicious politics. It was a trying time in my life, and I sometimes felt abandoned by God. Having made it through the ordeal with the support of my family and church community, I look back ashamed of my faith-lessness, thanking God for all his kindness. I have learned how important it is to remember that when life is difficult, we must remember that God has not left us.

Life is unpredictable and filled with change. Faith must be our anchor through our ups and downs, highs and lows. We must maintain our faith through our sadness just as through our joy.

Faith is a spiritual muscle; if not exercised, it grows weak. If our faith is to remain strong in times of crisis, it must be strengthened in times of composure. We cannot expect our faith to carry us through our suffering unless we regularly reaffirm our faith and constantly acknowledge God's guidance in our daily lives.

How are we to know when our faith is strong enough? We must find the answer to this question within ourselves. When we, as men, women, and children, realize that our faith is not belief but knowledge, then, and only then, is our faith strong enough. Faith is not merely hope, and it must be more than belief; faith is a *knowing* of the heart.

In this chapter, we can see how our mothers and our fathers, our brothers and our sisters help us develop and live by faith. When family members and those close to us are strong in faith, they can show us that faith allows us to endure our misfortunes and enjoy our prosperity. In reading these selections, we see that when we know we can move the mountains in our lives, we cannot fail.

Dr. Benjamin S. Carson

In 1987, Dr. Benjamin S. Carson made medical history by leading a medical team that separated West German conjoined twins; in 1997 he led a team of South African doctors in the first successful separation of vertically conjoined twins. However, like many Americans who have achieved phenomenal success, his childhood was far from easy. Carson and his brother were raised by their mother, a struggling single parent with a third-grade education. As a child, Carson was an underachiever who had frequent temper tantrums. But after his mother challenged him to succeed in school, he turned his life around and won academic scholarships to college and medical school. Today, Carson is director of the Division of Pediatric Neurosurgery at the Johns Hopkins Hospital in Baltimore, Maryland. In this excerpt from his autobiography, Gifted Hands, *Carson remembers the day his faith in God changed his life.*

from Gifted Hands

I stared at the ten-dollar bill on the table before me, knowing I had to make a choice. And since I had only one chance, I wanted to make sure I made the right one.

For days I'd considered the matter from every possible angle. I'd prayed for God to help me. But it still seemed to come down to making one single decision.

An ironic situation faced me in the fall of 1968, for most of the top colleges in the country had contacted me with offers and inducements. However, each college required a ten-dollar nonreturnable entrance fee sent with the application. I had exactly ten dollars, so I could apply only to one.

Looking back I realize that I could have borrowed the money to make several applications. Or, it's possible that if I'd talked to representatives from the schools they might have waived the fee. But my mother had pushed the concept of self-reliance for so long I didn't want to start out owing a school just to get accepted.

At that time the University of Michigan—a spectacular school and always in the top ten academically and in sports events—actively recruited black students. And the University of Michigan waived the fees for in-state students who couldn't afford to pay. However, I wanted to attend college farther away.

I looked hard at my future, knowing that I could get into any of the top schools but not knowing what to do. Graduating third in my class, I had excellent SAT scores, and most of the top colleges were scrambling to enroll blacks. After college, with a major in premed and minor in psychology, I'd be ready for medical school, and at last on the real road toward becoming a doctor.

For a long time it bothered me that I had graduated third in my senior high school class. It's probably a character flaw, but I can't help myself. It wasn't that I had to be first in everything, but I *should* have been number one. If I hadn't gotten so sidetracked by the need for peer approval, I would have been at the top of my class. In thinking toward college, I determined that would never happen again. From now on, I'd be the best student I was capable of being.

Several weeks flew by as I struggled over which college to send my application to, and by late spring I had narrowed the choice between Harvard and Yale. Either would have been great, which made the decision difficult. Strangely enough, my final decision hinged on a television program. As I watched *College Bowl* one Sunday night, the Yale students wiped the Harvard students off the face of the map with a fantastic score of something like 510 to 35. That game helped me to make my decision—I wanted to go to Yale.

In less than a month I not only had my acceptance at Yale to enter in the fall of 1969, but they offered me a 90 percent academic scholarship.

I suppose I should have been elated by the news. I was happy, but not surprised. Actually I took it calmly, and perhaps even a bit arrogantly, reminding myself that I had already accomplished just about everything I'd set out to do—a high scholastic record, top SAT scores, every kind of high school recognition possible, along with my long list of achievements with the ROTC program.

Campus accommodations befitted students of my stature. The student housing was luxurious, the rooms more like suites. The suites included a living room, fireplace, and built-in bookcases. Bedrooms branched off from the main room. Two to four students shared each suite. I had a room to myself.

I strode onto the campus, looked up at the tall, gothic-style buildings, and approved of the ivy-covered walls. I figured I'd take the place by storm. And why not? I was incredibly bright.

After less than a week on campus I discovered I wasn't that bright. All the students were bright, many of them extremely gifted and perceptive. Yale was a great leveler for me, because I now studied, worked, and lived with dozens of high-achieving students, and I didn't stand out among them.

One day I was sitting at the dining room table with several class members who were talking about their SAT scores. One of them said, "I blew the SAT test with a total of just a little over 1500 in both parts."

"That's not too bad," another one sympathized. "Not great, but not bad."

"What did you get?" the first student asked him.

"Oh, 1540 or 1550, total. I can't remember my exact math score."

It seemed perfectly natural to all of them to have scores in the high-90 percentile. I kept silent, realizing that I ranked lower than every student sitting around me. It was my first awareness of not being quite as bright as I thought, and the experience washed away a little of my cockiness. At the same time, the incident only slightly deterred me. It would be simple enough to show them. I'd do what I did at Southwestern and throw myself completely into my studies, learning as much as possible. Then my grades would put me right up in the top echelon.

But I quickly learned that the classwork at Yale was difficult, unlike anything I'd ever encountered at Southwestern High School. The professors expected us to have done our homework before we came to class, then used that information as the basis for the day's lectures. This was a foreign concept to me. I'd slid through semester after semester in high school studying only what I wanted, and then, being a good crammer, spent the last few days before exams memorizing like mad. It had worked at Southwestern. It was a shock to realize it wouldn't work at Yale.

Each day I slipped farther and farther behind in my classwork, especially in chemistry. Why I didn't work to keep up, I'm not sure. I could give myself a dozen excuses, but they didn't matter. What mattered was that I didn't know what was going on in chemistry class.

It all came to a head at the end of the first semester when I faced final examinations. The day before the exam I wandered around the campus, sick with dread. I couldn't deny it any longer: I was failing freshman chemistry, and failing it badly. My feet scuffed through the golden leaves carpeting the wide sidewalks. Sunlight and shadow danced on ivy-covered walls. But the beauty of that autumn day mocked me. I'd blown it. I didn't have the slightest hope of passing chemistry, because I hadn't kept up with the material. As the realization sunk in of my impending failure, this bright boy from Detroit also stared squarely into another horrible truth—if I failed chemistry I couldn't stay in the premed program.

Despair washed over me as memories of fifth grade flashed through my mind. "What score did you get, Carson?" "Hey, dummy, did you get any right today?" Years had passed, but I could still hear the taunting voices in my head.

What am I doing at Yale anyway? It was a legitimate question, and I couldn't push the thought away. *Who do I think I am? Just a dumb black kid from the poor side of Detroit who has no business trying to make it through Yale with all these intelligent, affluent students.* I kicked a stone and sent it flying into the brown grass. *Stop it*, I told myself. *You'll only make it worse.* I turned my memories back to those teachers who told me, "Benjamin, you're bright. You can go places."

There, walking alone in the darkness of my thoughts, I could hear Mother insist, "Bennie, you can do it! Why, son, you can do anything you want, and you can do it better than anybody else. I believe in you."

I turned and began walking between the tall, classic buildings back to the dorm. I had to study. *Stop thinking about failing*, I told myself. *You can still pull this off. Maybe.* I looked up through a scatter of fluttering leaves silhouetted against the rose autumn sunset. Doubts niggled at the back of my mind.

Finally I turned to God. "I need help," I prayed. "Being a doctor is all I've ever wanted to do, and now it looks like I can't. And, Lord, I've always had the impression you wanted me to be a doctor. I've worked hard and focused my life that way, assuming that's what I was going to do. But if I fail chemistry I'm going to have to find something else to do. Please help me know what else I should do."

Back in my room, I sank down on my bed. Dusk came early, and the room was dark. The evening sounds of campus filled the quiet room—cars passing, students' voices in the park below my window, gusts of wind rustling through the trees. Quiet sounds. I sat there, a tall, skinny kid, head in my hands. I had failed. I had finally faced a challenge I couldn't overcome; I was just too late.

Standing up, I flipped on the desk lamp. "Okay," I said as I paced my room, "I'm going to fail chemistry. So I'm not going to be a doctor. Then what is there for me?"

No matter how many other career choices I considered, I couldn't think of anything else in the whole world I wanted more than being a doctor. I remembered the scholarship offer from West Point. A teaching career? Business? None of these areas held any real interest.

My mind reached toward God—a desperate yearning, begging, clinging to him. "Either help me understand what kind of work I ought to do, or else perform some kind of miracle and help me to pass this exam."

From that moment on, I felt at peace. I had no answer. God didn't break through my haze of depression and flash a picture in front of me. Yet I knew that whatever happened, everything was going to be all right.

One glimmer of hope—a tiny one at that—shone through my seemingly impossible situation. Although I had been holding on to the bottom rung of the class from the first week at Yale, the professor had a rule that might save me. If failing students did well on the final exam, the teacher would throw out most of the semester's work and let the good final-test score count heavily toward the final grade. That presented the only possibility for me to pass chemistry.

It was nearly 10 P.M., and I was tired. I shook my head, knowing that between now and tomorrow morning I couldn't pull off that kind of miracle.

"Ben, you have to try," I said aloud. "You have to do everything you can."

I sat down for the next two hours and pored through my thick chemistry textbook, memorizing formulas and equations that I thought might help. No matter what happened during the exam, I would go into it determined to do the best I could. I'd fail but, I consoled myself, at least I'd have a high fail.

As I scribbled formulas on paper, forcing myself to memorize what had no meaning to me, I knew deep inside why I was failing. The course wasn't that tough. The truth lay in something much more basic. Despite my impressive academic record in high school, I really hadn't learned anything about studying. All the way through high school I'd relied on the same old methods—wasting my time during the semester, and then cramming for final exams.

Midnight. The words on the pages blurred, and my mind refused to take in any more information. I flopped into my bed and whispered in the darkness, "God, I'm sorry. Please forgive me for failing you and for failing myself." Then I slept.

While I slept I had a strange dream, and when I awakened in the morning it remained as vivid as if it had actually happened. In the dream I was sitting in the chemistry lecture hall, the only person there. The door opened, and a nebulous figure walked into the room, stopped at the board, and started working out chemistry problems. I took notes of everything he wrote.

When I awakened, I recalled most of the problems, and I hurriedly wrote them down before they faded from memory. A few of the answers actually did fade but, still remembering the problems, I looked them up in my textbook. I knew quite a bit about psychology so I assumed I was still trying to work out unresolved problems during my sleep.

I dressed, ate breakfast, and went to the chemistry lecture room with a feeling of resignation. I wasn't sure if I knew enough to pass, but I was numb from intensive cramming and despair. The lecture hall was huge, filled with individual fold-down wooden seats. It would seat about a thousand students. In the front of the room chalkboards faced us from a large stage. Also on the stage was a big desk with a countertop and sink for chemistry demonstrations. My steps sounded hollow on the wooden floor.

The professor came in and, without saying much, began to hand out the booklets of examination questions. My eyes followed him around the room. It took him a while to pass out the booklets to six hundred students. While I waited, I noticed the way the sun shone through the small panes of the arched windows along one wall. It was a beautiful morning to fail a test.

At last, heart pounding, I opened the booklet and read the first problem. In that instant, I could almost hear the discordant melody from *The Twilight Zone*. In fact, I felt I had entered that never-never land. Hurriedly I skimmed through the booklet, laughing silently, confirming what I suddenly knew. The exam problems were identical to those written by the shadowy dream figure in my sleep.

I knew the answer to every question on the first page. "Piece of cake," I mumbled as my pencil flew to write the solutions. The first page finished, I turned to the next page, and again the first problem was one I had seen written on the board in my dream. I could hardly believe it.

I didn't stop to analyze what was happening. I was so excited to know correct answers that I worked quickly, almost afraid I'd lose what I remembered. Near the end of the test, where my dream recall began to weaken, I didn't get every single problem. But it was enough. I knew I would pass.

"God, you pulled off a miracle," I told him as I left the classroom. "And I make a promise to you that I'll never put you into that situation again."

I walked around campus for over an hour, elated, yet needing to be alone, wanting to figure out what had happened. I'd never had a dream like that before. Neither had anyone I'd ever known. And that experience contradicted everything I'd read about dreams in my psychology studies.

The only explanation just blew me away. The one answer was humbling in its simplicity. For whatever reason, the God of the universe, the God who holds galaxies in his hands, had seen a reason to reach down to a campus room on Planet Earth and send a dream to a discouraged ghetto kid who wanted to become a doctor.

I gasped at the sure knowledge of what had happened. I felt small and humble. Finally I laughed out loud, remembering that the Bible had recorded such events, though they were few—times where God gave specific answers and directions to his people. God had done it for me in the twentieth century. Despite my failure, God had forgiven me and come through to pull off something marvelous for me.

"It's clear that you want me to be a doctor," I said to God. "I'm going to do everything within my power to be one. I'm going to learn to study. I promise you that I'll never do this to you again."

During my four years at Yale I did backslide a little, but never to the point of not being prepared. I started learning how to study, no longer concentrating on surface material and just what the professors were likely to ask on finals. I aimed to grasp everything in detail. In chemistry, for instance, I didn't want to just know answers but to understand the reasoning behind the formulas. From there, I applied the same principle to all my classes.

After this experience, I had no doubt that I would be a physician. I also had the sense that God not only wanted me to be a physician, but that he had special things for me to do. I'm not sure people always understand when I say that, but I had an inner certainty that I was on the right path in my life—the path God had chosen for me. Great things were going to happen in my life, and I had to do my part by preparing myself and being ready.

When the final chemistry grades came out, Benjamin S. Carson scored 97—right up there with the top of the class.

Exercise Faith:

- In high school, Dr. Carson is the sort of student who can cram for exams and pass with flying colors. He learns that his study strategy

will not work at Yale and, instead of taking action, becomes paralyzed with fear and self-doubt. We often see our children struggling
with these issues of self-doubt, especially during adolescence. Their
bouts with insecurity can lead them astray. As parents, we can instill
the sort of faith in our children that Carson's mother instilled in
him. Share Psalm 116:16 with your child or an adolescent in your
life who has lost faith in his or her abilities: "The Lord preserveth
the simple: I was brought low, and he helped me."

• Carson's prayers resulted in a seeming miracle. One thinks of
Matthew 14:31: "Oh thou of little faith, wherefore didst thou
doubt?" The experience of nearly flunking out of school—and Yale
at that—had a profound influence on the ways in which Carson
conducted himself in the future. In many ways the experience
seemed a test from God, much like the trials faced by Job; however,
Carson's trials were self-imposed. Have you had experiences in
which you lost your faith in God's goodness because you followed
your will and not God's?

• This excerpt is a wonderful example of the words of Matthew
17:20: "And Jesus said unto them, Because of your unbelief: for ver-
ily I say unto you, If ye have faith as a grain of mustard seed, ye
shall say unto this mountain, Remove hence to yonder place; and it
shall remove; and nothing shall be impossible unto you." What a
wonderful message to meditate on when our faith is shaky. Make
this passage a family motto.

• Carson's faith was affirmed through a powerful dream. Consider
keeping a dream journal, taking particular note of any spiritual
messages you receive during the night.

Cornelia Walker Bailey

*Born and raised on Sapelo Island off the Georgia coast, Cornelia Walker Bailey
lectures extensively about her unique childhood and the Geechee culture in which*

she was raised. In this charming tale of faith and family tradition, excerpted from her memoir, God, Dr. Buzzard, and the Bolito Man, *written with Christena Bledsoe, Bailey shows that our burdens become lighter when we have something to believe in.*

from God, Dr. Buzzard, and the Bolito Man

A MAKE-DO OR DO-WITHOUT FAMILY

At planting time on Sapelo, we relied on signs from nature that the soil was ready to receive new seed and on our beliefs about our bonds to the earth.

We were a make-do or do-without family, and the spring I was four I learned how much everything we had counted toward our survival. If our flour had weevils in it, Mama sifted it and used it anyway. Our sugar was kept in a container set in a pan of water with a greased rim so that the sugar ants wouldn't get to it. And you know that if our staples were that precious, our crops were more so. We depended on those crops. What we grew was what we ate, along with the fish we got from the sea and Papa's hunting, and the few staples we bought. So Mama and Papa were careful to do everything just right with our crop.

If there was a pregnant woman around at planting time, she dropped the seed. A pregnant woman was the best planter there was because she was carrying new life in her. Your seed would get up faster, your crops would grow faster and they would bear better, all because of her, and if she dropped the seed for watermelon, they would grow like crazy. Your field would practically explode; you would have watermelon everywhere. Ada was in the field dropping the seed this particular spring and if I had been a little older, it might have made me wonder if she was in the family way. But I was too young to know about things like that. Besides, I was in the fields too.

If you didn't have a pregnant woman around, you'd get a young child to drop the seed, the younger the better, because little hands were full of life. The seed would grow just as fast as a growing child. Sometimes a family would even borrow a young child if they didn't have one.

I was dropping the seed before I was two years old, before I could even talk. I was just big enough to walk that row. Mama had me in real bib overalls, a long shirt, and I was barefoot. The weather was warm and it was barefoot time.

Mama had patience with me galore. She would hold my hand in hers, give me three or four seeds, whatever was supposed to go in the hole, and show me just where to put them. She'd say, "Put it right there. That's fine. Go to the next one. Okay, now drop one right there." I got the hang of it and I would drop the seed and she would push and stamp it in the dirt. I was out there thinking I was as big as my mama and daddy. They let me plant the fields and it was neat.

Old hands were the worst to have around at planting time. We believed that old hands should never drop seed because your crop will always take longer to grow. They didn't have much planting life left in them; they were going back to the earth, not coming from it. The old people would say, "Yeah, girl, I'm going backwards every day," and that meant they were closer to death than you.

We had other rules for planting too. We never planted when the tide was out, we planted when the tide was coming in, because if the tide was low or going out, we believed it would stunt the growth of your plants. We always tried to plant on the new moon, just as it was beginning to grow and swell. If we didn't plant on the new moon, Papa would say, "We'll plant on the fullest of the moon," because that was the second-best time.

Our early crops went in the ground in February and March and then come Good Friday, Mama would say, "Okay, it's Good Friday, so I'm planting my lima beans." That day was blessed by God, so your beans would do better if you planted them then.

For certain crops, you had to be sure that danger of a late frost was over before you planted. Mama said nothing can fool the pecan trees so we watched the pecan trees and when they were putting out their blossoms, we knew it was safe to plant okra or anything else.

Papa would get everything ready. He would burn the fields off so he could get a plow through and spread lime over the soil to make it better. He made his own lime by burning oyster shells from a pile we kept near the house, and if he wanted to spread ashes too, he'd get them from a pile of ashes we saved from our wood stove and chimney. Then he would hitch our ox, Bully, to the plow and plow the fields.

Exercise Faith:

- What I love about this story is the family's faith in the seeds, faith in the goodness of the earth, and, poor as they are, faith that the tradition of planting will help them all "make do." Think about your own life and work. What are the things you place your faith in every day?

- As dictated by tradition, the family in this story much prefers the hand of a child or pregnant woman than that of an aging family member to plant the seeds. By contrast, today's fast-paced information age calls for science and fact, not tradition, to form the basis of our actions. This story is therefore an example of how our faith helps us live and "make do." What are some of the family traditions that you hold dear, and are they matters of faith?

Spiritual

It is crucial for men and women to have confidence in their abilities. Self-confidence is the key to success. Yet on the other hand, it is important to remember that our confidence in ourselves should be grounded in our reliance on God. Our relationship with

God empowers us so that we can achieve. We can believe in ourselves as long as we are connected to God. In reality, I believe in myself because I believe in the God in me. Apart from God, I do not have faith in myself. My prayer every day is that the Lord will "guide my feet" so that I can find the fulfillment in God's divine will and purpose in my life.

Guide My Feet

Guide my feet
While I run this race (yes, my Lord!)
Guide my feet
While I run this race (yes, my Lord!)
Guide my feet
While I run this race,
For I don't want to run this race in vain! (race in vain!)

Hold my hand
While I run this race (yes, my Lord!)
Hold my hand
While I run this race (yes, my Lord!)
Hold my hand
While I run this race,
For I don't want to run this race in vain! (race in vain!)

Stand by me
While I run this race (yes, my Lord!)
Stand by me
While I run this race (yes, my Lord!)
Stand by me
While I run this race,
For I don't want to run this race in vain! (race in vain!)

I'm your child
While I run this race (yes, my Lord!)
I'm your child
While I run this race (yes, my Lord!)
I'm your child
While I run this race,
For I don't want to run this race in vain! (race in vain!)

Search my heart
While I run this race (yes, my Lord!)
Search my heart
While I run this race (yes, my Lord!)
Search my heart
While I run this race,
For I don't want to run this race in vain! (race in vain!)

Exercise Faith:

* I love this song for its reminder, "I'm your child." Our faith is an acknowledgment that we are all children of God. We live faithfully when we acknowledge that we can't run this race on our own. From the most wizened of our senior citizens to the presidents of Fortune 500 companies to the most powerful of international leaders, we are all children of God. Add this refrain to your own prayers this week: "I'm your child while I run this race."

Julius Lester

*A*uthor, columnist, folksinger, and radio personality Julius Lester was born in 1939 in St. Louis. The great-grandson of slaves, he studied and wrote about slavery in numerous books for children, including the 1968 Newbery Medal runner-

up, To Be a Slave, *the 1969 collection* Black Folktales, *from which this story is taken, and* Why Heaven Is Far Away, *published in 2002.*

People Who Could Fly

It happened long, long ago, when black people were taken from their homes in Africa and forced to come here to work as slaves. They were put onto ships, and many died during the long voyage across the Atlantic Ocean. Those that survived stepped off the boats into a land they had never seen, a land they never knew existed, and they were put into the fields to work. Many refused, and they were killed. Others would work, but when the white man's whip lashed their backs to make them work harder, they would turn and fight. And some of them killed the white men with the whips. Others were killed by the white men. Some would run away and try to go back home, back to Africa where there were no white people, where they worked their own land for the good of each other, not for the good of white men. Some of those who tried to go back to Africa would walk until they came to the ocean, and then they would walk into the water, and no one knows if they did walk to Africa through the water or if they drowned. It didn't matter. At least they were no longer slaves.

Now when the white man forced Africans onto the slave-ships, he did not know, nor did he care, if he took the village musicians, artists, or witch doctors. As long as they were black and looked strong, he wanted them—men, women, and children. Thus, he did not know that sometimes there would be a witch doctor among those he had captured. If he had known, and had also known that the witch doctor was the medium of the gods, he would have thought twice. But he did not care. These black men and women were not people to him. He looked at them and counted each one as so much money for his pocket.

It was to a plantation in South Carolina that one boatload of Africans was brought. Among them was the son of a witch doctor who had not completed by many months studying the secrets of the gods from his father. This young man carried with him the secrets and powers of the generations of Africa.

One day, one hot day when the sun singed the very hair on the head, they were working in the fields. They had been in the fields since before the sun rose, and, as it made its journey to the highest part of the sky, the very air seemed to be on fire. A young woman, her body curved with the child that grew deep inside her, fainted.

Before her body struck the ground, the white man with the whip was riding toward her on his horse. He threw water in her face. "Get back to work, you lazy nigger! There ain't going to be no sitting down on the job as long as I'm here." He cracked the whip against her back and, screaming, she staggered to her feet.

All work had stopped as the Africans watched, saying nothing.

"If you niggers don't want a taste of the same, you'd better get to work!"

They lowered their heads and went back to work. The young witch doctor worked his way slowly toward the young mother-to-be, but before he could reach her, she collapsed again, and the white man with the whip was upon her, lashing her until her body was raised from the ground by the sheer violence of her sobs. The young witch doctor worked his way to her side and whispered to the person beside her. He told the next person, and on around the field it went. They did it so quickly and quietly that the white man with the whip noticed nothing.

A few moments later, someone else in the field fainted, and, as the white man with the whip rode toward him, the young witch doctor shouted, "Now!" He uttered a strange word, and the person who had fainted rose from the ground, and moving his arms like wings, he flew into the sky and out of sight.

The man with the whip looked around at the Africans, but they only stared into the distance, tiny smiles softening their lips. "Who did that? Who was that who yelled out?" No one said anything. "Well, just let me get my hands on him."

Not too many minutes had passed before the young woman fainted once again. The man was almost upon her when the young witch doctor shouted, "Now!" and uttered a strange word.

She, too, rose from the ground and, waving her arms like wings, she flew into the distance and out of sight.

This time the man with the whip knew who was responsible, and as he pulled back his arm to lash the young witch doctor, the young man yelled, "Now! Now! Everyone!" He uttered the strange word, and all of the Africans dropped their hoes, stretched out their arms, and flew away, back to their home, back to Africa.

That was long ago, and no one new remembers what word it was that the young witch doctor knew that could make people fly. But who knows? Maybe one morning someone will awake with a strange word on his tongue and, uttering it, we will all stretch out our arms and take to the air, leaving these blood-drenched fields of our misery.

Exercise Faith:

- In the time of slavery, telling stories like this one was a way for African Americans to keep their spirits alive. Those who were not able to escape told of those who were and so the hope for freedom was passed on through an oral history tradition. Your legacy could be a compilation of faith testimonies. Be generous in your telling of hopeful stories.

- For millions of oppressed people, faith in something better than a current circumstance can help to bring about change. Think of a way you can bring about a better reality for someone you know. Then act on your idea.

- Hebrews 11:1–3 tells us something of the meaning of faith: "Now faith is the substance of things hoped for, the evidence of things not seen. For by it the elders obtained a good report. Through faith we understand that the worlds were framed by the word of God, so that things which are seen were not made of things which do appear." Are you able to take action based on what cannot be seen?

Susan L. Taylor

Susan L. Taylor, *editorial director of* Essence, *has been inspiring African Americans to be their best since she joined the magazine in 1970. Taylor's words of wisdom, imparted in her column, "In the Spirit," come from the heart: She has survived divorce, single motherhood, abuse, and self-doubt. This excerpt from Taylor's collection* In the Spirit *speaks to the importance of exercising faith on a daily basis.*

from In the Spirit

We learn most about the unlimited breadth and depth of God's love for us when our faith is tested. Often it's when we are at the point of despair, when we have exhausted all of our limited human solutions, that we finally surrender to God and trust the Holy Spirit to have its way in us.

It has been so with me. During times of crisis my faith has been so shaken that I feared my life would never get better. But it's also been in my darkest hours—when my reasoning mind fails to see the larger spiritual cycles at work—that I've grown in awareness of God's unfailing love and infinite power. The seeds of faith are always alive in us, but sometimes it takes a crisis to provoke them to grow.

It's true that a worried mind saps energy, feeds the blues, and fuels a negative cycle. But sometimes a case of the blues is one of the ways God beckons us. My greatest insights have been shaped by my greatest challenges. The same is probably true for you. Life is very much like a schoolroom: It gives us the lessons and tests we need to develop and grow. Every crisis in our lives is a call toward the Holy One. If, early on, we can recognize the opportunity for growth inherent in each obstacle in our path, we will reduce the amount of energy expended and pain endured in repeating the same lessons.

We all want to avoid pain and suffering as much as possible, but they are intrinsic to life. Although we cannot totally avoid emotional pain, we can get a jump on handling it at the first symptom. Just as you might treat yourself with vitamin C to stave off a cold, treating yourself with a dose of active faith—making a conscious effort to stand firm and to put your faith in God—will stave off fear and lead you toward a new beginning.

Once a crisis is history, you can easily look back on it and see how the experience expanded your awareness and helped you to grow. But it is while you are at a critical juncture that you must resist giving your power to panic, anger, or fear. This is when you must use your power to tame your mind and have faith in the truth. Spirit is always at the center of your being; therefore, everything in your life, regardless of appearance, is in Divine Order. During any crisis, pause before you act and focus your energy inward to your highest state of consciousness, where infinite knowledge, wisdom, and strength abide.

Each time we face and grow through a painful situation, we are made stronger, wiser, whole again. Intellectual insecurity coaxed me to return to school. Financial and emotional struggles as a single mother compelled me to become more focused, more disciplined, to *get* up when I wanted to *give* up.

Our biggest problems in life come not so much from the difficulties we confront but from how we perceive and respond to them. I've stayed depressed for weeks before remembering I had a choice: I could continue to dwell on the problem and the many ways in which it could ruin my life, or I could take charge of my thoughts, uplift my faith, and move my feet in a positive direction. If we act with the confidence of faith when facing life's daily difficulties and frustrations, each day we will bring our faith forward, increasing and strengthening it. Then we will have the inner assurance and the emotional strength to surmount the big stuff. As you practice awareness of the Presence within you as a conscious moment-to-moment mental exercise, living your faith becomes a life habit.

The habit of faith is as simple as the habit of facing the light instead of the dark when you want to see. Toward the light is the truth. Everything you need to live fully will always be provided.

Exercise Faith:

- In contemporary society, we daily face challenges that can derail our faith: the threat of downsizings, unsafe schools, terrorism at home and abroad. These realities can pull our emotions into a downward spiral and we can lose sight of the fact that God has our back. In these trying times, exercising our faith is an essential act. When challenges are thrown in your path, take a breath, then take a "time-out" to remember the wisdom of 2 Corinthians 13:5: "Examine yourselves, whether ye be in the faith; prove your own selves. Know ye not your own selves, how that Jesus Christ is in you, except ye be reprobates?"

- Taylor writes, "The habit of faith is as simple as the habit of facing the light instead of the dark when you want to see. Toward the light is the truth. Everything you need to live fully will always be provided." The habit of faith *is* simple, but it does take some work. We all know that healthy habits, like going to the gym three times a week, take time to click. Remember that building your faith also takes work. Read James 2:14: "What does it profit, my brethren, though a man say he hath faith, and have not works? Can faith save him?" Work *at* your faith and add good works *to* your faith.

- What are your own habits of faith? Do you believe in what you cannot see? Do you look to the future and see more than what is present? Are there habits you need to change in order to have more faith? Reflect on the time when you failed to achieve something due to a lack of faith and then make a commitment never to lose your faith again. Think of ways that you can exercise faith in your life.

- Sometimes the only way to develop faith is by acting as if you have it. If you find your faith wavering or going through a dry spell, try setting aside a time each day to *practice* believing anyway.

Spiritual

T his African American spiritual is inspired by Jeremiah 8:21–23. In the scriptures, the Prophet Jeremiah bemoans the stubbornness of the people of Israel to
take advantage of the cures available to them. The land of Gilead was famous for the
medicinal plants and oils that were abundant there, but the actual "balm" to which this
song refers is the spiritual balm of Christ.

There Is a Balm in Gilead

There is a balm in Gilead
to make the wounded whole.
There is a balm in Gilead
to heal the sin-sick soul.

Sometimes I feel discouraged,
and think my work's in vain,
but then the Holy Spirit
revives my soul again.

Don't ever feel discouraged,
For Jesus is your friend,
And if you lack for knowledge,
He'll not refuse to lend.

If you cannot preach like Peter,
if you cannot pray like Paul,
you can tell the love of Jesus
and say, "He died for all."

Exercise Faith:

- Read Jeremiah 6–8. The people of Israel were told, "Stand ye in the ways, and see, and ask for the old paths, where is the good way, and walk therein, and ye shall find rest for your souls" (6:16). They said, "We will not hearken" [walk in it] (6:17). By rejecting the teachings, they seem to say that they do not need help and are autonomous. But in singing this hymn—and answering the prophet Jeremiah's call emphatically ("There is a balm in Gilead!")—we acknowledge that we do need help outside of ourselves. We cannot stand alone. We need our faith to sustain us.

- Spiritual and emotional healing is available to all who have faith. Our ancestors understood the power of faith and sang about its hope. Strive to exercise your faith when you are discouraged. Apply the balm of Gilead.

Bible

The woman in this passage is perhaps the most preached-about woman in the African American church. Her story has been told from pulpits and lecterns across this country. Even more than Mary, Esther, or Ruth, this woman seems to capture our attention.

For twelve long years, she has suffered and endured the tragedy of a broken and sick body, the victim of a disorder that the Gospel writers Mark and Luke describe as "an issue of blood." Weakened, poverty-stricken, and outcast, she nevertheless maintains such a strong faith that she eventually makes a demand on the power of God that brings total and immediate deliverance.

"The Woman with an Issue of Blood," retold here from Mark 5:25–34, speaks directly to our condition and our experience. Her desperation and frustration is the embodiment of black people's intense desire for wholeness and restoration to legitimate personhood. Because her faith and determination effected her healing, she is the woman who shows us how to turn our tragedies into triumph and sorrow into joy.

The Woman with an Issue of Blood

There was a certain woman who had an issue of blood for twelve years. She had suffered much under many physicians and had spent all that she had and had not gotten better, but rather, grew worse.

When she heard that Jesus was passing through town, she found the multitude of his followers and pressed up behind him until she was able to touch his garment.

For she said, "If only I may touch his clothes, I shall be made well."

Immediately, the fountain of her blood was dried up, and she felt in her body that she was healed of that plague.

But Jesus, knowing that power had gone forth from him, immediately turned around in the crowd and said, "Who touched my garments?"

His disciples said to him, "You see the crowd pressing around you, and yet you say, 'Who touched me?'"

But Jesus looked around to see who had done it.

And the woman, frightened and trembling, knowing what had occurred within her, came and fell down before him and told him the whole truth.

And he said to her, "Daughter, your faith has made you well; go in peace and be healed of your disease."

Exercise Faith:

- The woman in this story speaks openly about her faith. Are you comfortable with your faith in the same way? Make a list of things you believe in with all of your heart.

- Unlike the woman in this story, we may not be confronted with a tangible manifestation of God. Does this fact make it more difficult for us to express our faith? How do you express your faith in your everyday life? Are you able to be as persistent as this woman was?

- Jesus asks, "Who touched me?" and draws attention to the woman. Have you ever been called upon to make your faith public? If so, how did you respond? Was it easy or uncomfortable? Does it depend on the setting? Church need not be the only context for public displays of faith.

Nella Larsen

The daughter of a Danish mother and West Indian father, Nella Larsen was one of the most prolific writers of the Harlem Renaissance. Questions surrounding her African American heritage and an accusation of plagiarism, however, proved detrimental to her literary career. Scholars have noted that Nella Larsen herself was not particularly religious; nevertheless, this passage captures beautifully one woman's transcendent faith experience. This excerpt is from Larsen's novel Quicksand.

from Quicksand

The day was a rainy one. Helga Crane, stretched out on her bed, felt herself so broken physically, mentally, that she had given up thinking. But back and forth in her staggered brain wavering, incoherent thoughts shot shuttle-like. Her pride would have shut out these humiliating thoughts and painful visions of herself. The effort was too great. She felt alone, isolated from all other human beings, separated even from her own anterior existence by the disaster of yesterday. Over and over, she repeated: "There's nothing left but to go now." Her anguish seemed unbearable.

For days, for weeks, voluptuous visions had haunted her. Desire had burned in her flesh with uncontrollable violence. The wish to give herself had been so intense that Dr. Anderson's surprising, trivial apology loomed as a direct refusal of the offering. Whatever outcome she had expected, it had been something else than this, this mortification, this feeling of ridicule and self-loathing, this knowledge that she had deluded herself. It was all, she told herself, as unpleasant as possible. Almost she wished she could die. Not quite. It wasn't that she was afraid of death, which had, she thought, its picturesque aspects. It was rather that she knew she would not die. And death, after the debacle, would but intensify its absurdity. Also, it would reduce her, Helga Crane, to unimportance, to nothingness. Even in her unhappy present state, that did not appeal to her. Gradually, reluctantly, she began to know that the blow to her self-esteem, the certainty of having proved herself a silly fool, was perhaps the severest hurt which she had suffered. It was her self-assurance that had gone down in the crash. After all, what Dr. Anderson thought didn't matter. She could escape from the discomfort of his knowing gray eyes. But she couldn't escape from sure knowledge that she had made a fool of herself. This angered her further and she struck the wall with her hands and jumped up and began hastily to dress herself. She couldn't go on with the analysis. It was too hard. Why bother, when she could add nothing to the obvious fact that she had been a fool?

"I can't stay in this room any longer. I must get out or I'll choke." Her self-knowledge had increased her anguish. Distracted, agitated, incapable of containing herself, she tore open drawers and closets, trying desperately to take some interest in the selection of her apparel.

It was evening and still raining. In the streets, unusually deserted, the electric lights cast dull glows. Helga Crane, walking rapidly, aimlessly, could decide on no definite destination. She had not thought to take umbrella or even rubbers. Rain and wind whipped cruelly about her, drenching her garments and chilling her body. Soon the foolish little satin shoes which she wore were sopping wet. Unheeding these physical discomforts, she went on, but at the open corner of One Hundred and Thirty-eighth Street a sudden more ruthless gust of wind ripped the small hat from her head. In the next minute the black clouds opened wider and spilled their water with unusual fury. The streets became swirling rivers. Helga Crane, forgetting her mental torment, looked about anxiously for a sheltering taxi. A few taxis sped by, but inhabited, so she began desperately to struggle through wind and rain toward one of the buildings, where she could take shelter in a store or a doorway. But another whirl of wind lashed her and, scornful of her slight strength, tossed her into the swollen gutter.

Now she knew beyond all doubt that she had no desire to die, and certainly not there nor then. Not in such a messy, wet manner. Death had lost all of its picturesque aspects to the girl lying soaked and soiled in the flooded gutter. So, though she was very tired and very weak, she dragged herself up and succeeded finally in making her way to the store whose blurred light she had marked for her destination.

She had opened the door and had entered before she was aware that inside people were singing a song which she was conscious of having heard years ago—hundreds of years, it seemed. Repeated over and over, she made out the words:

> *. . . Showers of blessings,*
> *Showers of blessings . . .*

She was conscious too of a hundred pairs of eyes upon her and she stood there, drenched and disheveled, at the door of this improvised meeting-house.

> *. . . Showers of blessings . . .*

The appropriateness of the song, with its constant reference to showers, the ridiculousness of herself in such surroundings, was too much for Helga Crane's frayed nerves. She sat down on the floor, a dripping heap, and laughed and laughed and laughed.

It was into a shocked silence that she laughed. For at the first hysterical peal the words of the song had died in the singers' throats, and the wheezy organ had lapsed into stillness. But in a moment there were hushed solicitous voices; she was assisted to her feet and led haltingly to a chair near the low platform at the far end of the room. On one side of her a tall, angular black woman under a queer hat sat down, on the other a fattish yellow man with huge, outstanding ears and long, nervous hands.

The singing began again, this time a low wailing thing:

Oh, the bitter shame and sorrow
That a time could ever be,
When I let the Savior's pity
Plead in vain, and proudly answered:
"All of self and none of thee,
All of self and none of thee."

Yet he found me, I beheld him,
Bleeding on the cursed tree;
Heard him pray: "Forgive them, Father."
And my wistful heart said faintly,
"Some of self and some of thee,
Some of self and some of thee."

There were, it appeared, endless moaning verses. Behind Helga a woman had begun to cry audibly, and soon, somewhere else, another. Outside, the wind still bellowed. The wailing singing went on:

. . . *Less of self and more of thee,*
Less of self and more of thee.

Helga too began to weep, at first silently, softly; then with great racking sobs. Her nerves were so torn, so aching, her body so wet, so cold! It was a relief to cry unrestrainedly, and she gave herself freely to soothing tears, not noticing that the groaning and sobbing of those about her had increased, unaware that the grotesque ebony figure at her side had begun gently to pat her arm to the rhythm of the singing and to croon softly: "Yes, chile, yes, chile." Nor did she notice the furtive glances that the man on her other side cast at her between his fervent shouts of "Amen!" and "Praise God for a sinner!"

She did notice, though, that the tempo, the atmosphere of the place, had changed, and gradually she ceased to weep and gave her attention to what was happening about her. Now they were singing:

. . . Jesus knows all about my troubles. . . .

Men and women were swaying and clapping their hands, shouting and stamping their feet to the frankly irreverent melody of the song. Without warning the woman at her side threw off her hat, leaped to her feet, waved her long arms, and shouted shrilly: "Glory! Hallelujah!" and then, in a wild, ecstatic fury jumped up and down before Helga, clutching at the girl's soaked coat, and screamed: "Come to Jesus, you pore los' Jesebel!"

At this the short brown man on the platform raised a placating hand and sanctimoniously delivered himself of the words: "Remembah de words of our Mastah: 'Let him that is without sin cast de first stone.' Let us pray for our errin sistah."

Helga Crane was amused, angry, disdainful, as she sat there, listening to the preacher praying for her soul. But though she was contemptuous, she was being too well entertained to leave. And it was, at least, warm and dry. So she stayed, listening to the fervent exhortation to God to save her and to the zealous shoutings and groanings of the congregation. Particularly she was interested in the writhings and weepings of the feminine portion, which seemed to predominate. Little by little the performance took on an almost Bacchic vehemence. Behind her, before her, beside her, frenzied women gesticulated, screamed, wept, and tottered to the praying of the preacher, which had gradually become a cadenced chant. When at last he ended, another took up the plea in the same moaning chant, and then another. It went on and on without pause with the persistence of some unconquerable faith exalted beyond time and reality.

Fascinated, Helga Crane watched until there crept upon her an indistinct horror of an unknown world. She felt herself in the presence of a nameless people, observing rites of a remote obscure origin. The faces of the men and women took on the aspect of a dim vision. "This," she whispered to herself, "is terrible. I must get out of here." But the horror held her. She remained motionless, watching, as if she lacked the strength to leave the place—foul, vile, and terrible, with its mixture of breaths, its contact of bodies, its concerted convulsions, all in wild appeal for a single soul. Her soul.

And as Helga watched and listened, gradually a curious influence penetrated her; she felt an echo of the weird orgy resound in her own heart; she felt herself possessed by the same madness; she too felt a brutal desire to shout and fling herself about. Frightened at the strength of the obsession, she gathered herself for one last effort to escape, but vainly. In her rising, weakness and nausea from last night's unsuccessful attempt to make herself drunk overcame her. She had eaten nothing since yesterday. She fell forward against the crude railing which enclosed the little platform. For a single moment she remained there in silent stillness, because she was afraid she was going to be sick. And in that moment she was lost—or saved. The yelling figures about her pressed forward, closing her in on all sides. Maddened, she grasped at the railing, and with no previous intention began to yell like one insane, drowning every other clamor, while torrents of tears streamed down her face. She was unconscious of the words she uttered, or their meaning—"Oh, God, mercy, mercy. Have mercy on me!"—but she repeated them over and over.

From those about her came a thunderclap of joy. Arms were

stretched toward her with savage frenzy. The women dragged themselves upon their knees or crawled over the floor like reptiles, sobbing and pulling their hair and tearing off their clothing. Those who succeeded in getting near to her leaned forward to encourage the unfortunate sister, dropping hot tears and beads of sweat upon her bare arms and neck.

The thing became real. A miraculous calm came upon her. Life seemed to expand, and to become very easy. Helga Crane felt within her a supreme aspiration toward the regaining of simple happiness, a happiness unburdened by the complexities of the lives she had known. About her the tumult and the shouting continued, but in a lesser degree. Some of the more exuberant worshipers had fainted into inert masses, the voices of others were almost spent. Gradually the room grew quiet and almost solemn, and to the kneeling girl time seemed to sink back into the mysterious grandeur and holiness of far-off simpler centuries.

Exercise Faith:

- This passage is a vivid description of the transformative power of a moment of grace. Many Christians go their whole lives waiting for just such a moment to happen. And while the moment doesn't always happen for everyone, we should nevertheless be ready for it in case it does. As Helga Crane illustrates, even those of us who are "amused, angry, disdainful" are not outside the boundary of faith's calling.

- "The thing became real." What do you think this sentence means in the context of this story? In the context of faith?

- Helga Crane is miserable and unhappy, and while trying to escape the rain, she stumbles into a churchful of worshipers singing, "Showers of blessings." Helga is aware of the "ridiculousness" of the situation. The obvious metaphor of a church sanctuary in the middle of a rainstorm is almost more than she can bear. But the fact that Helga is aware of how crazy it all seems suggests that Larsen understands that faith is not a neat and tidy virtue. Are there ridiculous circumstances that have brought you to your own spiritual understanding?

- If we try to deconstruct or analyze faith, we will be disappointed. Instead, pray that your heart will be open to the "mysterious grandeur and holiness" of faith. Like Helga, you may be overcome with a "miraculous calm."

C. A. Tindley

Born into slavery in 1856, Charles Albert Tindley taught himself to read and write and eventually became a highly regarded pastor in the city of Philadelphia. Named in his honor in 1924, the Tindley Temple United Methodist Church is today a thriving ministry and a lasting testament to the power of faith. Church hymns are legendary in the African American faith experience. Without such hymns as Tindley's "Stand By Me," many of our brothers and sisters would not have made it through the trials in life.

Stand by Me

When the storms of life are raging,
Stand by me, stand by me.
When the storms of life are raging,
Stand by me, stand by me.

When the world is tossing me,
Like a ship out on the sea:
Thou who knowest all about it,
Stand by your child, stand by me.

In the midst of persecution,
Stand by me, stand by me.
In the midst of persecution,
Stand by me, stand by me.

When my foes in battle array
Undertake to stop my way,
Thou who rescued Paul and Silas,
Stand by me, stand by me.

When I'm growing old and feeble,
Stand by me, stand by me.
When I'm growing old and feeble,
Stand by me, stand by me.

When my life becomes a burden,
And I'm nearing chilly Jordan
O thou Lily of the Valley,
Stand by me, stand by me.

Exercise Faith:

- It has been written of C. A. Tindley that he composed gospel music because it lifted him like "angel wings." Listen to a gospel recording of "Stand by Me" in conjunction with Paul's assurances in Romans 8:37–39: "Nay, in all these things we are more than conquerors through him that loved us. For I am persuaded, that neither death, nor life, nor angels, nor principalities, nor powers, nor things present, nor things to come, nor height, nor depth, nor any other creature, shall be able to separate us from the love of God, which is in Christ Jesus our Lord."

- Gwendolyn Sims Warren, musical director at our Allen African Methodist Episcopal Church in Jamaica, Queens, and author of

Ev'ry Time I Feel the Spirit, has noted the significance of Tindley's beginning this hymn with the words "When the storms of life are raging." Storms in life are not a possibility; rather, they are an inevitability. A constant theme in Tindley's hymns is that it is only through struggle and adversity that we are really changed. How have storms in your life changed you?

- By asking God to "stand by us," we acknowledge our dependence as well as God's dependability. He will stand by us, if we ask, as Tindley does in this hymn. Talk about the related ideas of dependence and dependability with your family.

Carolyn M. Rodgers

Carolyn M. Rodgers was one of the leaders of the Chicago Black Arts Movement in the 1960s. Born in 1945, Rodgers is a graduate of Roosevelt University and the University of Chicago. She is a cofounder of Third World Press and the author of numerous books of poetry. The following is a selection from how i got ovah, which was first published in 1968.

how i got ovah II / It Is Deep II

just when i thought i had gotten away
my mother
called me on the phone
and did not ask,
but commanded me
to come to church with her.

and because i knew so much
and had "escaped"
i thought it a harmless enough act.

i was not prepared for the Holy Ghost.
i was not prepared to be covered by the
blood of Jesus.

    i was not ready to be dipped in
            the water. . . .
i could not drink the water turned wine.

and so i went back another day
trying to understand the mysteries
of mystical life the "intellectual"
purity of mystical light.
and that Sunday evening while i was
sitting there and the holy gospel choir
was singing
    "oh oh oh oh somebody touched me"
        somebody touched me.
           and when i turned around to
see what it was whoever touched me wanted
my mother leaned over and whispered in my ear
    "musta been the hand of the Lord"

Exercise Faith:

- After reading this poem and studying the Proverbs, what meaning does the title hold for you? Ask your family how Rodgers plays with the expression "getting ovah." Can one "get over" on God? If we are faithful, perhaps we'll never think we need to try.
- Our African-American experience has always been rooted in faith. In spite of events during the course of the week, despite discrimination, disrespect, and discouragement, when Sunday came, it was off to church. There we entered the worship service with the singing of "We've Come This Far by Faith." Our faith was strengthened and

our resolve to remain strong in the face of obstacles was strengthened. Whether or not you go to church, try to set aside Sunday morning for faith renewal.

- In "how i got ovah," the narrator's mother has clearly been supportive and patient with her daughter's experimentation with a nonreligious lifestyle, but she continues to stress the importance of religion; in fact, she commands her daughter to attend church with her. Because her daughter thinks she is above it all, she decides to attend, dismissing the visit as a "harmless enough act." Her mother's invitation, however, leads to another visit—and this time she is touched by the Holy Ghost. Read Proverbs 1. How does the passage parallel the themes in Rodgers' poem?

- "how i got ovah" speaks to the cultural schism between a black militant daughter and her traditional, churchgoing mother. The daughter, who "knew so much and had 'escaped,'" is not prepared to be touched by the hand of the Lord. But her mother is not surprised. Have you experienced a time in your life when you left the church but were encouraged to "come home" by the elders in your life? Do you think we can ever be truly prepared for God?

Forbearance

An ability to withstand provocation and endure difficulties,
FORBEARANCE grows from our knowledge that patience
will ultimately earn its proper reward.

We must accept that in every human life, some rain will fall. We cannot escape sadness and suffering. We must stop asking ourselves what we can do to avoid the rain and start asking what we can do to weather the storm.

From 1987 to 1988, I endured a series of legal attacks, including false charges of sexual harassment and financial improprieties. With my integrity called into question, pending legal challenges, and high visibility in the media, it was very difficult for me to fulfill my responsibilities as husband, father, pastor, and congressman. The stressful situation soon began affecting my health. Occasional chest pains and nervous stomach slowed me down for a while, but I had to persevere in the midst of discomfort. I tried to maintain a regular schedule. Preaching on Sunday, traveling to Washington as a United States congressman, and remaining focused enough to help my children study for spelling and social studies tests in the midst of media attacks and a trial was one of the biggest challenges of my life. I believed, though, that the key to authentic living was embracing and continuing in my purpose even in the midst of a storm. So I persevered and endured the hardships of that season until I was ultimately cleared of all charges.

The ability to withstand life's hardships without abandoning dreams and purpose is a skill that we all must work to develop. Forbearance, which is the "ability to withstand provocation and endure difficulties" with patience and hope, becomes the very essence of survival. When we get knocked down, it is essential that we know how to get back up. Because hardship and persecution do not exempt us from living with integrity and compassion, our goal must always be to maintain the right attitude in times of trial. Revenge is never the solution; you cannot pick yourself up by putting your adversaries down.

In Jesus' day, the proper method of disciplining those whom you saw as your inferiors was to slap them on the cheek with the open palm of your right hand. In turning the other cheek, Jesus forced his attacker to commit a taboo act, because the attacker would then have to use his left hand or the back of his right hand. In essence, he was challenging them not to respond violently in any way whatsoever. This is the same method that worked so effectively when Dr. Martin Luther King, Jr., led nonviolent protests during the civil rights era.

This explanation is important, because we must not misunderstand the concept of forbearance. It is *enduring* in spite of injustice and economic upheaval, *persevering* while surrounded by trouble and distress, and *surviving* despite hardship.

The entries in this chapter are written by men and women who lived through difficult times and survived despite overwhelming burdens. As African Americans, we can understand the necessity of forbearance, because our experience in this country has been one riddled with harsh treatment and oppression, yet our history as a people is replete with individuals, families, and communities that refused to be crushed by external pressure. Our past is filled with instances in which we fought injustice with truth, love, and justice. We must never forget how our people responded to violence with dignity and determination as they sat at lunch counters, rode on buses, demonstrated on the streets, and sat in jails.

As African Americans, we also know how difficult it is to practice forbearance in our daily lives. It is not easy to follow Jesus' teaching and turn the other cheek when our enemies strike us; it is not easy to keep running the race when obstacles are continually placed in our path. But, as this chapter shows, we must learn from our predecessors, who have kept the spirit of our black soul shining through centuries of stormy weather.

Maya Angelou

P oet and playwright Maya Angelou has chronicled her rich life in no fewer than six memoirs. The following excerpt is from the first volume, I Know Why the Caged Bird Sings, *published in 1970. In this passage, Angelou, as a young girl, learns an object lesson from her grandmother. A strong, religious individual, Angelou's grandmother owned a small country store in Arkansas, where the Ku Klux Klan, segregation, and insults from school-age white girls provided plenty of opportunities to practice the virtue of forbearance.*

from I Know Why the Caged Bird Sings

O ne summer morning, after I had swept the dirt yard of leaves, spearmint-gum wrappers, and Vienna-sausage labels, I raked the yellow-red dirt, and made half-moons carefully, so that the design stood out clearly and masklike. I put the rake behind the Store and came through the back of the house to find Grandmother on the front porch in her big, wide white apron. The apron was so stiff by virtue of the starch that it could have stood alone. Momma was admiring the yard, so I joined her. It truly looked like a flat redhead that had been raked with a big-toothed comb. Momma didn't say anything but I knew she liked it. She looked over toward the school principal's house and to the right at Mr. McElroy's. She was hoping one of those community pillars would see the design before the day's business wiped it out. Then she looked upward to the school. My head had swung with hers, so at just about the same time we saw a troop of the powhite-trash kids marching over the hill and down by the side of the school.

I looked to Momma for direction. She did an excellent job of sagging from her waist down, but from the waist up she seemed to be pulling for the top of the oak tree across the road. Then she began to moan a hymn. Maybe not to moan, but the tune was so slow and the meter so strange that she could have been moaning. She didn't look at me again. When the children reached halfway down the hill, halfway to the Store, she said without turning, "Sister, go on inside."

I wanted to beg her, "Momma, don't wait for them. Come on inside with me. If they come in the Store, you go to the bedroom and let me wait on them. They only frighten me if you're around. Alone I know how to handle them." But of course I couldn't say anything, so I went in and stood behind the screen door.

Before the girls got to the porch I heard their laughter crackling and popping like pine logs in a cooking stove. I suppose my lifelong paranoia was born in those cold, molasses-slow minutes. They came finally to stand on the ground in front of Momma. At first they pretended seriousness. Then one of them wrapped her right arm in the crook of her left, pushed out her mouth, and started to hum. I realized that she was aping my grandmother. Another said, "Naw, Helen, you ain't standing like her. This here's it." Then she lifted her chest, folded her arms, and mocked that strange carriage that was Annie Handerson. Another laughed, "Naw, you can't do it. Your mouth ain't pooched out enough. It's like this."

I thought about the rifle behind the door, but I knew I'd never be able to hold it straight, and the .410, our sawed-off shotgun, which stayed loaded and was fired every New Year's night, was locked in the trunk and Uncle Willie had the key on his chain. Through the fly-specked screen-door, I could see that the arms of Momma's apron jiggled from the vibrations of her humming. But her knees seemed to have locked as if they would never bend again.

She sang on. No louder than before, but no softer either. No slower or faster.

The dirt of the girls' cotton dresses continued on their legs, feet, arms, and faces to make them all of a piece. Their greasy uncolored hair hung down, uncombed, with a grim finality. I knelt to see them better, to remember them for all time. The tears that had slipped down my dress left unsurprising dark spots, and made the front yard blurry and even more unreal. The world had taken a deep breath and was having doubts about continuing to revolve.

The girls had tired of mocking Momma and turned to other means of agitation. One crossed her eyes, stuck her thumbs in both sides of her mouth, and said, "Look here, Annie." Grandmother hummed on and the apron strings trembled. I wanted to throw a handful of black pepper in their faces, to throw lye on them, to scream that they were dirty, scummy peckerwoods, but I knew I was as clearly imprisoned behind the scene as the actors outside were confined to their roles.

One of the smaller girls did a kind of puppet dance while her fellow clowns laughed at her. But the tall one, who was almost a woman, said something very quietly, which I couldn't hear. They all moved backward from the porch, still watching Momma. For an awful second I thought they were going to throw a rock at Momma, who seemed (except for the apron strings) to have turned into stone herself. But the big girl turned her back, bent down, and put her hands flat on the ground—she didn't pick up anything. She simply shifted her weight and did a handstand.

Her dirty bare feet and long legs went straight for the sky. Her dress fell down around her shoulders, and she had on no drawers. The slick pubic hair made a brown triangle where her legs came together. She hung in the vacuum of that lifeless morning for only a few seconds, then wavered and tumbled. The other girls clapped her on the back and slapped their hands.

Momma changed her song to "bread of Heaven, bread of Heaven, feed me till I want no more."

I found that I was praying too. How long could Momma hold out? What new indignity would they think of to subject her to? Would I be able to stay out of it? What would Momma really like me to do?

Then they were moving out of the yard, on their way to town. They bobbed their heads and shook their slack behinds and turned, one at a time:

"Bye, Annie."

"Bye, Annie."

"Bye, Annie."

Momma never turned her head or unfolded her arms, but she stopped singing and said, "Bye, Miz Helen, bye, Miz Ruth, bye, Miz Eloise."

I burst. A firecracker July-the-Fourth burst. How could Momma call them Miz? The mean nasty things. Why couldn't she have come inside the sweet, cool Store when we saw them breasting the hill? What did she prove? And then if they were dirty, mean, and impudent, why did Momma have to call them Miz?

She stood another whole song through and then opened the screen door to look down on me crying in rage. She looked until I looked up.

Her face was a brown moon that shone on me. She was beautiful. Something had happened out there, which I couldn't completely understand, but I could see that she was happy. Then she bent down and touched me as mothers of the church "lay hands on the sick and afflicted" and I quieted.

"Go wash your face, Sister." And she went behind the candy counter and hummed, "Glory, glory, hallelujah, when I lay my burden down."

I threw the well water on my face and used the weekday handkerchief to blow my nose. Whatever the contest had been out front, I knew Momma had won.

I took the rake back to the front yard. The smudged footprints were easy to erase. I worked for a long time on my new design and laid the rake behind the wash pot. When I came back in the Store, I took Momma's hand and we both walked outside to look at the pattern.

It was a large heart with lots of hearts growing smaller inside, and piercing from the outside rim to the smallest heart was an arrow. Momma said, "Sister, that's right pretty." Then she turned back to the Store and resumed, "Glory, glory, hallelujah, when I lay my burden down."

Exercise Forbearance:

- In our daily lives, we regularly have to face the cruelty of others, and we are often tempted to respond in rage, anger, or violence. As we see in this story, Momma refuses to let herself be provoked by harassment. Do you think Momma acted as a hero or a coward?
- Think of a time when you were ridiculed or made fun of. How did you react? If you were faced with the same situation again, would you react differently?
- Despite being mocked and derided, Momma maintains a respectful demeanor. Do you believe that being kind and polite to your enemies can sometimes be the best form of defense, or even offense?

Linda Brent

Harriet Jacobs was one of the very few slave women to write about the slavery experience. Using the pseudonym Linda Brent to protect her relatives, Jacobs wrote Incidents in the Life of a Slave Girl *in 1861 with the help of Lydia Marie Child, a Northern abolitionist. Some of the most harrowing details reported in* Incidents in the Life of a Slave Girl *address the losses she suffered as a child and the unjust treatment of her family.*

from Incidents in the Life of a Slave Girl

I was born a slave, but I never knew it till six years of happy childhood had passed away. My father was a carpenter, and considered so intelligent and skillful in his trade, that, when buildings out of the common line were to be erected, he was sent for from long distances, to be head workman. On condition of paying his mistress two hundred dollars a year, and supporting himself, he was allowed to work at his trade, and manage his own affairs. His strongest wish was to purchase his children; but, though he several times offered his hard earnings for that purpose, he never succeeded. In complexion my parents were a light shade of brownish yellow, and were termed mulattos. They lived together in a comfortable home; and, though we were all slaves, I was so fondly shielded that I never dreamed I was a piece of merchandise, trusted to them for safekeeping, and liable to be demanded of them at any moment. I had one brother, William, who was two years younger than myself—a bright, affectionate child. I had also a great treasure in my maternal grandmother, who was a remarkable woman in many respects. She was the daughter of a planter in South Carolina, who, at his death, left her mother and his three children free, with money to go to St. Augustine, where they had relatives.

It was during the Revolutionary War; and they were captured on their passage, carried back, and sold to different purchasers. Such was the story my grandmother used to tell me; but I do not remember all the particulars. She was a little girl when she was captured and sold to the keeper of a large hotel. I have often heard her tell how hard she fared during childhood. But as she grew older she evinced so much intelligence, and was so faithful, that her master and mistress could not help seeing it was for their interest to take care of such a valuable piece of property. She became an indispensable personage in the household, officiating in all capacities, from cook and wet nurse to seamstress. She was much praised for her cooking; and her nice crackers became so famous in the neighborhood that many people were desirous of obtaining them. In consequence of numerous requests of this kind, she asked permission of her mistress to bake crackers at night, after all the household work was done; and she obtained leave to do it, provided she would clothe herself and her children from the profits. Upon these terms, after working hard all day for her mistress, she began her midnight bakings, assisted by her two oldest children. The business proved profitable; and each year she laid by a little, which was saved for a fund to purchase her children. Her master died, and the property was divided among his heirs. The widow had her dower in the hotel, which she continued to keep open. My grandmother remained in her service as a slave; but her children were divided among her master's children. As she had five, Benjamin, the youngest one, was sold, in order that each heir might have an equal portion of dollars and cents. There was so little difference in our ages that he seemed more like my brother than my uncle. He was a bright, handsome lad, nearly white; for he inherited the complexion my grandmother had derived from Anglo-Saxon ancestors. Though he was only ten years old, seven hundred and twenty dollars were paid for him. His sale was a terrible blow to my grandmother; but she was naturally hopeful, and she went to work with renewed energy, trusting in time to be able to purchase some of her children. She had laid up three hundred dollars, which her mistress one day begged as a loan, promising to pay her soon. The reader probably knows that no promise or writing given to a slave is legally binding; for, according to Southern laws, a slave, being property, can hold no property. When my grandmother lent her hard earning to her mistress, she trusted solely to her honor. The honor of a slaveholder to a slave!

To this good grandmother I was indebted for many comforts. My brother Willie and I often received portions of the crackers, cakes, and preserves she made to sell; and after we ceased to be children we were indebted to her for many more important services.

Such were the unusually fortunate circumstances of my early childhood. When I was six years old, my mother died; and then for the first time, I learned, by the talk around me, that I was a slave. My mother's mistress was the daughter of my grandmother's mistress. She was the foster sister of my mother; they were both nourished at my grandmother's breast. In fact, my mother had been weaned at three months old, that the babe of the mistress might obtain sufficient food. They played together as children; and, when they became women, my mother was a most faithful servant to her whiter foster sister. On her deathbed her mistress promised that her children should never suffer for any thing; and during her lifetime she kept her word. They all spoke kindly of my dead mother, who had been a slave merely in name, but in nature was noble and womanly. I grieved for her, and my young mind was troubled with the thought of who would now take care of me and my little brother. I was told that my home was now to be with her mistress; and I found it a happy one. No toilsome or disagreeable duties were imposed on me. My mistress was so kind to me that I was always glad to do her bidding, and proud to labor for her as much as my young years would permit. I would sit by her side for hours, sewing diligently, with a heart as free from care as that of any free-born white child. When she thought I was tired, she would send me out to run and jump; and away I bounded, to gather berries or flowers to decorate her room. Those were happy days—too happy to last. The slave child had no thought for the morrow; but there came that blight, which too surely waits on every human being born to be a chattel.

When I was nearly twelve years old, my kind mistress sickened and died. As I saw the cheek grow paler, and the eye more glassy, how earnestly I prayed in my heart that she might live! I loved her; for she had been almost like a mother to me. My prayers were not answered. She died, and they buried her in the little churchyard, where, day after day, my tears fell upon her grave.

I was sent to spend a week with my grandmother. I was now old enough to begin to think of the future; and again and again I asked myself what they would do with me. I felt sure I should never find another mistress so kind as the one who was gone. She had promised my dying mother that her children should never suffer for any thing; and when I remembered that, and recalled her many proofs of attachment to me, I could not help having some hope that she had left me free. My friends were almost certain it would be so. They thought she would be sure to do it, on account of my mother's love and faithful service. But, alas! we all know that the memory of a faithful slave does not avail much to save her children from the auction block.

After a brief period of suspense, the will of my mistress was read, and we learned that she had bequeathed me to her sister's daughter, a child of five years old. So vanished our hopes. My mistress had taught me the precepts of God's Word: "Thou shalt love thy neighbor as thyself. Whatsoever ye would that men should do unto you, do ye even so unto them." But I was her slave, and I suppose she did not recognize me as her neighbor. I would give much to blot out from my memory that one great wrong. As a child, I loved my mistress; and, looking back on the happy days I spent with her, I try to think with less bitterness of this act of injustice. While I was with her, she taught me to read and spell; and for this privilege, which so rarely falls to the lot of a slave, I bless her memory.

She possessed but few slaves; and at her death those were all distributed among her relatives. Five of them were my grandmother's children, and had shared the same milk that nourished her mother's children. Notwithstanding my grandmother's long and faithful service to her owners, not one of her children escaped the auction block. These God-breathing machines are no more, in the sight of their masters, than the cotton they plant, or the horses they tend.

Exercise Forbearance:

* Our slave foremothers suffered injustices that are difficult to fathom. Reading Harriet Jacobs's account reminds us that our people were hardworking, industrious, and wanted more than anything to escape slavery and racism. Although their masters and mistresses may have been fond of them (and, in many cases, close relatives), they did not view them as human beings but saw them simply as "God-breathing machines" who were "no more, in the sight of their masters, than the cotton they plant, or the horses they tend." Reading *Incidents in the Life of a Slave Girl* is an emotional experience. Take a moment to contemplate the forbearance of Jacobs and her family and of our brothers and sisters who endured slavery so that we could live today.

* Jacobs writes, "My mistress had taught me the precepts of God's Word: 'Thou shalt love thy neighbor as thyself. Whatsoever ye would that men should do unto you, do ye even so unto them.' But I was her slave, and I suppose she did not recognize me as her neighbor." During slavery, biblical passages, like those in Ephesians 6:5–9, were used to support the enslavement of Africans, which would justify the actions of Jacobs's mistress. However, our ancestors and abolitionists such as Lydia Maria Child also turned to the Bible for its messages of freedom, justice, and righteousness. In fact, the Bible was an instrumental tool in the fight to end slavery (interestingly, others looked to the Bible to justify slavery's continuation and expansion). Consider our ancestors' forbearance in their belief

that it was God's will that they would one day be free as you read 2 Samuel 22:3–4: "The God of my rock; in him will I trust: he is my shield, and the horn of my salvation, my high tower, and my refuge, my saviour; thou savest me from violence. I will call on the Lord, who is worthy to be praised: so shall I be saved from mine enemies."

- Nehemiah 4:9 reads, "...we made our prayer unto our God, and set a watch against them day and night." Discuss how this passage parallels the experiences Jacobs and her ancestors faced under slavery. Today, we often take our families for granted and do not appreciate the fact that we are allowed to legally marry and can keep our families together without the threat of enslavement. However, enslavement often comes in the form of economic and educational disparity, media misrepresentation, and job discrimination. In what ways should our communities counter systems of discrimination and exercise forbearance?

Sterling A. Brown

*S*terling A. Brown, one of the most renowned poets of the Harlem Renaissance, was born in Washington, D.C., in 1901, to a Howard professor and a Fisk graduate. He received an academic scholarship to Williams College and graduated Phi Beta Kappa. He went on to receive a master's degree from Harvard University. After graduation, Brown became a teacher and worked at Virginia Seminary and College, Fisk University, and Howard University, where he taught for forty years. He authored The Southern Road; The Negro in American Fiction; Negro Poetry and Drama; The Negro Caravan; and The Last Ride of Wild Bill and Eleven Narrative Poems. Brown wrote about the lives of blacks in the South during the Harlem Renaissance, a period which focused on the lives of black migrants who had made the long journey to Northern cities. "Strong Men" was first published in The Book of American Negro Poetry, edited by James Weldon Johnson, in 1931. Brown died in 1989.

Strong Men

They dragged you from homeland,
They chained you in coffles,
They huddled you spoon-fashion in filthy hatches,
They sold you to give a few gentlemen ease.

They broke you in like oxen,
They scourged you,
They branded you,
They made your women breeders,
They swelled your numbers with bastards. . . .
They taught you the religion they disgraced.

You sang:

    Keep a-inchin' along
    Lak a po' inch worm. . . .
You sang:
    Bye and bye
    I'm gonna lay down dis heaby load. . . .

You sang:
    Walk togedder, chillen,
    Dontcha git weary. . . .
        The strong men keep a-comin' on
        The strong men git stronger.

They point with pride to the roads you built for them,
They ride in comfort over the rails you laid for them,
They put hammers in your hands
And said—Drive so much before sundown.

You sang:
> Ain't no hammah
> In dis lan',
> Strikes lak mine, bebby,
> Strikes lak mine.

They cooped you in their kitchens,
They penned you in their factories,
They gave you the jobs that they were too good for,
They tried to guarantee happiness to themselves
By shunting dirt and misery to you.

You sang:
> Me an' muh baby gonna shine, shine
> Me an' muh baby gonna shine.
>> The strong men keep a-comin' on
>> The strong men git stronger. . . .

They bought off some of your leaders
You stumbled, as blind men will. . . .
They coaxed you, unwontedly soft-voiced. . . .
You followed a way,
Then laughed as usual.

They heard the laugh and wondered:
Uncomfortable;
Unadmitting a deeper terror . . .
> The strong men keep a-comin' on
> Gittin' stronger. . . .
What, from the slums
Where they have hemmed you,
What, from the tiny huts
They could not keep from you—

What reaches them
Making them ill at ease, fearful?
Today they shout prohibition at you
"Thou shalt not this"
"Thou shalt not that"
"Reserved for whites only"
You laugh.

One thing they cannot prohibit—
    The strong men . . . coming on
The strong men gittin' stronger.
    Strong men . . .
    Stronger . . .

Exercise Forbearance:

- I can think of nothing more inspiring than the image of strong men who keep getting stronger. As painful as the slavery legacy is, Sterling Brown reminds us of the incredible strength and determination of our ancestors. How might we instill the kind of determination celebrated in this poem to current generations of young African American men?

- I love the line "Me an' muh baby gonna shine, shine," because it suggests that couples can work as a team as they begin their lives together. No matter the difficulties, together they will forbear and succeed. How have members of your own family helped you "shine" in difficult times? What has been the impact of forbearance on your marriage and other relationships?

- The African American male, who some say is an endangered species today, must reclaim the spirit of forbearance to avoid this potentially self-fulfilling prophecy. Our future rests upon the acquisition of the forbearance skills our foreparents had. They had an indomitable sense of power in the face of long odds for survival. Their spirit mirrors the assertion of Paul in Romans 8:37: "Nay, in all these things we are more than conquerors through him that loved us." What are some of the forbearance skills necessary for our future survival?

Anne Moody

C ivil rights activist Anne Moody was born in rural Mississippi in 1940, the *daughter of sharecroppers. Her autobiography,* Coming of Age in Mississippi, *published in 1969, describes growing up on a plantation, becoming a civil rights activist at Tougaloo College, and eventually moving to New York. This excerpt details how Moody helped integrate Woolworth's lunch counter in Jackson, Mississippi.*

from Coming of Age in Mississippi

I had counted on graduating in the spring of 1963, but as it turned out, I couldn't because some of my credits still had to be cleared with Natchez College. A year before, this would have seemed like a terrible disaster, but now I hardly even felt disappointed. I had a good excuse to stay on campus for the summer and work with the Movement, and this was what I really wanted to do. I couldn't go home again anyway, and I couldn't go to New Orleans—I didn't have money enough for bus fare.

During my senior year at Tougaloo, my family hadn't sent me one penny. I had only the small amount of money I had earned at Maple Hill. I couldn't afford to eat at school or live in the dorms, so I had gotten permission to move off campus. I had to prove that I could finish school, even if I had to go hungry every day. I knew Raymond and Miss Pearl were just waiting to see me drop out. But something happened to me as I got more and more involved in the Movement. It no longer seemed important to prove anything. I had found something outside myself that gave meaning to my life.

I had become very friendly with my social science professor, John Salter, who was in charge of NAACP activities on campus. All during the year, while the NAACP conducted a boycott of the downtown stores in Jackson, I had been one of Salter's most faithful canvassers and church speakers. During the last week of school, he told me that sit-in demonstrations were about to start in Jackson and that he wanted me to be the spokesman for a team that would sit in at Woolworth's lunch counter. The two other demonstrators would be classmates of mine, Memphis and Pearlena. Pearlena was a dedicated NAACP worker, but Memphis had not been very involved in the Movement on campus. It seemed that the organization had had a rough time finding students who were in a position to go to jail. I had nothing to lose one way or the other. Around ten o'clock the morning of the demonstrations, NAACP headquarters alerted the news services. As a result, the police department was also informed, but neither the policemen nor the newsmen knew exactly where or when the demonstrations would start. They stationed themselves along Capitol Street and waited.

To divert attention from the sit-in at Woolworth, the picketing started at JCPenney a good fifteen minutes before. The pickets were allowed to walk up and down in front of the store three or four times before they were arrested. At exactly 11 A.M., Pearlena, Memphis, and I entered Woolworth's from the rear entrance. We separated as soon as we stepped into the store, and made small purchases from various counters. Pearlena had given Memphis her watch. He was to let us know when it was 11:14. At 11:14 we were to join him near the lunch counter and at exactly 11:15 we were to take seats at it.

Seconds before 11:15 we were occupying three seats at the previously segregated Woolworth's lunch counter. In the beginning the waitresses seemed to ignore us, as if they really didn't know what was going on. Our waitress walked past us a couple of times before she noticed we had started to write our own orders down and realized we wanted service. She asked us what we wanted. We began to read to her from our order slips. She told us that we would be served at the back counter, which was for Negroes.

"We would like to be served here," I said.

The waitress started to repeat what she had said, then stopped in the middle of the sentence. She turned the lights out behind the counter, and she and the other waitresses almost ran to the back of the store, deserting all their white customers. I guess they thought that violence would start immediately after the whites at the counter realized what was going on. There were five or six other people at the counter. A couple of them just got up and walked away. A girl sitting next to me finished her banana split before leaving. A middle-aged white woman who had not yet been served rose from her seat and came over to us. "I'd like to stay here with you," she said, "but my husband is waiting."

The newsmen came in just as she was leaving. They must have discovered what was going on shortly after some of the people began to leave the store. One of the newsmen ran behind the woman who spoke to us and asked her to identify herself. She refused to give her name, but said she was a native of Vicksburg and a former resident of California. When asked why she had said what she had said to us, she replied, "I am in sympathy with the Negro movement." By this time a crowd of cameramen and reporters had gathered around us taking pictures and asking questions, such as Where were we from? Why did we sit in? What organization sponsored it? Were we students? From what school? How were we classified?

I told them that we were all students at Tougaloo College, that we were represented by no particular organization, and that we planned to stay there even after the store closed. "All we want is service" was my reply to one of them. After they had finished probing for about twenty minutes, they were almost ready to leave.

At noon, students from a nearby white high school started pouring in to Woolworth's. When they first saw us they were sort of surprised. They didn't know how to react. A few started to heckle and the newsmen became interested again. Then the white students started chanting all kinds of anti-Negro slogans. We were called a little bit of everything. The rest of the seats except the three we were occupying had been roped off to prevent others from sitting down. A couple of the boys took one end of the rope and made it into a hangman's noose. Several attempts were made to put it around our necks. The crowds grew as more students and adults came in for lunch.

We kept our eyes straight forward and did not look at the crowd except for occasional glances to see what was going on.... Memphis suggested that we pray. We bowed our heads, and all hell broke loose. A man rushed forward, threw Memphis from his seat, and slapped my face. Then another man who worked in the store threw me against an adjoining counter.

Down on my knees on the floor, I saw Memphis lying near the lunch counter with blood running out of the corners of his mouth. As he tried to protect his face, the man who'd thrown him down kept kicking him against the head. If he had worn hard-soled shoes instead of sneakers, the first kick probably would have killed Memphis. Finally a man dressed in plain clothes identified himself as a police officer and arrested Memphis and his attacker.

Pearlena had been thrown to the floor. She and I got back on our stools after Memphis was arrested. There were some white Tougaloo teachers in the crowd. They asked Pearlena and me if we wanted to leave. They said that things were getting too rough. We didn't know what to do. While we were trying to make up our minds, we were joined by Joan Trumpauer. Now there were three of us and we were integrated. The crowd began to chant, "Communists, Communists, Communists." Some old man in the crowd ordered the students to take us off the stools.

"Which one should I get first?" a big husky boy said.

"That white nigger," the old man said.

The boy lifted Joan from the counter by her waist and carried her out of the store. Simultaneously, I was snatched from my stool by two high school students. I was dragged about thirty feet toward the door by my hair when someone made them turn me loose. As I was getting up off the floor, I saw Joan coming back inside. We started back to the center of the counter to join Pearlena. Lois Chaffee, a white Tougaloo faculty member, was now sitting next to her. So Joan and I just climbed across the rope at the front end of the counter and sat down. There were now four of us, two whites and two Negroes, all women. The mob started smearing us with ketchup, mustard, sugar, pies, and everything on the counter. Soon Joan and I were joined by John Salter, but the moment he sat down he was hit on the jaw with what appeared to be brass knuckles. Blood gushed from his face and someone threw salt into the open wound. Ed King, Tougaloo's chaplain, rushed to him.

At the other end of the counter, Lois and Pearlena were joined by George Raymond, a CORE field-worker and a student from Jackson State College. Then a Negro high school boy sat down next to me. The mob took spray paint from the counter and sprayed it on the new demonstrators. The high school student had on a white shirt; the word "nigger" was written on his back with red spray paint.

We sat there for three hours taking a beating when the manager decided to close the store because the mob had begun to go wild with stuff from other counters. He begged and begged everyone to leave. But even after fifteen minutes of begging, no one budged. They would not leave until we did. Then Dr. Beittel, the president of Tougaloo College, came running in. He said he had just heard what was happening.

About ninety policemen were standing outside the store; they had been watching the whole thing through the windows, but had not come in to stop the mob or do anything. President Beittel went outside and asked Captain Ray to come and escort us out. The captain refused, stating the manager had to invite him in before he could enter the premises, so Dr. Beittel himself brought us out. He had told the police that they had better protect us after we were outside the store. When we got outside, the policemen formed a single line that blocked the mob from us. However, they were allowed to throw at us everything they had collected. Within ten minutes, we were picked up by Reverend King in his station wagon and taken to the NAACP headquarters on Lynch Street.

After the sit-in, all I could think of was how sick Mississippi whites were. They believed so much in the segregated Southern way of life, they would kill to preserve it. I sat there in the NAACP office and thought of how many times they had killed when this way of life was threatened. I knew that the killing had just begun. "Many more will die before it is over with," I thought. Before the sit-in, I had always hated the whites in Mississippi. Now I knew it was impossible for me to hate sickness. The whites had a disease, an incurable disease in its final stage. What were our chances against such a disease? I thought of the students, the young Negroes who had just begun to protest, as young interns. When these young interns got older, I thought, they would be the best doctors in the world for social problems.

Before we were taken back to campus, I wanted to get my hair washed. It was stiff with dried mustard, ketchup, and sugar. I stopped in at a beauty shop across the street from the NAACP ofice. I didn't have on any shoes because I had lost them when I was dragged across the floor at Woolworth's. My stockings were sticking to my legs from the mustard that had dried on them. The hairdresser took one look at me and said, "My land, you were in the sit-in, huh?"

"Yes," I answered. "Do you have time to wash my hair and style it?"

"Right away," she said, and she meant right away. There were three other ladies already waiting, but they seemed glad to let me go ahead of them. The hairdresser was real nice. She even took my stockings off and washed my legs while my hair was drying.

There was a mass rally that night at the Pearl Street Church in Jackson, and the place was packed. People were standing two abreast in the aisles. Before the speakers began, all the sit-inners walked out on the stage and were introduced by Medgar Evers. People stood and applauded for what seemed like thirty minutes or more. Medgar told the audience that this was just the beginning of such demonstrations. He asked them to pledge themselves to unite in a massive offensive against segregation in Jackson, and throughout the state. The rally ended with "We Shall Overcome" and sent home hundreds of determined people. It seemed as though Mississippi Negroes were about to get together at last.

Exercise Forbearance:

- In the 1960s, our black mothers and fathers led the fight for civil rights against overwhelming forces. They wanted to entirely overhaul a deep-rooted social system of racism and segregation. Did they succeed? Was the tactic of nonviolence effective? Would there have been a better way to fight injustice? What are some techniques presently available to us for fighting injustice?
- Imagine you were a demonstrator in this same Woolworth's. How might you have reacted?
- Make a list of things you think are unfair in your life and in our society. Then discuss how, with the help of your family and community, you might be able to change those things.

Bible

Our nation's judicial system, with its disproportionate sentencing practices and unfair treatment of African Americans, has instilled into our community a deep sense of injustice. In this story retold from Matthew 26:59–68, we identify with Jesus' predicament when he is put on trial before Pontius Pilate and the high priest and elders. In Jesus' trial, there are no witnesses to any crime, and those who speak out against him provide false testimony. Jesus' silence in the face of contrived accusations demonstrates his strength, confidence, and forbearance.

Jesus Before the High Priest

Jesus, accused of having broken the law, was brought before the scribes, the elders, and all the council members. The high priest sought to prove that Jesus had committed crimes punishable by death.

Lacking evidence, the council searched for false testimony to use against Jesus. Finally, two false witnesses came forward, claiming that Jesus had said, "I am able to destroy the temple of God and to build it in three days."

The high priest rose and asked Jesus whether the claims were true. "What is this testimony that these men are bringing against you? Have you no answer to make?"

But Jesus held his peace and remained silent.

Angered, the high priest said to Jesus, "I charge you under oath by the living God: Tell us if you are Christ, the Son of God."

"Yes, it is as you say," Jesus replied. "But I say to you all: In the future, you will see the Son of man sitting aside the right hand of the Mighty One and coming on the clouds of heaven."

The high priest then tore his clothes and said, "He has spoken blasphemy! What further need have we of witnesses? You have all heard his blasphemy. What is your judgment?"

The council members answered, "He deserves death."

Then, they spat in his face and struck him with their fists. Others slapped him with the palms of their hands, saying, "Prophesy to us, Christ. Who hit you?"

Exercise Forbearance:

- With the truth on his side, Jesus refuses to answer the men who bring false charges against him. What are some reasons that Jesus does not speak up? Does it make you angry that Jesus does not speak up on his own behalf? Do you think that he was silent because he understood that the sacrifice of his life would have a greater impact on love and justice than mere rhetoric?

- As African Americans, we have long had our voices silenced, and we have sometimes been deprived of our basic right to free speech. Is it dangerous to keep quiet when we are asked to speak out in situations in which no answer is the correct one? Can we still find power in holding our peace and remaining silent? What is the difference between submission and forbearance?

Paul Laurence Dunbar

Maya Angelou found the title of her autobiography in "Sympathy" by Paul Laurence Dunbar. The powerful and unforgettable imagery of a caged bird singing is an idea even younger family members can appreciate when considering the virtue of forbearance. Laurence wrote this poem when he was working as an assistant at the Library of Congress, where, according to his wife, the iron grilling of the book stacks looked to him like prison bars.

Sympathy

I know what the caged bird feels, alas!
　　When the sun is bright on the upland slopes;
When the wind stirs soft through the springing grass,
And the river flows like a stream of glass;

When the first bird sings and the first bud opes,
And the faint perfume from its chalice steals—
I know what the caged bird feels!

I know why the caged bird beats his wing
        Till its blood is red on the cruel bars;
For he must fly back to his perch and cling
When he fain would be on the bough a-swing;
        And a pain still throbs in the old, old scars
And they pulse again with a keener sting—
I know why he beats his wing!

I know why the caged bird sings, ah me,
        When his wing is bruised and his bosom sore—
When he beats his bars and he would be free;
It is not a carol of joy or glee,
        But a prayer that he sends from his heart's deep core,
But a plea, that upward to Heaven he flings—
I know why the caged bird sings!

Exercise Forbearance:

- Why do you think the caged bird sings "when his wing is bruised and his bosom sore"?
- The idea that an artist's work, likened in the poem to the song of a bird, is something that will find its way out is an incredibly powerful message. How else besides in art might we let our spirits soar in the face of cruelty or injustice? Can art be a means of forbearance?
- Might the song of the bird also be likened to faith? How easy or difficult would it be for someone to constrain your faith? Can your faith soar beyond the bars imposed by our society and culture? How might your faith be a tool for forbearance?

Spiritual

D r. Martin Luther King, Jr., referred to this favorite old spiritual in his speech at the end of the Selma-to-Montgomery march on March 25, 1965. Joshua 6 relates how the men of Joshua walked around the city of Jericho blowing their trumpets, and from that force alone, the walls of the city were felled. God's strategy of waiting and walking is a message of both patience and forbearance: Joshua 6:3 tells, "And ye shall compass the city, all ye men of war, and go round about the city once. Thus shalt thou do six days." In Dr. King's words, "The battle is in our hands. And we can answer with creative nonviolence the call to higher ground to which the new directions of our struggle summons us."

Joshua Fit de Battle of Jericho

Joshua fit de battle of Jericho, Jericho, Jericho,
Joshua fit de battle of Jericho,
And the walls came a tumbalin' down, down, down.

You may talk about your men of Gideon,
You may talk about your men of Saul,
But there's none like good old Josh-u-a,
At the battle of Jericho, that morning;

Joshua rose early in the morning,
That is when the trumpets blew,
They marched around the city,
At the battle of Jericho.

Right up to the walls of Jericho,
He marched with spear in hand,

Joshua commanded the children to shout,
And the walls came a tumbalin' down, down, down;

Joshua fit de battle of Jericho, Jericho, Jericho,
Joshua fit de battle of Jericho, the trumpets they did blow, so,
Joshua fit de battle of Jericho, and the walls came a-tumbalin' down.

Exercise Forbearance:

- When you were faced with a great challenge, were you tempted to scream, shout, or react violently? Did you feel called upon to keep silent? How did you handle it?
- This song reminds us of the joy that comes from winning a battle not by the spear but through forbearance. It's tempting to think there is great satisfaction to be gained from lashing out when we are angry or faced with obstacles, but think about how a moment of patience can bring about an even more meaningful victory. As 2 Corinthians 10:4 reminds us, "For the weapons of our warfare are not carnal, but mighty through God to the pulling down of strong holds."

Olaudah Equiano

Kidnapped at age eleven from his African village, Olaudah Equiano was shipped to the West Indies and sold to a Virginia planter. He was later purchased by a Royal Navy officer, who renamed him Gustavus Vassa—ironically, the name of a sixteenth-century Swedish nobleman-turned-king whom the Swedes viewed as their liberator from Danish oppression. After ten years of enslavement working as a seaman, Equiano bought his freedom. He became involved in the London movement to abolish the slave trade, inspiring him to write his autobiography in 1779. Equiano's narrative is one of the first works written in English by a former slave and was the first of what became known as the slave narrative. While many scholars have suggested *that Equiano wove the experiences of many slaves into his book, his story is still unique in that unlike most slaves, Equiano traveled the world as a seaman, was literate, and was able to pay for his freedom. He died in London in 1797. This excerpt describes his experience of what has become known as the "middle passage," the leg of the slave trade route that transported human cargo from Africa to North and South America and the Caribbean.*

from The Interesting Narrative of the Life of Olaudah Equiano, or Gustavus Vassa, The African, Written by Himself

The first object which saluted my eyes when I arrived on the coast was the sea, and a slave ship, which was then riding at anchor, and waiting for its cargo. These filled me with astonishment, which was soon converted into terror when I was carried on board. I was immediately handled and tossed up to see if I were sound by some of the crew; and I was now persuaded that I had gotten into a world of bad spirits, and that they were going to kill me. Their complexions too differing so much from ours, their long hair, and the language they spoke (which was very different from any I had ever heard), united to confirm me in this belief. Indeed such were the horrors of my views and fears at the moment, that, if ten thousand worlds had been my own, I would have freely parted with them all to have exchanged my condition with that of the meanest slave in my own country. When I looked round the ship too and saw a large furnace or copper boiling, and a multitude of black people of every description chained together, every one of their countenances expressing dejection and sorrow, I no longer doubted of my fate; and, quite overpowered with horror and anguish, I fell motionless on the deck and fainted. When I recovered a little I found some black people about me, who I believed were some of those who brought me on board, and had been receiving their pay; they talked to me in order to cheer me, but all in vain. I asked them if we were not to be eaten by those white men with horrible looks, red faces, and loose hair. They told me I was not; and one of the crew brought me a small portion of spirituous liquor in a wine glass; but, being afraid of him, I would not take it out of his hand. One of the blacks therefore took it from him and gave it to me, and I took a little down my palate, which, instead of reviving me, as they thought it would, threw me into the greatest consternation at the strange feeling it produced, having never tasted any such liquor before. Soon after this the blacks who brought me on board went off, and left me abandoned to despair.

I now saw myself deprived of all chance of returning to my native country, or even the least glimpse of hope of gaining the shore, which I now considered as friendly; and I even wished for my former slavery in preference to my present situation, which was filled with horrors of every kind, still heightened by my ignorance of what I was to undergo. I was not long suffered to indulge my grief; I was soon put down under the decks, and there I received such a salutation in my nostrils as I had never experienced in my life: so that, with the loathsomeness of the stench, and crying together, I became so sick and low that I was not able to eat, nor had I the least desire to taste any thing. I now wished for the last friend, death, to relieve me; but soon, to my grief, two of the white men offered me eatables; and, on my refusing to eat, one of them held me fast by the hands, and laid me across I think the windlass, and tied my feet, while the other flogged me severely. I had never experienced any thing of this kind before; and although, not being used to the water, I naturally feared that element the first time I saw it, yet nevertheless, could I have got over the nettings, I would have jumped over the side, but I could not; and, besides, the crew used to watch us very closely who were not chained down to the decks, lest we should leap into the water: and I have seen some of these poor African prisoners most severely cut for attempting to do so, and hourly whipped for not eating. This indeed was often the case with myself. In a little time after, amongst the poor chained men, I found some of my

own nation, which in a small degree gave ease to my mind. I inquired
of these what was to be done with us; they gave me to understand we
were to be carried to these white people's country to work for them. I
then was a little revived, and thought, if it were no worse than working, my situation was not so desperate: but still I feared I should be
put to death, the white people looked and acted, as I thought, in so
savage a manner; for I had never seen among any people such instances
of brutal cruelty; and this not only shown towards us blacks, but also
to some of the whites themselves. One white man in particular I saw,
when we were permitted to be on deck, flogged so unmercifully with a
large rope near the foremast, that he died in consequence of it; and
they tossed him over the side as they would have done a brute. This
made me fear these people the more; and I expected nothing less than
to be treated in the same manner. I could not help expressing my fears
and apprehensions to some of my countrymen: I asked them if these
people had no country, but lived in this hollow place (the ship): they
told me they did not, but came from a distant one. "Then," said I,
"how comes it in all our country we never heard of them?" They told
me because they lived so very far off. I then asked where were their
women? had they any like themselves? I was told they had: "and why,"
said I, "do we not see them?" they answered, because they were left
behind. I asked how the vessel could go? they told me they could not
tell; but that there were cloths put upon the masts by the help of the
ropes I saw, and then the vessel went on; and the white men had some
spell or magic they put in the water when they liked in order to stop the
vessel. I was exceedingly amazed at this account, and really thought they
were spirits. I therefore wished much to be from amongst them, for I
expected they would sacrifice me: but my wishes were vain; for we were
so quartered that it was impossible for any of us to make our escape.

While we stayed on the coast I was mostly on deck; and one day, to
my great astonishment, I saw one of these vessels coming in with the
sails up. As soon as the whites saw it, they gave a great shout, at which
we were amazed; and the more so as the vessel appeared larger by

approaching nearer. At last she came to an anchor in my sight, and when the anchor was let go I and my countrymen who saw it were lost in astonishment to observe the vessel stop; and were now convinced it was done by magic. Soon after this the other ship got her boats out, and they came on board of us, and the people of both ships seemed very glad to see each other. Several of the strangers also shook hands with us black people, and made motions with their hands, signifying I suppose we were to go to their country; but we did not understand them.

At last, when the ship we were in had got in all her cargo, they made ready with many fearful noises, and we were all put under deck, so that we could not see how they managed the vessel. But this disappointment was the least of my sorrow. The stench of the hold while we were on the coast was so intolerably loathsome, that it was dangerous to remain there for any time, and some of us had been permitted to stay on the deck for the fresh air; but now that the whole ship's cargo were confined together, it became absolutely pestilential. The closeness of the place, and the heat of the climate, added to the number in the ship, which was so crowded that each had scarcely room to turn himself, almost suffocated us. This produced copious perspirations, so that the air soon became unfit for respiration, from a variety of loathsome smells, and brought on a sickness among the slaves, of which many died, thus falling victims to the improvident avarice, as I may call it, of their purchasers. This wretched situation was again aggravated by the galling of the chains, now become insupportable; and the filth of the necessary tubs, into which the children often fell, and were almost suffocated. The shrieks of the women, and the groans of the dying, rendered the whole a scene of horror almost inconceivable. Happily perhaps for myself I was soon reduced so low here that it was thought necessary to keep me almost always on deck; and from my extreme youth I was not put in fetters. In this situation I expected every hour to share the fate of my companions, some of whom were almost daily brought upon deck at the point of death, which I began to hope would soon put an end to my miseries. Often did I think many of the inhabitants of the deep much more happy than myself. I envied them the freedom they enjoyed, and as often wished I could change my condition for theirs. Every circumstance I met with served only to render my state more painful, and heighten my apprehensions, and my opinion of the cruelty of the whites.

One day they had taken a number of fishes; and when they had killed and satisfied themselves with as many as they thought fit, to our astonishment who were on the deck, rather than give any of them to us to eat as we expected, they tossed the remaining fish into the sea again, although we begged and prayed for some as well as we could, but in vain; and some of my countrymen, being pressed by hunger, took an opportunity, when they thought no one saw them, of trying to get a little privately; but they were discovered, and the attempt procured them some very severe floggings. One day, when we had a smooth sea and moderate wind, two of my wearied countrymen who were chained together (I was near them at the time), preferring death to such a life of misery, somehow made through the nettings and jumped into the sea: immediately another quite dejected fellow, who, on account of his illness, was suffered to be out of irons, also followed their example; and I believe many more would very soon have done the same if they had not been prevented by the ship's crew, who were instantly alarmed. Those of us that were the most active were in a moment put down under the deck, and there was such a noise and confusion amongst the people of the ship as I never heard before, to stop her, and get the boat out to go after the slaves. However two of the wretches were drowned, but they got the other, and afterwards flogged him unmercifully for thus attempting to prefer death to slavery. In this manner we continued to undergo more hardships than I can now relate, hardships which are inseparable from this accursed trade. Many a time we were near suffocation from the want of fresh air, which we were often without for whole days together. This, and the stench of the necessary tubs, carried off many.

During our passage I first saw flying fishes, which surprised me very much: they used frequently to fly across the ship, and many of them fell on the deck. I also now first saw the use of the quadrant; I had often with astonishment seen the mariners make observations with it, and I could not think what it meant. They at last took notice of my surprise; and one of them, willing to increase it, as well as to gratify my curiosity, made me one day look through it. The clouds appeared to me to be land, which disappeared as they passed along. This heightened my wonder; and I was now more persuaded than ever that I was in another world, and that every thing about me was magic. At last we came in sight of the island of Barbadoes, at which the whites on board gave a great shout, and made many signs of joy to us. We did not know what to think of this; but as the vessel drew nearer we plainly saw the harbour, and other ships of different kinds and sizes; and we soon anchored amongst them off Bridge Town. Many merchants and planters now came on board, though it was in the evening. They put us in separate parcels, and examined us attentively. They also made us jump, and pointed to the land, signifying we were to go there. We thought by this we should be eaten by these ugly men, as they appeared to us; and, when soon after we were all put down under the deck again, there was much dread and trembling among us, and nothing but bitter cries to be heard all the night from these apprehensions, insomuch that at last the white people got some old slaves from the land to pacify us. They told us we were not to be eaten, but to work, and were soon to go on land, where we should see many of our country-people. This report eased us much; and sure enough, soon after we were landed, there came to us Africans of all languages.

We were conducted immediately to the merchant's yard, where we were all pent up together like so many sheep in a fold, without regard to sex or age. As every object was new to me every thing I saw filled me with surprise. What struck me first was that the houses were built with stories, and in every other respect different from those in Africa: but I was still more astonished on seeing people on horseback. I did not know what this could mean; and indeed I thought these people were full of nothing but magical arts. While I was in this astonishment one of my fellow prisoners spoke to a countryman of his about the horses, who said they were the same kind they had in their country. I understood them, though they were from a distant part of Africa, and I thought it odd I had not seen any horses there; but afterwards, when I came to converse with different Africans, I found they had many horses amongst them, and much larger than those I then saw.

We were not many days in the merchant's custody before we were sold after their usual manner, which is this:——On a signal given (as the beat of a drum), the buyers rush at once into the yard where the slaves are confined, and make choice of that parcel they like best. The noise and clamour with which this is attended, and the eagerness visible in the countenances of the buyers, serve not a little to increase the apprehensions of the terrified Africans, who may well be supposed to consider them as the ministers of that destruction to which they think themselves devoted. In this manner, without scruple, are relations and friends separated, most of them never to see each other again. I remember in the vessel in which I was brought over, in the men's apartment, there were several brothers, who, in the sale, were sold in different lots; and it was very moving on this occasion to see and hear their cries at parting. O, ye nominal Christians! might not an African ask you, Learned you this from your God, who says unto you, Do unto all men as you would men should do unto you? Is it not enough that we are torn from our country and friends to toil for your luxury and lust of gain? Must every tender feeling be likewise sacrificed to your avarice? Are the dearest friends and relations, now rendered more dear by their separation from their kindred, still to be parted from each other, and thus prevented from cheering the gloom of slavery with the small comfort of being together and mingling their sufferings and sorrows? Why are parents to lose their children, brothers their sisters, or husbands their wives? Surely this is a new refinement in cruelty, which, while it has no advantage to atone for it, thus aggravates distress, and adds fresh horrors even to the wretchedness of slavery.

Exercise Forbearance:

- Olaudah Equiano was kidnapped from his home, his family, and his friends. He survived the horrors of the middle passage and slave "seasoning" in the West Indies, and was sold to two different masters. But his spirit was strong and his desire for freedom even stronger. Equiano employed the seafaring skills he picked up as a slave to save money to buy his freedom and used his literacy as a means to show the public how terrible the institution of slavery was. Think about the ways in which trying times have forced you to be resourceful and the ways in which they have forced you to exercise forbearance.

- Ask your family to describe three situations in Equiano's narrative in which he exercised forbearance. Then read Jeremiah 15. What does God promise to Jeremiah for his forbearance?

Alice Wine

Alice Wine was one of the first graduates, in 1956, of the voter education schools on Johns Island, South Carolina. "Keep Your Eyes on the Prize," a song she based on the age-old spiritual "Keep Your Hand on the Plow," became one of the anthems of the civil rights movement.

Keep Your Eyes on the Prize

Paul and Silas, bound in jail,
Had no money for to go their bail,
Keep your eyes on the prize, hold on, hold on.

Hold on, hold on,
Keep your eyes on the prize,
Hold on, hold on.

Paul and Silas began to shout,
The jail door opened and they walked on out.
Keep your eyes on the prize, hold on, hold on.

Freedom's name is mighty sweet,
Soon one day we're gonna meet.

Got my hand on the Gospel plow,
I woudn't take nothing for my journey now.

The only chain that a man can stand,
Is that chain of hand in hand.

The only thing we did wrong,
Stayed in the wilderness a day too long.

The only thing we did right,
Was the day we started to fight.

We're gonna board that big Greyhound,
Carryin' love from town to town.

We're gonna ride for civil rights,
We're gonna ride both black and white.

We've met jail and violence too,
But God's love has seen us through.

Haven't been to heaven but I've been told,
Streets up there are paved with gold.

Exercise Forbearance:

- Since slavery, the Bible has served as our guide to freedom. And it has served us well. During the civil rights movement, many of our religious leaders turned to Acts 16:25 and Acts 16:36, which tell the story of Paul and Silas's imprisonment and release for preaching the Gospel. In considering these passages, think about other stories that speak to our forbearance in our struggle for freedom in this country.

- Think about the ways in which the Reverend Martin Luther King's imprisonment in the Birmingham jail compares with Paul and Silas's imprisonment and treatment in Acts 16. Listen to Mahalia Jackson's recording of "Keep Your Hand on the Plow" and the Freedomways' version of "Keep Your Eyes on the Prize" with your children. Ask them to describe how the Reverend Martin Luther King and Paul and Silas exhibited the virtue of forbearance.

Forgiveness

A merciful disposition to pardon the mistakes of others,
FORGIVENESS is an active compassion arising
from the knowledge that no human being is perfect.

How many black men and women in America have been murdered? How many of our ancestors were beaten? How many lynched? How many enslaved? For centuries, we have been the targets of persecution, the victims of segregation, the prey of hatred. And then, when we are suffering from abuse and mistreatment, cruelty and contempt, we are asked to forgive. We are told to contain our outrage and to repress our fury. This task seems virtually impossible.

But as difficult as it is to forgive, it is essential that we respond to injustice with justice. There are times when we are called upon to prove our morality. We must never let our virtue dissolve in the face of evil.

In my personal life there have been many times when it was necessary for me to exercise the virtue of forgiveness. An instance that stands out was after my first marriage became troubled and eventually fell apart. If I had not had the capacity to forgive, I am convinced that the Lord would not have blessed me with such a wonderful wife the second time around. It was the realization that no one person could wreck a marriage that made it possible for me to forgive my wife while praying that she would also forgive me.

In the second instance, the false accusations of friends and trusted church leadership ended in a federal trial. Even before the Justice Department dropped its case due to a lack of evidence, the only way that I could continue to function through this ordeal without wallowing in anger and desire for retribution was by praying for the power to forgive. I had to forgive not only my accusers, but also the Justice Department, for assuming that being black meant being guilty until proven innocent. My life is better for having forgiven them.

Retaliation is a mark of weakness; forgiveness is a badge of strength. By refusing to give in to our vengeful impulses, we demonstrate how the power of love and restraint can redeem our lives so that we can live in peace and productivity. Rather than let our enemies lead us to hatred, we must lead our enemies to love.

To forgive is really an act of giving. It is giving another chance to those who have wronged us. It is giving them the benefits of God's love and compassion. It is giving them the opportunity to find God by following the light that your example provides. Indeed, forgiveness may be the most benevolent act of giving.

When considering whether or not to forgive others, we must always remember that at some point, we will inevitably be asking others to forgive us. The Bible tells of an adulterous woman whose neighbors were prepared to throw stones at her as punishment for her transgression. Assembling with stones in hand, the villagers planned to murder this woman. But Jesus saved her, standing up and proclaiming, "If anyone is without sin, let him cast the first stone."

We are all sinners and we all have the capacity to wound others. We have all made mistakes and have all asked for forgiveness. While our ability to forgive illustrates our capacity for morality, it is also an admission of the fact that we are not perfect. By forgiving, we acknowledge that we too have sinned, will sin again, and will need to beg forgiveness of others. If we ask for compassion, we must also provide it; if we hope to be forgiven, we must also forgive.

Forgiveness, however, is not a remedy. Some people tend to perversely believe that it is okay to sin or hurt now because their transgressions can be forgiven in the future. They count on the forgiveness of God and those who love them. But the likelihood of forgiveness does not remove the need for integrity and accountability. Sins and misdeeds may be pardoned, but forgiveness does not always remove the consequences of the act.

Even so, it is our responsibility to forgive the crimes committed against us. We spend too much time condemning others and too little time redeeming ourselves. Holding grudges only suffocates our minds and binds our hearts. Seeking revenge consumes our hearts with negative energy that renders us unproductive and frustrated. Forgiveness frees us from the shackles of hatred and instills in us a conscience of compassion. Forgiveness does not always come easily; it is a feat that may take months or years to accomplish. It is, however, a goal that should be pursued with persistence, for once achieved, it frees us up to live beyond the limitations of ill will.

John Newton

John Newton's story is one I preach often. He spent many a day on the sea working the slave trade—abusing, oppressing, murdering. The captain of his own slave ship before the age of twenty-three, he was a man of little conscience who felt justified in the way that he treated men and women of color. In his eyes, Africans were not humans at all. Then one day a storm rose on the sea, and Newton and the entire ship almost died. Newton was also stricken with a serious fever. His life was at its lowest point, and he was emotionally and spiritually in the depths of despair. But one day, Newton met Jesus. He who had been wild, belligerent, and decadent became a new creation in Christ. His past was purged by the blood of Jesus, and his sins were obliterated by God's mercy and grace. He left that slave ship, and after teaching himself to read and devoting himself to years of religious study, he mounted the pulpit. So appreciative and so overwhelmed was he by his new life that he wrote a hymn about it that would live throughout the ages.

Amazing Grace

Amazing grace! How sweet the sound,
That saved a wretch like me!
I once was lost, but now am found,
Was blind, but now I see.

'Twas grace that taught my heart to fear,
And grace my fears relieved;
How precious did that grace appear
The hour I first believed.

Through many dangers, toils and snares,
I have already come;
'Tis grace hath brought me safe thus far,
And grace will lead me home.

The Lord has promised good to me,
His Word my hope secures;
He will my Shield and Portion be,
As long as life endures.

When we've been there ten thousand years,
Bright shining as the sun,
We've no less days to sing God's praise
Than when we'd first begun.*

Exercise Forgiveness:

- How and why is John Newton included in a book that aims to describe virtue from an African American perspective? Clearly our perspectives are not the same; in fact, his life before salvation is a painful reminder of the horrendous sins against our people. But Newton's sins were transformed by God and the grace bestowed upon him is manifest in the artistry of the hymn. We've included it here because it is a consummate meditation on forgiveness, because it is enormously popular in the African American church, and because it is perhaps as powerful a testament to turning one's life around that has ever been written. I hope you will sing "Amazing Grace" to your heart's content.

- John Newton was not killed aboard that slave ship—he was saved. He was not wiped out in that raging storm, but was cleaned up and ultimately became a minister of the Gospel. It truly was amazing grace. Unmerited favor. Unearned pardon. Undeserved blessing. This is the forgiveness we as Christians can expect from our relationship with God. Do you know about amazing grace?

- We might also have included this hymn as a meditation on faith. " 'Twas grace that taught my heart to fear / And grace my fears relieved." Think about your faith as the thing that causes you to be fearful and at once relieved of fear.

- It is a miracle when you are forgiven. In what ways might you turn your own life around, as John Newton did, to honor God and that miracle?

*Note: The last stanza is by an unknown author.

Charles W. Chesnutt

Charles W. Chesnutt was born in 1858 in Cleveland, the child of free blacks from North Carolina. After pursuing a literary career, in 1906 he became involved in social and political activities. Along with prominent activists, such as Booker T. Washington and W. E. B. DuBois, Chesnutt lobbied for reform and better treatment of blacks, particularly in the South. He continued to run a successful business throughout his writing life. Originally published in 1901 in Southern Workman magazine, this post—Civil War story suggests that only through friendship and economic partnership can we prosper and succeed. Chesnutt's message is one of charity and brotherly love, but also a compelling example of forgiveness.

The Partners

Among the human flotsam and jetsam that followed in the wake of the Civil War, there drifted into a certain Southern town, shortly after the surrender, two young colored men, named respectively William Cain and Rufus Green. They had made each other's acquaintance in a refugee camp attached to an army cantonment, and when the soldiers went away, William and Rufus were thrown upon their own resources. They were fast friends, and discussed with each other the subject of their future.

"Well, ez fer me," said William, "my marster had put me ter de bricklayer's an' plasterer's trade, an' I'd wukked at it six weeks befo' I come away. I hadn' larnt eve'ything, but I reckon I knows ernuff ter make a livin' at it."

"Ez fer me," returned Rufus gloomily—he was not of the most cheerful temperament—"I don' know how ter use nuffin' but a hoe."

"I has ter use de hoe in my bizness too," rejoined William. "De mo'tar has ter be mix' wid a hoe. W'y can't we go in podners? You kin mix de mo'tar, an' I'll put it on, tel I've larnt you all I knows. We'll keep ou' money tergether, an' w'at I makes shill be ez much yo'n ez mine, an' w'at you makes shill be ez much mine ez yo'n, an' w'at we bofe makes shill belong ter bofe of us. How would dat 'rangement suit you?"

Rufus, having felt some alarm at the prospect of facing the world alone—slavery had not been a good school for training in self-reliance—found this proposition a very agreeable one, and promptly expressed his willingness to accept it.

"And now," said William, who thus early in the affair assumed the initiative, "we ought to hab somethin' ter show ou' agreement—dat's de way w'ite folks does bizness, an' we'll hafter do de same. I knows a man roun' here w'at kin write, an' we'll git some paper an' hab him draw up de articles."

The scribe and the paper were found, and William dictated the following agreement, the phraseology of which is reminiscent of certain solemn forms which he had heard used from time to time, being town-bred and accustomed to the ways of the world:

"William Cain an' Rufus Green is gone in partners this day to work at whatever their hands find to do. What they makes shall belong to one as much as the other, and they shall stand by each other in sickness and in health, in good luck and in bad, till death shall us part, and the Lord have mercy on our souls. Amen."

This was written in a doubtful hand, on each of two sheets of foolscap paper, and signed by the partners with their respective marks. Each received a copy of the agreement, and they promised the man a half-dollar for his services, to be paid out of their first earnings.

Having found a place to live, William and Rufus settled down as well as their uncertain fortunes would permit. It soon became apparent that William was the more capable of the two, and equally clear—to his patrons at least—that he had not worked at his trade long enough to learn to do fine work. In consequence of the discovery, the partners soon themselves engaged almost solely in the whitewashing and patching business, at which they were fairly successful. Even here, however, William's relative superiority manifested itself, and he generally wielded the brush while Rufus mixed the whitewash. When business was slack, they engaged in such manual labor as they could find. They ate together, slept together, and had a common purse, from which they supplied their necessities and had a little left for amusements and tobacco.

They were living thus, in a hand-to-mouth way, but with the cheerful contentment characteristic of their race, when a Northern philanthropist, filled with the fine, postbellum zeal for the freedmen, purchased at a low price an extensive plantation in the vicinity of the town, which he cut up into small farms, and, for the encouragement of industry and thrift among the Negroes, sold to them at prices little more than nominal. All but two of the farms had been disposed of before he discovered William and Rufus. Learning that they lived in what they called partnership, he informed them that such a relation was incompatible with the development of self-reliance and strength of character, and that their best interests would be promoted by their learning each to fight his own battle. A thoughtful student of history might have suggested to the philanthropist that the power of highly developed races lies mainly in their ability to combine for the better accomplishment of a common purpose. The good man meant well, however, and his method was admirably adapted to separate the wheat from the chaff. His arguments, or his liberal offer, proved effective; William and Rufus put away the whitewash pails and brushes and became freeholders and farmers upon adjoining tracts of land.

The soil was fertile, and the new owners were filled with the buoyant hopefulness and zeal which characterized the colored people immediately after their emancipation, when there seemed to be a rosy future for their race, not in some distant generation, when the memory of their bondage should have become dim and legendary, but for themselves and their children. The good philanthropist, waiving for the moment his theory of self-reliance—of which indeed his whole generous scheme was a contradiction—gave his beneficiaries advice and oversight for several years, during which William and Rufus, in company with their neighbors, throve apace. In much less time than even the philanthropist had anticipated, both farms were paid for, and William and Rufus tasted the pleasures which any healthy-minded man feels when he first knows himself owner, in fee simple, by metes and bounds, of a piece of the soil which, in a broader sense, is the common heritage of mankind.

During the first years of their separation William and Rufus remained fast friends. The friendship, like their former partnership, was of more practical benefit to Rufus than to William. It was largely due to William's advice about plowing and planting and harvesting, to William's superior knowledge of horses and cattle and hogs, and his more trustworthy intuitions about wind and weather, that Rufus had been able to pay for his farm and procure his deed at the same time with William. This aid, too, was rendered spontaneously, and so much as a matter of course, that Rufus, who was a man of slow perceptions, flattered himself upon being a very successful farmer, and on the high-road to substantial wealth.

Nevertheless, as the years rolled on, William's greater prosperity became apparent even to Rufus, who began gradually to appreciate the fact that William's fields bore larger crops, that his cows calved oftener and gave more milk, that his hogs were fatter and better bred, that his hens laid more eggs and suffered less from fox or hawk or other thieves.

Shortly after becoming a landowner Rufus had married a wife, who in time bore him several children. William, too, had selected a help-meet, with a like effect upon his household. The first rift in the long friendship came one day when one of William's children and one of Rufus' had a juvenile dispute, which, if left to themselves, they would have forgotten in an hour. Their mothers, however, took up the quarrel, and having longer memories, became somewhat estranged over it. Since the families were near neighbors and had long been dependent upon one another for the exchange of neighborly courtesies, a quarrel

was irksome to say the least. At first William and Rufus paid no attention to the misunderstanding, its only effect upon them being that
they met and talked along the turnrows and across fences rather than
by each other's firesides. As it was, the trouble would probably soon
have been smoothed over, had not the demon Envy, with its train of
malice and all uncharitableness, taken possession of Rufus' wife and
passed from her to her husband.

Mrs. William Cain came out to church one Sunday in a new frock.
Rufus was unable, at the moment, to buy his wife a garment equally
handsome. To make matters worse, William drove Mrs. Cain to church
the same day in a new buggy, a luxury in which Rufus, who, like
William himself, had hitherto walked to church or driven thither in
his cart, could not as yet afford to indulge.

"Dat Cain 'oman is puttin' on mo' airs 'n ef she own' somebody,"
sniffed Mrs. Rufus. "She jes' displayin' dem clo's, an' he's jes' bought
dat buggy—he must 'a' got it on credit—jes' ter show off an' make us
feel po' an' mean. Rufus, ef you are de man I take you fer, you won'
have nuthin' mo' ter do wid dem people!"

When William next saw Rufus working near the fence and walked
down to pass the time of day, Rufus saw him coming and moved farther away. For the first few times that this occurred, William supposed
it to be a mere coincidence; but when Rufus one day passed him on
the road without speaking, even the pretense of deep absorption in
thought did not deceive William. His old friend had turned against
him, and he felt sore at heart. Surely a friendship of such long standing ought not to be broken because of a few hard words by two quick-
tempered women on account of a children's quarrel.

It occurred to William that perhaps he might pour oil upon the
troubled waters. One Saturday evening he sent his hired man over to
Rufus' house with a message.

"My boss wants ter know," said the messenger, "ef you wouldn't lack
ter borry his buggy ter-morrer afternoon an' take a ride somewhar."

This seemed to Rufus very kind of William, and he was on the point of accepting the offer, when Mrs. Green broke in: "You kin go an' tell William Cain dat we don' go ridin' in borried buggies; dat w'en we git able ter pay fer a buggy, we'll ride, an' not be trapesin' roun' de country showin' off in buggies w'at ain't paid fer!"

This message, delivered with fidelity both to language and spirit, aroused some righteous resentment in William's bosom. If Rufus preferred enmity to friendship, William concluded that he would at least not force his good offices upon his neighbor, but would hereafter wait until they were requested. He knew from past experience that Rufus would need them sooner or later. As a consequence of this mutual coolness, the breach between the neighbors became, if not wider, at least more pronounced.

The purchase of the buggy and the incidents growing out of it had taken place in the autumn, after the crops had been gathered and sold. During the following winter Rufus' sweet potatoes, which had not been properly put up, began to rot, and almost his entire supply was spoiled before he became aware of their condition. During any other winter, William, whose potatoes always kept well, would have lent him, at a nominal price, enough potatoes to tide him over the season. This time, however, Rufus was compelled to pay winter prices for his potatoes, and cart them home from the town, five miles away.

Henceforth misfortune seemed to follow Rufus. His cows went dry, and the family had to get along without milk, while they could see, as they drove along the road, William's pigs feeding upon the surplus of his dairy. One of Rufus' two horses was taken sick. Upon a similar occasion, the winter before, William had suggested treatment which had cured the complaint. Rufus administered the same remedy for a different disease, and the horse died. So far had the ill-feeling toward his neighbor gone that Rufus ascribed the death of the horse to William, instead of to his own folly in giving the medicine without a proper understanding of the ailment.

William would have been willing at any moment to resume their former relations, upon proper advances from Rufus, of whose misfortunes he was indeed not fully informed, for intercourse between the two families had entirely ceased and even the children were forbidden to play together. The line that separated their farms marked as well the boundary between two school districts, and the children went in opposite directions to different schools. But there came a time when even William's patience was exhausted, and he began to feel something like anger toward his whilom friend.

The rear part of William's farm consisted of a low meadow, through which ran a small stream. With the instinct of a wise farmer seeking to diversify his crops to the best advantage, William had planted this meadow in rice, with very good results. In the cultivation of this cereal it was necessary, now and then, to flood the meadow. This had heretofore been accomplished easily by damming up the stream at the point where it left William's land, whereby it overspread its banks and overflowed the low ground. This had resulted also in flooding Rufus' meadow, which was of similar location and extent, and through which the stream flowed before reaching William's land; but as Rufus had hitherto followed William's advice and example in the matter of planting rice, this overflow was mutually satisfactory and profitable to both.

In the season that followed the beginning of this alienation of an old friendship, Rufus planted his meadow in rice; but lacking William's wisdom, and not having the benefit of his advice, Rufus's crop proved a failure, and the following year he determined to plant the meadow in corn. Having received no notice of his neighbor's intention to change the crop, William planted rice as usual, and in due time dammed up the stream in order to flood the meadow. When Rufus saw the water coming upon his corn, he said nothing to William, but went to consult a lawyer, who advised an injunction. A lawsuit was accordingly begun, and William restrained from backing up the water on the adjoining land.

It was this unneighborly conduct on the part of Rufus that turned the milk of William's friendship into the gall of enmity. He employed the best lawyer in the county, and instructed him to fight the lawsuit to the bitter end.

A quarrel between adjoining landowners is usually a tedious affair, with many collateral complications, and the law's delays are proverbial. In the course of the next year or two it became necessary, at a certain stage of the proceedings, to make a detailed plat of Rufus' farm, for which purpose a surveyor was employed. In order to perform his work properly, the surveyor went to the county records and procured an exact copy of the description in Rufus' deed. When with his instruments he went to survey Rufus' lines he made a remarkable discovery—the deed did not convey that piece of land at all, but contained a repetition of the description of another parcel in the philanthropist's allotment, previously sold to a different purchaser.

The surveyor was—he believed unjustly—a poor man. His ancestors had once been rich in land and slaves. His grandfather had once owned the very plantation out of which Rufus' farm had been carved. The family had been ruined by the war. Driving past these flourishing farms, the surveyor had often thought they ought to be his own. Now he had discovered that one of the best of them was occupied by a Negro who held it under a clouded title. After a very brief struggle with his conscience, the surveyor made a long journey. In a distant Northern city he found a descendant of the philanthropist, who had met with reverses and had died in comparative poverty. Upon certain plausible representations the surveyor procured, for a small sum, a quit-claim deed of all the right, title, and interest of the philanthropist's heir in the land occupied and improved for many years by Rufus. Armed with this document, he returned home and began an action in ejectment.

The writ served upon Rufus fell like a bombshell in the heart of his household. Never had he so needed the advice and moral support of his former friend as when he first comprehended the import of the proceedings now begun against him. If he had followed his first impulse, he would have gone and begged his friend's pardon for his own past conduct, to which, he obscurely realized, the alienation of recent years was almost entirely due. Some such suggestion to his wife evoked, however, a torrent of indignant protest.

"Beg his pa'don indeed!" she cried. "He's 'sponsible fer all ou' troubles. Ef he had n' dammed up dat creek you never would 'a' gone ter de law, an' den you would n' 'a' h'ed no su'veyor, an' all dis trouble would n' 'a' come on us. He's 'sponsible fer it all, an' you sha' n't go nigh 'im."

So Rufus went for advice to his lawyer, who tried the case and lost it on a technicality. A better advocate might have won it. A rich man, properly advised, might have taken the case to a higher court with a fair prospect of ultimate success. But Rufus' misfortunes, including the expenses of litigation, had exhausted his cash and his credit, both of which had been derived from the property now decreed to be no longer his. He lost the spring of hope, and yielded to what seemed the inevitable. His wife took the blow as hard, but in a different manner.

"You're no 'count at all," she said to Rufus bitterly. "I ma'ied a man wid land an' hosses an' cows an' hawgs. Now after ten years er slavin', w'at is I got? A man wid nuthin', an' not much er dat! I've wukked myse'f ter skin an' bone, fer who? Fer a w'ite man! I mought as well never 'a' be'n freed. But I'll do so no longer! Hencefo'th you c'n go yo' way an' I'll go mine."

She went away in anger, taking her two children and moving to the neighboring town, where she rented a small room and took in washing for a living. Rufus still lingered at the farm, which he had received a two-weeks' notice to vacate. Several times during the first week he had seen William near the line fence, looking toward the house that must soon be occupied by strangers. Perhaps William was sorry for his old friend—more likely he was gloating over his fallen enemy. Rufus hardened his heart and stiffened his neck, and when he saw William, looked the other way.

On the last day of the second week Rufus harnessed up the old sore-backed horse, his sole remaining beast of burden, to the rickety spring wagon which in the apathy of hopelessness he had not cleaned or repaired for several months. Only the day before he had seen the new owner riding along the road with his wife, inspecting their future domain. Rufus had rented an abandoned log cabin in the woods not far away, where he could hide his diminished head in shame; and he hoped to procure days' work on the neighboring farms, whereby to keep body and soul together. He would resign his deaconship in the church, and henceforth lead the life of obscurity for which alone his meager talents qualified him. It was hard, nevertheless, to leave the land that he had labored upon for so many years, the house he had built with his own hands, and in which he had expected to spend his declining years in peaceful comfort—it was very, very hard.

He loaded the wagon with his few remaining chattels—his wife had taken some, and others had been sold. When he had brought the last piece out of the house, he sat down upon the doorstep and buried his face in his hands. In that moment of self-examination the true source of his misfortunes became entirely clear to him. Long he sat there, until even the sore-backed horse turned his head with an air of mild surprise in his lack-luster eye.

"Rufus!"

So deeply had Rufus been absorbed in his own somber thoughts that he had not seen William climb over the fence and approach the house. At the sound of his voice so near at hand, Rufus looked up and saw William standing before him with outstretched hand.

"No, William," said Rufus, shaking his head slowly, "I could n' shake han's wid you."

"Stop yo' foolishness, Rufus, an' listen ter me? Gimme yo' han'!"

"No, William," returned Rufus sadly, "I ain' fitten fer ter tech yo' han'. You wuz my bes' frien'; you made me w'at I wuz; an' I tu'ned my back on you, an' ha'dened my heart lak Farro of ole Egyp' ter de child'en er Is'ael. You had never done me nuthin' but good; but I went ter de law 'ginst you, an' den de law come ter me—an' I've be'n sarved right! I ain' fitten' ter tech yo' han', William. Go 'long an' leave me ter my punishment!"

"You has spoke de truf, Rufus, de Lord's truf! But ef I kin fergive w'at you done ter me, dey ain' no 'casion fer you ter bear malice 'ginst yo'se'f. Git up f'm dere, man, an' gimme yo' han', an' den listen ter my wo'ds!"

Rufus rose slowly, and taking each other's hands they buried their enmity in a prolonged and fervent clasp.

"An' now, Rufus," said William, drawing from his pocket an old yellow paper, through which the light shone along the seams where it had been folded, "does you reco'nize dat paper?"

"No, William, you 'member I never l'arned ter read."

"Well, I has, an' I'll read dis paper ter you:

"'William Cain an' Rufus Green is gone in partners this day to work at whatever their hands find to do. What they makes shall belong to one as much as the other, and they shall stand by each other in sickness and in health, in good luck and in bad, till death shall us part, and the Lord have mercy on our souls. Amen.'

"Ou' ole podnership paper, William," said Rufus sadly, "ou' ole podnership, w'at wuz broke up ten years ago!"

"Broke up? Who said it wuz broke up?" exclaimed William. "It says 'in good luck an' in bad, till death shall us part,' an' it means w'at it says! Do you suppose de Lord would have mussy on my soul ef I wuz ter fersake my ole podner at de time er his greates' trouble? He would n' be a jes' God ef he did! Come 'long now, Rufus, an' we'll put dem things back in yo' house, an' onhitch dat hoss. You ain' gwine ter stir one foot f'm dis place, onless it's ter go home ter dinner wid me. I've seen my lawyer, an' he says you got plenty er time yit ter 'peal you' case an' take it ter de upper co't, wid eve'y chance ter win it—an' he's a hones' man, w'at knows de law. I've got money in de bank, an' w'at's mine is yo'n till yo' troubles is ended, an' f'm dis time fo'th we is podners 'till death shall us part.'"

Exercise Forgiveness:

- William's act of forgiving Rufus is completely selfless, and it's clear as soon as they are reconciled that the future is turning for both of them in ways that only moments before had seemed impossible. Are you capable of the kind of unqualified forgiveness depicted in this story?
- Is there an estranged friendship in your own life whose resolution might bring about a similar transformation in your life? Think about why you are holding on to any unresolved conflicts . . . and then let them melt away in the crucible of forgiveness.
- William recognizes that Rufus must also forgive himself in order for the friendship to move forward. He doesn't make Rufus feel bad about past history in the moment that he extends his forgiveness. Practice this same generosity of spirit when you are next in a position to forgive someone. Recognize the importance of encouraging your friend to forgive himself.

Itabari Njeri

Raised in Brooklyn, Itabari Njeri is a journalist and author of the autobiographical novel Every Good-bye Ain't Gone. *In this passage from the novel, Njeri travels to the small Southern town where her beloved grandfather was killed in a car accident many years before. She seeks closure on her grandfather's death, a tragedy that has nagged her for her entire adult life. But rather than bringing her peace, the visit makes the circumstances surrounding her grandfather's death even more painful.*

from Every Good-Bye Ain't Gone

I drove along a road in southern Georgia. It was a night without a moon. Beyond the pine trees and farmland I could see fire in the distance. Farmers had torched their fields to clear the earth for planting. Bark and grass smoldered at the edge of the road. I saw a tall pine ablaze, and I could not suppress the thought of a burning cross as I drove to the house of the man who killed my grandfather twenty-three years ago.

I had heard the tale all of my life: Drunken white boys drag racing through a small Southern town in 1960 had killed my granddaddy. Nobody, I was told, knew their names. Nobody, I was told, knew what happened to them. Things were hushed up. Those were the rumors. What everyone knew was this: Granddaddy was a black doctor in Bainbridge, Georgia. Late on the night of October 30 his phone rang. It was an emergency. A patient was gravely ill. Granddaddy left his home in his robe and pajamas, drove to the small infirmary he ran in town, and treated his patient. As he was returning home, a car collided with his. My grandfather was thrown to the pavement. His ribs were broken; his skull was cracked.

Several hours later, the telephone call came to my parents' apartment in Harlem. Granddaddy was dead.

During my childhood, my grandfather was the only adult male I remember openly loving me. Yet, oddly, I seemed unable to absorb the meaning of his death. I felt no grief. Nineteen sixty had been filled with confusing events that disturbed the calm childhood I had known. The distant and accidental violence that took my grandfather's life could not compete with the psychological terror that had begun to engulf my own. The year my grandfather died, my own father returned, and I began to sleep each night with a knife under my pillow.

As I grew older, my grandfather assumed mythic proportions in my imagination. Even in absence, he filled my room like music and watched over me when I was fearful. His fantasized presence diverted thoughts of my father's drunken rages. With age, my fantasizing ceased, the image of my grandfather faded. What lingered was the memory of his caress, the pain of something missing in my life, wrenched away by reckless white youths. I had a growing sense—the beginning of an inevitable comprehension—that this society deals blacks a disproportionate share of pain and denial.

With time, I felt compelled to find out what really happened in Bainbridge that night in 1960.

My family wasn't much help. My stepgrandmother, Madelyn, had suffered a nervous breakdown after the accident and to this day is unyielding in her refusal to discuss it. "It's been twenty-three years," she says. "It took me a long time to get past that. I don't want to open old wounds."

She also feared that, if I stirred things up, "they might desecrate" my granddaddy's grave. If she still held such fears after so much time, I needed no other reason to return to Bainbridge, and so I did. . . .

Black people in Bainbridge had told me my grandfather was buried in Pineview Cemetery. "It's the black cemetery in the white part of town," said Anne Smith, seventy-eight, an elegant, retired school-teacher. Granddaddy had delivered her baby. "The white cemetery is in the black part of town," she said.

I headed for the white part of town.

The streets were unfamiliar. I had only been to Bainbridge twice before, in 1957 and 1958.

Mama and I had flown to Tallahassee from New York City. Grand-daddy had picked us up and driven the forty-two miles north to Bain-bridge, Georgia's "first inland port," population 12,714, then. The town lies in the southwest corner of the state, north of Attapulgus, south of Camilla.

My grandfather had moved there in 1935 after his residency at Brewster Hospital in Jacksonville, Florida. Shortly before, he'd divorced my Jamaican-born grandmother, Ruby Duncombe Lord, to marry Madelyn Parsons, a much younger woman. Ruby never had a kind word to say about Granddaddy. Their marital problems were myriad, but among them was her refusal to move to the Jim Crow South from New York. "I'll not step aside for any white people," she boldly claimed. What she really felt, I suspect, was justifiable fear of a life filled with terrorism. But Bainbridge needed a black doctor, so Granddaddy went.

I spent two summers with my grandfather, and a few holidays. I was about four the first time we met, and properly outfitted for the occasion in a brilliant yellow, silk-and-satin-trimmed peignoir. I believed myself devastating. But the straps kept slipping. The sleeves kept sliding. I didn't care. Granddaddy hugged me and chased me in circles around the house till we fell down laughing on the floor.

"Oh, Granddaddy, I don't feel so well," I'd tease.

"We can't have that," he'd say, then run and get his black bag and pretend to prepare an injection.

"No, no. I'm fine, Grandpa." He'd chase me again.

"Sure you're fine now?"

"I'm sure." I squealed and ran myself silly. He'd catch me, hug me, and tickle me to tears.

Now I was searching for his grave.

The weather was windy, cold, very gray. In the car, outside the cemetery, I sat searching for my sunglasses. I kept fumbling for them, in my purse, under the seat. I had not cried once.

It was my third day in town. I had talked to dozens of people who knew him, trying to reconstruct his life and death. I wanted to be professionally detached, unemotional. I cursed the missing sunglasses.

Thirteen minutes later I gave up and stepped out of the rented car.

I began walking around the southern rim of the graveyard. His would be a big tombstone, I was sure.

"Was he good?" repeated L. H. B. Foote incredulously. "One of the best. He never stopped trying to learn medicine, and that makes any doctor good." Leonard Hobson Buchanan Foote, M.D., did not look

his eighty-five years. We had sat in his Tallahassee home on the Florida
A&M University campus. For forty years he had been the director of
student medical services there. He had been one of my grandfather's
closest friends.

They entered Howard University the same year. "The freshman class
of 1918," Foote said. The year before, my grandfather had immigrated
to the United States from Georgetown, Guyana, then a British colony.

"I was just a boy from Maryland," Foote said, "born and reared
just north of Baltimore." Granddaddy, he recalled, "was tall, slender,
a nice-looking young colored man with a foreign accent. I'd say, 'Man,
I can't understand you. What are you saying?' He'd say, 'You just listen
real good. I speak the King's English.' I said, 'What king?' He said,
'The King of England.' 'You're one of those West Indians, huh?' 'Yeah,
what's wrong with that?' 'Not a thing,' I said. 'Welcome here, brother.'

"I felt like I had lost a brother when he died. He had a lot of whites
who were his friends, some of them were his patients."

But, he said, Granddaddy had been the object of some resentment.
There are, explained Foote, "three things that the Southern white man
has tried over the years to keep out of the hands of blacks—education, money, and social rank. Your grandfather had all that."

As I walked to the western edge of the graveyard, I heard voices
nearby. Several houses lined the western perimeter of the cemetery. I
stared at the windows looking out on the tombstones.

"Rumor was, one of the boys in the car could look out of his
kitchen window and see Daddy's grave," my aunt Earlyne had told me.

I searched for nearly an hour. Finally, I reached the north end.
About fifty feet ahead of me I spotted a gray marble headstone.

I stepped closer to the tombstone, a solitary monument in a
twenty-foot-square plot. It was the biggest headstone in the cemetery:
THE FAMILY OF DR. E A R LORD.

I stared standing in the cold. I wiped my nose. In the crevice of the
chiseled letters that formed the word "of," dirt and rain had left a
sooty streak. It was the only smudge on the stone. Unconsciously, I

leaned forward and began to wipe the stain with the pink Kleenex in my hand. I rubbed hard against the marble. The tissue frayed and disintegrated in the wind.

On the slab of marble that covered his grave was the symbol of the medical profession, the caduceus with its entwined serpents on a winged staff. Engraved in the stone was his full name: EDWARD ADOLPHUS RUFUS LORD SR. M.D.

They called him Earl Lord for short. He was born July 26, 1897, in Georgetown, Guyana. He died October 30, 1960, in Bainbridge, Georgia.

"Wasn't from around here," Bernice Busbee drawled. The man across from her stood gnomelike behind the rocking chair in his office, smiled like Puck, and softly proclaimed himself "the oldest living white person in Bainbridge." Then Mortimer Alfred Ehrlich, M.D., eighty-nine, sat down and rocked.

He was retired. As a younger man Dr. Ehrlich had often come to my grandfather's infirmary to help with surgery. He was one of the few whites in Bainbridge whom my family thought of as a genuine friend.

I told him only that I was a newspaper reporter doing a story about small-town doctors; I wanted him to speak freely. Then I asked him about Dr. Lord.

Dr. Ehrlich regarded me thoughtfully.

"I don't want to talk bad of the dead," he said. I switched off the tape recorder and smiled my encouragement.

"He was a bad man," Ehrlich finally said. The old chair groaned with each rock.

"Blacks didn't like him either," Busbee offered. She had been Ehrlich's receptionist for thirty-one years. Now they spent their days making quilts for comfort when it's cold. "He was an undermining, sneaky fellow," she said. "He tried to bring the NAACP in here."

"Lord was for integration," Ehrlich elaborated.

"He just didn't fit in," she said, "didn't understand the people. Didn't know our ways. We were all glad when he was gone."

My smile was beginning to ache.

"If he hadn't been killed in the accident, he would have been shot," Ehrlich said. "Better he was killed that way so we didn't have the bother of a trial for whoever shot him."

We spoke for a few more minutes. Then I rose to leave and shake his hand. He offered the tips of his fingers.

I left him rocking.

Exercise Forgiveness:

- In the midst of his despair, the Prophet Habakkuk cried out: "O Lord, how long shall I cry, and thou wilt not hear! even cry out unto thee of violence, and thou wilt not save!/Why dost thou shew me iniquity, and cause me to behold grievance? for spoiling and violence are before me: and there are that raise up strife and contention. Therefore the law is slacked, and judgment doth never go forth: for the wicked doth compass about the righteous; therefore wrong judgment proceedeth." (Habakkuk: I 2–4). Likewise, Njeri cannot reconcile a great injustice: the inability of the whites in Bainbridge to admit that the driver of the car who killed Dr. Lord should have been brought to justice. We all have stories about ancestors who were murdered or harassed by racists. But holding on to these wounds can be self-annihilating. Although Njeri holds on to the notion that every good-bye ain't gone, acknowledging the memory of her grandfather by working to bring meaning and justice to the circumstances surrounding his death, her inability to lay the incident to rest is preventing her from truly living in the present.

- In Habakkuk I, the Lord assures Habakkuk that justice will prevail. And in Matthew 6:14, he asks us to forgive those who sin against us: "For if ye forgive men their trespasses, your heavenly Father will also forgive you." How might Njeri's forgiveness provide her with the peace she seeks? How might this forgiveness truly bring closure to her grandfather's death?

* Are there people in your life who have committed acts against you that keep you mired in the past and prevent you from living your life to the fullest today? By not forgiving those who have committed wrongs against us, we remain victimized by their acts. Forgiveness does not mean that the act was not wrong or that we were not harmed by it; however, forgiveness gives us power. Consider Psalm 30:1: "I will extol thee, O Lord; for thou hast lifted me up, and hast not made my foes rejoice over me." In light of this story and the stories your family may carry about injustices suffered at the hands of racism, consider the meaning of this passage.

Sterling A. Brown

Onetime *poet laureate of the District of Columbia Sterling A. Brown graduated from Williams College in 1922 and did graduate work at Harvard. He died in 1989. His poetry was influenced by jazz, the blues, and spirituals and he was known for using African American folklore and contemporary idiom. Originally published in* Crisis *magazine in April 1927, "After the Storm" is not about forgiveness in a literal sense, but it captures the sentiment perfectly.*

After the Storm

There is pathetic beauty in it all,
  O'erhead the murky, sullen rain clouds pass,
  The sun's first darting rays have pierced the mass,
Just now so grim, so gray. Again the call
Is heard of storm hushed robins. Maples tall,
  To show the regal silver of their class,
  Rustle their thirst-slaked leaves and on the grass,
Drenched into higher color, some last drops fall.

'Tis like that heart, whose happiness excelled
    All others, which, with its gay threshold crossed

       At last by sorrow's gloom, has fitly learned
To stifle throes of pain, has ne'er rebelled

       In angry bitterness, has merely turned
    Gayness to pathos, with no beauty lost.

Exercise Forgiveness:

- Sterling Brown's poem captures the frenzy of the storm and its aftermath. It's funny how our anger can mirror that of a raging storm. When our personal storm is in progress we can say some terrible things for which we may need to seek forgiveness. Think about the ways in which a storm's aftermath is like forgiveness.

- Sometimes our anger at our children can come to a boil and we can react in ways that are overblown. But after these tumultuous times are over, we often realize that we could have reacted differently. Like a storm's fury, these times are temporary. When you find yourself becoming angry with your children, remember this passage from 2 Corinthians 2:7: "So that contrariwise ye ought to forgive him, and comfort him, lest perhaps such a one should be swallowed up with overmuch sorrow."

- Think about a time when your child scribbled on a freshly painted wall or spilled a bowl of spaghetti sauce. How did you handle the situation? Your children are precious and fragile souls who look to you for love, acceptance, and, yes, forgiveness. Read 1 John 2:12 and consider the way in which children have a special place in God's eyes. "I write unto you, little children, because your sins are forgiven for his name's sake."

Bible

I have often found it difficult to forgive those who wound me. I have felt that they did not deserve to be forgiven, especially if the offense was malicious. Sometime ago, a relative betrayed my trust by making a fraudulent transaction in my name. When the scheme was discovered, I was furious: The idea of one's committing such an intentional and potentially damaging transgression was more than I could fathom. However, my anger was quelled when I stood before God and cried out for him to forgive my own pride and arrogance. Realizing how much I needed God's mercy for my own ungodly attitude and actions, I had to grant that same mercy to my relative. Whether it is a case of family matters, race relations, or affairs of the heart, many of us are guilty of asking for the same forgiveness that we arrogantly withhold from others. The parable of "The Unforgiving Slave," retold from Matthew 18:21–35 reminds us that because we must all ask God for forgiveness at some point in our lives, we must therefore show compassion to our fellow human beings even when they have wronged us.

The Unforgiving Slave

Peter came to Jesus and questioned, "Lord, how many times ought my brother sin against me, and I forgive him? Till seven times?"

Jesus answered, "I tell you, not seven times, but seventy times seven times.

"Consequently, the kingdom of heaven can be likened to a certain king who sought to settle debts with his servants. When he had begun the settlements, a slave who owed him a sizable sum was brought to him. As he was unable to pay, his master demanded that he, his wife, his children, and all his possessions be sold to make the payment.

"The servant fell to his knees before the king. 'Exercise patience with me,' he pleaded, 'and I will repay you the entirety of my debts.' His master released him out of pity and waived the debt.

"As the servant left his master, he came across a fellow servant who owed him a small sum. He clutched the slave's throat and ordered, 'Pay back what you owe me.'

"The fellow servant dropped down before his feet and beseeched him, 'Be patient with me, and I will pay back all I owe you.'

"But he rebuffed him, and had the servant cast into prison until he could repay his debt. Disturbed by what they had witnessed, the other slaves reported the incident to their master.

"The king sent for the servant. 'You wicked slave! I canceled your debts because you pleaded with me to. Should you not have shown compassion to your fellow servant as I did to you?' Outraged, the king gave the slave over to be tortured until he could repay his debts entirely.

"My heavenly father shall do unto you in this way unless you forgive your brother and sister within your heart."

Exercise Forgiveness:

* As your sins are pardoned by God, you should also forgive your brothers and sisters. Further, God's forgiving us our sins should put us in the proper frame of mind to forgive one another, and unless we forgive from this position of the heart, we are not forgiving in the right way. To exercise true forgiveness means we count on the mercy of God to teach us how to forgive. We humbly ask forgiveness for ourselves and at the same time seek to forgive others as we are forgiven. The next time you are in a position to forgive someone who has wronged you, try to think consciously not about your position with this person—that he has wronged you and you deserve better and you are angry—but instead about your position with the one who ultimately forgives you. Only then do you move toward the spirit of forgiveness.

* It is often tempting to seek revenge or to act against someone who has wronged us. This parable teaches us to bring those affronts to God. For today, leave behind forever at least one grievance you have against another.

- In the parable of "The Unforgiving Slave," Peter asks Jesus if he
  ought to forgive his brother for sins. Jesus instructs Peter to exercise
  forgiveness far more than seven times; the King James Version of the
  Bible calls for forgiveness up to "seventy times seven" times. More
  recent translations of the Bible, however, interpret "seventy times
  seven" as 77 times. Is this interpretation merely a language update
  for contemporary readers, or does it reflect an unwillingness among
  those of us today to forgive others when we have been wronged?
  Would you be able to exercise forgiveness 490, or even 77 times?
  Consider the language of the King James Version the next time you
  feel a person has wronged you more than once.

Honesty

Straightforwardness of speech and integrity of conduct,
HONESTY paves the path to sincere and upright living.

It often seems as though human beings are afraid of the truth. We spend hours dreaming up good excuses and inventing intricate stories to hide reality. If only we would all open our eyes to the value of honesty. Why don't we realize that our lies only deceive us and taint our spirits?

America's economic well-being was damaged by corporate deception. Enron, Tyco, Global Crossings, and Arthur Anderson are companies that will be forever tainted because of their dishonesty. We have felt the consequences of such widespread dishonesty on a personal level. Our retirement account was invested in Enron, Tyco, and Global Crossings stock. Along with thousands of others, we now face an uncertain financial future due to the dishonesty of those we trusted.

What do we have to gain by obscuring the truth? When will we understand that an honest existence affords us a richer life? Lying often seems the easiest path to take, but dishonesty is in fact a trap, not a road. Beware of the "innocent" lie, for even the smallest masking of the truth only feeds the fire of deception. We all know that one lie leads to another. Do not let yourself reach the point at which you become terrified of the truth.

But honesty, I tell you, is more than just not lying. It is a way of life. To be honest is to be both open and unselfish; it is to share your life with those you love. Honesty is telling what must be told, giving what must be given, and doing what must be done. Honesty is a generosity of the heart upon which our relationships must be built.

Too often we neglect to be honest with ourselves. By concealing our weaknesses, we are only made weaker. We hope that by ignoring our problems, they will simply disappear. It is time we admit that they won't. Once you have mustered the strength to acknowledge your shortcomings and face your fears, the heavy burden of powerlessness will be lifted.

Resist the impulse to be dishonest. Find the courage to live your life according to God's commandment. As Leviticus 19:11 instructs, "Ye shall not steal, neither deal falsely, neither lie one to another." The Bible illustrates that dishonesty is a mark of poor intentions and selfish decision-making.

A life of honesty is a life of integrity. We must learn to be upright and righteous in all our relationships. Truthfulness must guide our actions as well as our thoughts. Always remember that those who lie suffer the consequences of their dishonesty, while those who tell the truth reap the benefits of honest living.

Booker T. Washington

It's possible to find an illustration of one of our virtues on just about every page of Booker T. Washington's 1901 autobiography, Up from Slavery. *I love this passage as an example of honesty.*

from Up from Slavery

At the end of my first year at Hampton I was confronted with another difficulty. Most of the students went home to spend their vacation. I had no money with which to go home, but I had to go somewhere. In those days very few students were permitted to remain at the school during vacation. It made me feel very sad and homesick to see the other students preparing to leave and starting for home. I not only had no money with which to go home, but I had none with which to go anywhere.

In some way, however, I had gotten hold of an extra, secondhand coat which I thought was a pretty valuable coat. This I decided to sell, in order to get a little money for traveling expenses. I had a good deal of boyish pride, and I tried to hide, as far as I could, from the other students the fact that I had no money and nowhere to go. I made it known to a few people in the town of Hampton that I had this coat to sell, and, after a good deal of persuading, one colored man promised to come to my room to look the coat over and consider the matter of buying it. This cheered my drooping spirits considerably. Early the next morning my prospective customer appeared. After looking the garment over carefully, he asked me how much I wanted for it. I told him I thought it was worth three dollars. He seemed to agree with me as to price, but remarked in the most matter-of-fact way: "I tell you what I will do: I will take the coat, and I will pay you five cents, cash down, and pay you the rest of the money just as soon as I can get it." It is not hard to imagine what my feelings were at the time.

With this disappointment I gave up all hope of getting out of the town of Hampton for my vacation work. I wanted very much to go where I might secure work that would at least pay me enough to purchase some much-needed clothing and other necessities. In a few days practically all the students and teachers had left for their homes, and this served to depress my spirits even more.

After trying for several days in and near the town of Hampton, I finally secured work in a restaurant at Fortress Monroe. The wages, however, were very little more than my board. At night, and between meals, I found considerable time for study and reading; and in this direction I improved myself very much during the summer.

When I left school at the end of my first year, I owed the institution sixteen dollars that I had not been able to work out. It was my greatest ambition during the summer to save money enough with which to pay this debt. I felt that this was a debt of honor, and that I could hardly bring myself to the point of even trying to enter school again till it was paid. I economized in every way that I could think of—did my own washing, and went without necessary garments—but still I found my summer vacation ending and I did not have the sixteen dollars.

One day, during the last week of my stay in the restaurant, I found under one of the tables a crisp, new ten-dollar bill. I could hardly contain myself, I was so happy. As it was not my place of business I felt it to be the proper thing to show the money to the proprietor. This I did. He seemed as glad as I was, but he coolly explained to me that, as it was his place of business, he had a right to keep the money, and he proceeded to do so.

This, I confess, was another pretty hard blow to me. I will not say that I became discouraged, for as I now look back over my life I do not recall that I ever became discouraged over anything that I set out to accomplish. I have begun everything with the idea that I could succeed, and I never had much patience with the multitudes of people who are always ready to explain why one cannot succeed.

Exercise Honesty:

- A visitor to our office happened in while we were working on this excerpt, and when he noticed this passage on the desk he picked it up to read. Now this was an educated man, a Stanford MBA, but I don't think he'd ever read Booker T. Washington. He was actually upset by the passage, and said fervently that he hoped that Washington somehow got another ten dollars. He also said he thought Washington had no obligation to return the ten dollars to the owner of the restaurant, since it clearly wasn't the owner's money, but was left behind by a customer. Washington's stringent honesty is an anathema for most of us today. Would you have returned the money to the owner of the restaurant? Do you know anyone who would have? The point of this example is not that the money belonged to this one or that one, but rather that Washington cared more about doing the right and honest thing, whatever that was, than anything else. Whether Washington gets another ten dollars is also not the point—because virtue really is its own reward.

- We probably see more examples of dishonesty in life than we do real, honest-to-goodness honesty: plagiarism by acclaimed historians, rampant cheating at major universities, the Enron scandal, teenagers downloading artists' songs off the Internet. There are more egregious crimes in the world than downloading an unauthorized copy of a copyrighted song, but the cumulative effect of all these infractions is an erosion of one of our most useful virtues. Look for honest moments. Look for opportunities to be honest and to point out honest moments to your children. Model honesty proactively in your home.

Dorothy West

Harlem Renaissance author and journalist Dorothy West was best known for her short stories. "Jack in the Pot," published in the collection The Richer, The Poorer, illustrates the consequences that ensued when Mrs. Edmunds lied "as she had not lied before in all her life."

Jack in the Pot

When she walked down the aisle of the theater, clutching the money in her hand, hearing the applause and laughter, seeing, dimly, the grinning black faces, she was trembling so violently that she did not know how she could ever regain her seat.

It was unbelievable. Week after week she had come on Wednesday afternoon to this smelly, third-run neighborhood movie house, paid her dime, received her beano card, and gone inside to wait through an indifferent feature until the house lights came on, and a too jovial white man wheeled a board onto the stage and busily fished in a bowl for numbers.

Today it had happened. As the too jovial white man called each number, she found a corresponding one on her card. When he called the seventh number and explained dramatically that whoever had punched five numbers in a row had won the jackpot of fifty-five dollars, she listened in smiling disbelief that there was that much money in his pocket. It was then that the woman beside her leaned toward her and said excitedly, "Look, lady, you got it!"

She did not remember going down the aisle. Undoubtedly her neighbor had prodded her to her feet. When it was over, she tottered dazedly to her seat, and sat in a dreamy stupor, scarcely able to believe her good fortune.

The drawing continued, the last dollar was given away, the theater darkened, and the afternoon crowd filed out. The little gray woman, collecting her wits, followed them.

She revived in the sharp air. Her head cleared and happiness swelled in her throat. She had fifty-five dollars in her purse. It was wonderful to think about.

She reached her own intersection and paused before Mr. Spiro's general market. Here she regularly shopped, settling part of her bill fortnightly out of her relief check. When Mr. Spiro put in inferior stock because most of his customers were poor-paying reliefers, she had wanted to shop elsewhere. But she could never get paid up.

Excitement smote her. She would go in, settle her account, and say good-bye to Mr. Spiro forever. Resolutely she turned into the market.

Mr. Spiro, broad and unkempt, began to boom heartily, from behind the counter, "Hello, Mrs. Edmunds."

She lowered her eyes and asked diffidently, "How much is my bill, Mr. Spiro?"

He recoiled in horror. "Do I worry about your bill, Mrs. Edmunds? Don't you pay something when you get your relief check? Ain't you one of my best customers?"

"I'd like to settle," said Mrs. Edmunds breathlessly.

Mr. Spiro eyed her shrewdly. His voice was soft and insinuating. "You got cash, Mrs. Edmunds? You hit the number? Every other week you give me something on account. This week you want to settle. Am I losing your trade? Ain't I always treated you right?

"Sure, Mr. Spiro," she answered nervously. "I was telling my husband just last night, ain't another man treats me like Mr. Spiro. And I said I wished I could settle my bill."

"Gee," he said triumphantly, "it's like I said. You're one of my best customers. Worrying about your bill when I ain't even worrying. I was telling your investigator..." he paused significantly: "When Mr. Edmunds gets a job, I know I'll get the balance. Mr. Edmunds got himself a job maybe?"

She was stiff with fright. "No, I'd have told you right off, and her, too. I ain't one to cheat on relief. I was only saying how I wished I could settle. I wasn't saying that I was."

"Well, then, what you want for supper?" Mr. Spiro asked soothingly.

"Loaf of bread," she answered gratefully, "two pork chops, one kinda thick, can of spaghetti, little can of milk."

The purchases were itemized. Mrs. Edmunds said good night and left the store. She felt sick and ashamed, for she had turned tail in the moment that was to have been her triumph over tyranny.

A little boy came toward her in the familiar rags of the neighborhood children. Suddenly Mrs. Edmunds could bear no longer the intolerable weight of her mean provisions.

"Little boy," she said.

"Ma'am?" He stopped and stared at her.

"Here." She held out the bag to him. "Take it home to your mama. It's food. It's clean."

He blinked, then snatched the bag from her hands, and turned and ran very fast in the direction from which he had come.

Mrs. Edmunds felt better at once. Now she could buy a really good supper. She walked ten blocks to a better neighborhood and the cold did not bother her. Her misshapen shoes were winged.

She pushed inside a resplendent store and marched to the meat counter. A porterhouse steak caught her eye. She could not look past it. It was big and thick and beautiful.

The clerk leaned toward her. "Steak, moddom?"

"That one."

It was glorious not to care about the cost of things. She bought mushrooms, fresh peas, cauliflower, tomatoes, a pound of good coffee, a pint of real cream, a dozen dinner rolls, and a maple walnut layer cake.

The winter stars were pricking the sky when she entered the dimly lit hallway of the old-law tenement building in which she lived. The dank smell smote her instantly after the long walk in the brisk, clear air. The Smith boy's dog had dirtied the hall again. Mr. Johnson, the janitor, was mournfully mopping up.

"Evenin', Mis' Edmunds, ma'am," he said plaintively.

"Evening," Mrs. Edmunds said coldly. Suddenly she hated Mr. Johnson. He was so humble.

Five young children shared the uninhabitable basement with him.

They were always half sick, and he was always neglecting his duties to tend to them. The tenants were continually deciding to report him to the agent, and then at the last moment deciding not to.

"I'll be up tomorrow to see 'bout them windows, Mis' Edmunds, ma'am. My baby kep' frettin' today, and I been so busy doctorin'."

"Those children need a mother," said Mrs. Edmunds severely. "You ought to get married again."

"My wife ain' daid," cried Mr. Johnson, shocked out of his servility. "She's in that T.B. home. Been there two years and 'bout on the road to health."

"Well," said Mrs. Edmunds inconclusively, and then added briskly, "I been waiting weeks and weeks for them window strips. Winter's half over. If the place was kept warm—"

"Yes'm, Mis' Edmunds," he said hastily, his bloodshot eyes imploring. "It's that o' furnace. I done tol' the agent time and again but they ain' fixin' to fix up this house 'long as you all is relief folks."

The steak was sizzling on the stove when Mr. Edmunds' key turned in the lock of the tiny three-room flat. His step dragged down the hall. Mrs. Edmunds knew what that meant: "No man wanted." Two years ago Mrs. Edmunds had begun, doggedly, to canvass the city for work, leaving home soon after breakfast and rarely returning before supper.

Once he had had a little stationery store. After losing it, he had spent his small savings and sold or pawned every decent article of furniture and clothing before applying for relief. Even so, there had been a long investigation while he and his wife slowly starved. Fear had been implanted in Mrs. Edmunds. Thereafter she was never wholly unafraid. Mr. Edmunds had had to stand by and watch his wife starve. He never got over being ashamed.

Mr. Edmunds stood in the kitchen doorway, holding his rain-streaked hat in his knotted hand. He was forty-nine, and he looked like an old man.

"I'm back," he said. "Cooking supper."

It was not a question. He seemed unaware of the intoxicating odors. She smiled at him brightly. "Smell good?"

He shook suddenly with the cold that was still in him. He was too cold, and their supper was too fine.

"Things'll pick up in the spring," she said soothingly.

"Not for me," he answered gloomily. "Look how I look. Like a bum. I wouldn't hire me, myself."

"What you want me to do about it?" she asked furiously.

"Nothing," he said with wry humor, "unless you can make money, and make me just about fifty dollars."

She caught her breath and stared at his shabbiness. She had seen him look like this so long that she had forgotten that clothes would make a difference.

She nodded toward the stove. "That steak and all. Guess you think I got a fortune. Well, I won a little old measly dollar at the movies."

His face lightened, and his eyes grew soft with affection. "You shouldn't have bought a steak," he said. "Wish you'd bought yourself something you been wanting. Like gloves. Some good warm gloves. Hurts my heart when I see you with cold hands."

She was ashamed, and wished she knew how to cross the room to kiss him. "Go wash," she said gruffly. "Steak's 'most too done already."

It was a wonderful dinner. Both of them had been starved for fresh meat. Mrs. Edmunds' face was flushed, and there was color in her lips, as if the good blood of the meat had filtered through her skin. Mr. Edmunds ate a pound and a half of the two-pound steak, and his hands seemed steadier with each sharp thrust of the knife.

Over the coffee and cake they talked contentedly. Mrs. Edmunds wanted to tell the truth about the money, and waited for an opening.

"We'll move out of this hole someday soon," said Mr. Edmunds.

"Things won't be like this always." He was full and warm and confident.

"If I had fifty dollars," Mrs. Edmunds began cautiously, "I believe I'd move tomorrow. Pay up these people what I owe, and get me a fit place to live in."

"Fifty dollars would be a drop in the bucket. You got to have something coming in steady."

He had hurt her again. "Fifty dollars is more than you got," she said meanly.

"It's more than you got, too," he said mildly. "Look at it like this. If you had fifty dollars and made a change, them relief folks would worry you like a pack of wolves. But say, f'instance, you had fifty dollars, and I had a job, we could walk out of here without a howdy-do to anybody."

It would have been anticlimactic to tell him about the money. She got up. "I'll do the dishes. You sit still."

He noticed no change in her and went on earnestly, "Lord's bound to put something in my way soon. Things is got to break for us. We don't live human. I never see a paper 'cept when I pick one up at the subway. I ain't had a cigarette in three years. We ain't got a radio. We don't have no company. All the pleasure you get is a ten-cent movie one day a week. I don't even get that."

Presently Mrs. Edmunds ventured, "You think the investigator would notice if we got a little radio for the bedroom?"

"Somebody got one to give away?" His voice was eager.

"Maybe."

"Well, seeing how she could check with the party what give it to you, I think it would be all right."

"Well, ne'mind . . ." her voice petered out.

It was his turn to try. "Want to play me a game of cards?"

He had not asked her for months. She cleared her throat. "I'll play a hand or two."

He stretched luxuriously. "I feel so good. Feeling like this, bet I'll land something tomorrow."

She said very gently, "The investigator comes tomorrow."

He smiled quickly to hide his disappointment. "Clean forgot. It don't matter. That meal was so good it'll carry me straight through Friday."

She opened her mouth to tell him about the jackpot, to promise him as many meals as there was money. Suddenly someone upstairs pounded on the radiator for heat. In a moment someone downstairs pounded. Presently their side of the house resounded. It was maddening. Mrs. Edmunds was bitterly aware that her hands and feet were like ice.

" 'Tisn't no use," she cried wildly to the walls. She burst into tears. " 'Tisn't nothing no use."

Her husband crossed quickly to her. He kissed her cheek. "I'm going to make all this up to you. You'll see."

By half past eight they were in bed. By quarter to nine Mrs. Edmunds was quietly sleeping. Mr. Edmunds lay staring at the ceiling as it kept coming closer.

Mrs. Edmunds waked first and decided to go again to the grand market. She dressed and went out into the street. An ambulance stood in front of the door. In a minute an intern emerged from the basement, carrying a bundled child. Mr. Johnson followed, his eyes more bleary and bloodshot than ever.

Mrs. Edmunds rushed up to him. "The baby?" she asked anxiously.

His face worked pitifully. "Yes, ma'am, Mis' Edmunds. Pneumonia. I heard you folks knockin' for heat last night but my hands was too full. I ain't forgot about them windows, though. I'll be up tomorrow bright and early."

Mr. Edmunds stood in the kitchen door. "I smell meat in the morning?" he asked incredulously. He sat down, and she spread the feast—kidneys, an omelet, hot buttered rolls, and strawberry jam. "You mind," he said happily, "explaining this mystery? Was that dollar of yours made out of elastic?"

"It wasn't a dollar like I said. It was five. I wanted to surprise you."

She did not look at him and her voice was breathless. She had decided to wait until after the investigator's visit to tell him the whole truth about the money. Otherwise they might both be nervous and betray themselves by their guilty knowledge.

"We got chicken for dinner," she added shyly.

"Lord, I don't know when I had a piece of chicken."

They ate, and the morning passed glowingly. With Mr. Edmunds' help, Mrs. Edmunds moved the furniture and gave the flat a thorough cleaning. She liked for the investigator to find her busy. She felt less embarrassed about being on relief when it could be seen that she occupied her time.

The afternoon waned. The Edmundses sat in the living room, and there was nothing to do. They were hungry but dared not start dinner. With activity suspended, they became aware of the penetrating cold and the rattling windows. Mr. Edmunds began to have that wild look of waiting for the investigator.

Mrs. Edmunds suddenly had an idea. She would go and get a newspaper and a package of cigarettes for him.

At the corner, she ran into Mr. Johnson. Rather he ran into her, for he turned the corner with his head down, and his gait as unsteady as if he had been drinking.

"That you, Mr. Johnson?" she said sharply.

He raised his head, and she saw that he was not drunk.

"Yes, ma'am, Mis' Edmunds."

"The baby—is she worse?"

Tears welled out of his eyes. "The Lord done took her."

Tears stood in her own eyes. "God knows I'm sorry to hear that. Let me know if there's anything I can do."

"Thank you, Mis' Edmunds, ma'am. But ain't nothin' nobody can do. I been pricin' funerals. I can get one for fifty dollars. But I been to my brother, and he ain't got it. I been everywhere. Couldn't raise no more than ten dollars." He was suddenly embarrassed. "I know all you tenants is on relief. I wasn't fixin' to ask you all."

"Fifty dollars," she said strainedly, "is a lot of money."

"God'd have to pass a miracle for me to raise it. Guess the city'll have to bury her. You reckon they'll let me take flowers?"

"You being the father, I guess they would," she said weakly.

When she returned home the flat was a little warmer. She entered the living room. Her husband's face brightened.

"You bought a paper!"

She held out the cigarettes. "You smoke this kind?" she asked lifelessly.

He jumped up and crossed to her. "I declare I don't know how to thank you! Wish that investigator'd come. I sure want to taste them."

"Go ahead and smoke," she cried fiercely. "It's none of her business. We got our rights same as working people."

She turned into the bedroom. She was utterly spent. Too much had happened in the last twenty-four hours.

"Guess I'll stretch out for a bit. I'm not going to sleep. If I do drop off, listen out for the investigator. The bell needs fixing. She might have to knock."

At half past five Mr. Edmunds put down the newspaper and tiptoed to the bedroom door. His wife was still asleep. He stood for a moment in indecision, then decided it was long past the hour when the investigator usually called, and went down the hall to the kitchen. He wanted to prepare supper as a surprise. He opened the window, took the foodstuffs out of the crate that in winter served as icebox, and set them on the table.

The doorbell tinkled faintly.

He went to the door and opened it. The investigator stepped inside. She was small and young and white.

"Good evening, miss," he said.

"I'm sorry to call so late," she apologized. "I've been busy all day with an evicted family. But I knew you were expecting me, and I didn't want you to stay in tomorrow."

"You come on up front, miss," he said. "I'll wake up my wife. She wasn't feeling so well and went to lie down."

She saw the light from the kitchen, and the dark rooms beyond.

"Don't wake Mrs. Edmunds," she said kindly, "if she isn't well. I'll just sit in the kitchen for a minute with you."

He looked down at her, but her open, honest face did not disarm him. He braced himself for whatever was to follow.

"Go right on in, miss," he said.

He took the dish towel and dusted the clean chair. "Sit down, miss."

He stood facing her with a furrow between his brows, and his arms folded. There was an awkward pause. She cast about for something to say, and saw the table.

"I interrupted your dinner preparations."

His voice and his face hardened for the blow.

"I was getting dinner for my wife. It's chicken."

"It looks like a nice one," she said pleasantly.

He was baffled. "We ain't had chicken once in three years."

"I understand," she said sincerely. "Sometimes I spend my whole salary on something I want very much."

"You ain't much like an investigator," he said in surprise. "One we had before you woulda raised Ned." He sat down suddenly, his defenses down. "Miss, I been wanting to ask you for this for a long time. You ever have any men's clothes?"

Her voice was distressed. "Every once in a while. But with so many people needing assistance, we can only give them to our employables. But I'll keep your request in mind."

He did not answer. He just sat staring at the floor, presenting an adjustment problem. There was nothing else to say to him.

She rose. "I'll be going now, Mr. Edmunds."

"I'll tell my wife you was here, miss."

A voice called from the bedroom. "Is that you talking?"

"It's the investigator lady," he said. "She's just going."

Mrs. Edmunds came hurrying down the hall, the sleep in her face and tousled hair.

"I was just lying down, ma'am. I didn't mean to go to sleep. My husband should've called me."

"I didn't want him to wake you."

"And he kept you sitting in the kitchen."

She glanced inside to assure herself that it was sufficiently spotless for the fine clothes of the investigator. She saw the laden table, and felt so ill that water welled into her mouth.

"The investigator lady knows about the chicken," Mr. Edmunds said quickly. "She—"

"It was only five dollars," his wife interrupted, wringing her hands.

"Five dollars for a chicken?" The investigator was shocked and incredulous.

"She didn't buy that chicken out of none of your relief money," Mr. Edmunds said defiantly. "It was money she won at a movie."

"It was only five dollars," Mrs. Edmunds repeated tearfully.

"We ain't trying to conceal nothing," Mr. Edmunds snarled. He was cornered and fighting. "If you'd asked me how we come by the chicken, I'd have told you."

"For God's sake, ma'am, don't cut us off," Mrs. Edmunds moaned.

"I'll never go to another movie. It was only ten cents. I didn't know I was doing wrong." She burst into tears.

The investigator stood tense. They had both been screaming at her. She was tired and so irritated that she wanted to scream back.

"Mrs. Edmunds," she said sharply, "get hold of yourself. I'm not going to cut you off. That's ridiculous. You won five dollars at a movie and you bought some food. That's fine. I wish my family could win five dollars for food."

She turned and tore out of the flat. They heard her stumbling and sobbing down the stairs.

"You feel like eating?" Mrs. Edmunds asked dully.

"I guess we're both hungry. That's why we got so upset."

"Maybe we'd better eat, then."

"Let me fix it."

"No." She entered the kitchen. "I kinda want to see you just sitting and smoking a cigarette."

He sat down and reached in his pocket with some eagerness. "I ain't had one yet." He lit a cigarette, inhaled, and felt better immediately.

"You think," she said bleakly, "she'll write that up in our case?"

"I don't know, dear."

"You think they'll close our case if she does?"

"I don't know that neither, dear."

She clutched the sink for support. "My God, what would we do?"

The smoke curled around him luxuriously. "Don't think about it till it happens."

"I got to think about it. The rent, the gas, the light, the food."

"They wouldn't hardly close our case for five dollars."

"Maybe they'd think it was more."

"You could prove it by the movie manager."

She went numb all over. Then suddenly she got mad about it.

It was nine o'clock when they sat down in the living room. The heat came up grudgingly. Mrs. Edmunds wrapped herself in her sweater and read the funnies. Mr. Edmunds was happily inhaling his second cigarette. They were both replete and in good humor.

The window rattled and Mr. Edmunds looked around at it lazily. "Been about two months since you asked Mr. Johnson for weather strips."

The paper shook in her hand. She did not look up. "He promised to fix it this morning, but his baby died."

"His baby! You don't say!"

She kept her eyes glued to the paper. "Pneumonia."

His voice filled with sympathy. He crushed out his cigarette. "Believe I'll go down and sit with him a while."

"He's not there," she said hastily. "I met him when I was going to the store. He said he'd be out all evening."

"I bet the poor man's trying to raise some money."

She let the paper fall in her lap, and clasped her hands to keep them from trembling. She lied again, as she had been lying steadily in the past twenty-four hours, as she had not lied before in all her life.

"He didn't say nothing to me about raising money."

"Wasn't no need to. Where would you get the first five cents to give him?"

I guess," she cried jealously, "you want me to give him the rest of my money."

"No," he said, "I want you to spend what little's left on yourself. Me, I wish I had fifty dollars to give him."

"As poor as you are," she asked angrily, "you'd give him that much money? That's easy to say when you haven't got it."

"I look at it this way," he said simply. "I think how I'd feel in his shoes."

"You got your own troubles," she argued heatedly. "The Johnson baby is better off dead. You'd be a fool to put fifty dollars in the ground. I'd spend my fifty dollars on the living."

" 'Tain't no use to work yourself up," he said. "You ain't got fifty dollars, and neither have I. We'll be quarreling in a minute over make-believe money. Let's go to bed."

Mrs. Edmunds waked at seven and tried to lie quietly by her husband's side, but lying still was torture. She dressed and went into the kitchen, and felt too listless to make her coffee. She sat down at the table and dropped her head on her folded arms. No tears came. There was only the burning in her throat and behind her eyes.

She sat in this manner for half an hour. Suddenly she heard a man's slow tread outside her front door. Terror gripped her. The steps moved on down the hall, but for a moment her knees were water. When she could control her trembling, she stood up and knew that she had to get out of the house. It could not contain her and Mr. Johnson.

She walked quickly away from her neighborhood. It was a raw day, and her feet and hands were beginning to grow numb. She felt sorry for herself. Other people were hurrying past in overshoes and heavy gloves. There were fifty-one dollars in her purse. It was her right to do what she pleased with them. Determinedly she turned into the subway.

In a downtown department store she rode the escalator to the dress department. She walked up and down the rows of lovely garments, stopping to finger critically, standing back to admire.

A salesgirl came toward her, looking straight at her with soft, expectant eyes.

"Do you wish to be waited on, madam?"

Mrs. Edmunds opened her mouth to say "Yes," but the word would not come. She stared at the girl stupidly. "I was just looking," she said.

In the shoe department, she saw a pair of comfort shoes and sat down timidly in a fine leather chair.

A salesman lounged toward her. "Something in shoes?"

"Yes, sir. That comfort shoe."

"Size?" His voice was bored.

"I don't know," she said.

"I'll have to measure you," he said reproachfully. "Give me your foot." He sat down on a stool and held out his hand.

She dragged her eyes up to his face. "How much you say those shoes cost?"

"I didn't say. Eight dollars."

She rose with acute relief. "I ain't got that much with me."

She retreated unsteadily. Something was making her knees weak and her head light.

Her legs steadied. She went quickly to the down escalator. She reached the third floor and was briskly crossing to the next down escalator when she saw the little dresses. A banner screamed that they were selling at the sacrifice price of one dollar. She decided to examine them.

She pushed through the crowd of women, and emerged triumphantly within reach of the dresses. She searched carefully. There were pinks and blues and yellows. She was looking for white. She pushed back through the crowd. In her careful hands lay a little white dress. It was spun gold and gossamer.

Boldly she beckoned a salesgirl. "I'll take this, miss," she said.

All the way home she was excited and close to tears. She was in a fever to see Mr. Johnson. She would let the regret come later. A child lay dead and waiting burial.

She turned her corner at a run. Going down the rickety basement stairs, she prayed that Mr. Johnson was on the premises.

She pounded on his door and he opened it. The agony in his face told her instantly that he had been unable to borrow the money. She tried to speak, and her tongue tripped over her eagerness.

Fear took hold of her and rattled her teeth. "Mr. Johnson, what about the funeral?"

"I give the baby to the student doctors."

"Oh my God, Mr. Johnson! Oh my God!"

"I bought her some flowers."

She turned and went blindly up the stairs. Drooping in the front doorway was a frost-nipped bunch of white flowers. She dragged herself up to her flat. Once she stopped to hide the package under her coat. She would never look at that little white dress again. The ten five-dollar bills were ten five-pound stones in her purse. They almost hurled her backward.

She turned the key in her lock. Mr. Edmunds stood at the door. He looked rested and confident.

"I been waiting for you. I just started to go."

"You had any breakfast?" she asked tonelessly.

"I made some coffee. It was all I wanted."

"I shoulda made some oatmeal before I went out."

"You have on the big pot time I come home. Bet I'll land something good," he boasted. "You brought good luck in this house. We ain't seen the last of it." He pecked her cheek and went out, hurrying as if he were late for work.

She plodded into the bedroom. The steam was coming up fine. She sank down on the side of the bed and unbuttoned her coat. The package fell on her lap. She took the ten five-dollar bills and pushed them between a fold of the package. It was burial money. She could never use it for anything else. She hid the package under the mattress.

Wearily she buttoned up her coat and opened her purse again. It was empty, for the few cents remaining from her last relief check had been spent indiscriminately with her prize money.

She went into the kitchen to take stock of her needs. There was nothing left from their feasts. She felt the coffeepot. It was still hot, but her throat was too constricted for her to attempt to swallow.

She took her paper shopping bag and started out to Mr. Spiro's.

Exercise Honesty:

- Mrs. Edmunds does not seem like a dishonest person, but once she holds back on the truth, she finds that it becomes harder and harder to be honest with her husband—and herself. Can you understand why she held back on telling Mr. Edmunds about the money? Are her actions excusable?

- At the moment Mrs. Edmunds is about to tell her husband about the jackpot—"to promise him as many meals as there was money"—the other tenants start pounding on the radiator for heat and she becomes distracted by the coldness in her own hands and feet. Mr. Edmunds kisses her and tells her he'll make it up to her. What does the story make you feel about Mrs. Edmunds at that moment?

- How would the events of Mrs. Edmunds' day have changed had she revealed the truth about the money she won from the beginning?
- The money in this story stands for the things not said. But honesty is more than the things you don't say—honesty is the truth that needs to come alive in a relationship. What are the truths that can be said out loud in your own relationships to make them more honest?
- Some examples of honesty are easy to understand, such as not telling a lie or being true to your word. Telling a difficult truth even when you can avoid explicit lying is much more uncommon—and valuable. How can we create a more proactive honesty in our own lives? How can we practice the opposite of sins of omission?
- Do something honest for honesty's sake. Maybe no one knows about it and no one gains anything by it, but the act itself is an expression of honesty that is proactive and alive.

Shirley Caesar

Shirley Caesar, an ordained pastor at the Mount Calvary Word of Faith Church in Raleigh, North Carolina, is better known as the "First Lady of Gospel." Caesar was born in Durham, North Carolina, in 1938 and as a young child began singing in her church. In 1971 she won her first Grammy, followed by nine more, as well as a special award from the NAACP. Her acclaimed 1987 single "Hold My Mule" is about the lack of virtues and values in modern America. In the following excerpt from her autobiography, she describes a key childhood incident that solidified her belief both in God and the importance of honesty.

from The Lady, the Melody, and the Word

Like most children, I didn't always want to hear instruction or receive correction. There were times when I even rebelled against going to church. At the age of twelve, I was a bit sassy. I wasn't cruel, but I was prone to the occasional mischief. I got into arguments with my brothers and sisters, went outside to play when Mama told me to do chores, did not pay attention as much as I should have while in church, and did not want to do my homework.

The worst of my waywardness occurred because I had an incredible love for Popsicles—those juicy, fruity, cold sticks of frozen ice. I had a habit of stopping by a store on the way home from school. Like so many other kids, I did not have much money, so I would stand around the store looking and talking with my friends, imagining that I could buy whatever I wanted. One day, I went beyond imagining. I did something about what I wanted. I took something that was not mine.

Once the owner of the store turned his back, I reached down into the freezer and grabbed a handful of those delightful, tasty treats. Before he turned back around, I stuffed them under my coat and walked out.

Wanting to keep what I had done a secret and not wanting to share the Popsicles with any of the other kids, I walked home slowly, taking the longest route through an old graveyard. That way I would not run into anybody. Step by step I walked and ate each and every single one of those Popsicles—grape, orange, lemon, and banana. The juice dripped down my chin and onto my fingers and my dress. I didn't care. Nothing had ever tasted quite so good.

Having finished the Popsicles, I hastened home, thinking I had gotten away with my wrongdoing. But by the time I reached home and walked onto the porch, word of what I had done had somehow reached Mama. "Girl, get in here," she yelled out to me.

Pretending to be innocent, I opened the door and walked into the house. "What's wrong?" I asked.

Mama said, "I hear you've been stealing."

"Me?" I replied, trying to look shocked. "I didn't steal anything, Mama."

"Stick out your tongue," she said, her voice stern.

Meekly, I obeyed. My tongue had Popsicle stains all over it.

"Now look at your dress."

Though I hated to do it, I stared down and saw all the stains. I had sticky hands, too. I had done a bad thing, and Mama knew it.

"I'm going to whip you for lying and stealing," Mama said. "Now, come to me like you came into the world."

I knew what that meant. She wanted me to come to her naked. I was due for a whipping like I would never forget. Mama had a stern sense of right and wrong, and I had crossed the line. After that whipping, I never stole another Popsicle—or anything else, for that matter.

I had a desire to do better. Although I did not really think about it all the time, my lying and stealing could have led to real trouble in later life. If the Lord had not saved me, I don't know how I would have ended up.

Exercise Honesty:

- The definition we've employed for honesty in this book is as much about the quality of being upright as it is about telling the truth. Share Shirley Caesar's story with a young person in your life. Talk about what it means to be upright.

- Children must learn to be accountable for the decisions they make. My parents often said, "I am punishing you now so that the law will not punish you later." Shirley Caesar was held accountable for stealing the Popsicles and lying, and she attributes her honesty going forward in life to the punishment received at the hand of her mother, and, more important, to God. Strive to convey to your children by example that we must all deal with the repercussions of the choices we make. Know, too, that God can help keep you honest.

Chester Himes

*C*hester Himes was born in Jefferson City, Missouri, in 1909. He experienced a rough adolescence and was sentenced to twenty years in prison for armed robbery. Writing from behind bars proved to be a very positive outlet, saving him from his self-destructive tendencies. In his lifetime he wrote six books, nine detective novels (two of which, Cotton Comes to Harlem and A Rage in Harlem, were made into films), an autobiography, and a collection of stories. In the 1950s, Himes moved to Europe permanently; he died in Spain in 1984. "Mama's Missionary Money" is one of his most anthologized stories—after reading it, you will understand why!

Mama's Missionary Money

Y ou Lem-u-wellllllll! You-u-uuuu Lem-u-wellllllLLLLLLLLLLL!"

Lemuel heard his ma call him. Always wanting him to go to the store. He squirmed back into the corner of the chicken house, out of sight of the yard. He felt damp where he had sat in some fresh chicken manure, and he cursed.

Through a chink in the wall he saw his ma come out of the house, shading the sun from her eyes with her hand, looking for him. Let her find Ella, his little sister, or get somebody else. Tired of going to the store all the time. If it wasn't for his ma it was for Miss Mittybelle next door. Most every morning soon's he started out the house here she come to her door. "Lem-u-well, would you lak t' go the sto' for me lak a darlin' li'l boy?" Just as soon's he got his glove and started out to play. Why din she just say, "Here, go to the sto'." Why'd she have to come on with that old "would you lak t' go" stuff? She knew his ma 'ud beat the stuffin's outen him if he refused.

He watched his ma looking around for him. She didn't call any-more, trying to slip up on him. Old chicken came in the door and looked at him. "Goway, you old tattle tale," he thought, but he was scared to move, scared to breathe. His ma went on off, 'round the house; he saw her going down the picket fence by Miss Mittybelle's sun flowers, going on to the store herself.

He got up and peeped out the door, looked around. He felt like old Daniel Boone. Wasn't nobody in sight. He went out in the yard. The dust was deep where the hens had burrowed hollows. It oozed up twixt the toes of his bare feet and felt hot and soft as flour. His long dark feet were dust-powdered to a tan color. The dust was thick on his ankles, thinning up his legs. There were numerous small scars on the black skin. He was always getting bruised or scratched or cut. There were scars on his hands too and on his long black arms.

He wondered where everybody was. Sonny done gone fishing with his pa. More like Bubber's ma kept him in 'cause he was feeling a little sick. From over toward Mulberry Street came sounds of yelling and screaming. He cocked his long egg-shaped head to listen; his narrow black face was stolid, black skin dusty dry in the noonday sun. Burr-head was getting a licking. Everybody knew everybody else's cry. He was trying to tell whether it was Burrhead's ma or pa beating him.

Old rooster walked by and looked at him. "Goan, old buzzard!" he whispered, kicking dust at it. The rooster scrambled back, ruffling up, ready to fight.

Lemuel went on to the house, opened and shut the screen door softly, and stood for a moment in the kitchen. His ma'd be gone about fifteen minutes. He wiped the dust off his feet with his hands and started going through the house, searching each room systemat-ically, just looking to see what he could find. He went upstairs to his ma and pa's room, sniffed around in the closet, feeling in the pockets of his pa's Sunday suit, then knelt down and looked under-neath the bed. He stopped and peeped out the front window, cau-tiously pulling back the curtains. Old Mr. Diggers was out in his yard 'cross the street, fooling 'round his fence. His ma wasn't nowhere in sight.

He turned back into the room and pulled open the top dresser drawer. There was a big rusty black pocketbook with a snap fastener back in the corner. He poked it with a finger. It felt hard. He lifted it up. It was heavy. He opened it. There was money inside, all kinds of money, nickels and dimes and quarters and paper dollars and even ten-dollar bills. He closed it up, shoved it back into the corner, slammed shut the drawer, and ran and looked out the front window. Then he ran and looked out the back window. He ran downstairs and went from room to room, looking out all the windows in the house. No one was in sight. Everybody stayed inside during the hot part of the day.

He ran back upstairs, opened the drawer, and got to the pocket-book. He opened it, took out a quarter, closed it, put it away, closed the drawer, ran downstairs and out the back door and across the vacant lot to Mulberry Street. He started downtown, walking fast as he could without running. When he came to the paved sidewalks, they were hot on his feet and he walked half dancing, lifting his feet quickly from the pavement. At the Bijou he handed up his quarter, got a dime in change, and went into the small, hot theater to watch a gangster film. Pow! Pow! Pow! That was him shooting down the cops. Pow! Pow! Pow!

"Where you been all day, Lem-u-well?" his ma asked as she bustled 'round the kitchen fixing supper.

"Over tuh the bayou. Fishin'. Me 'n Bluebelly went."

His ma backhanded at him but he ducked out of range. "Told you t' call Francis by his name."

"Yas'm. Francis, me 'n Francis."

His pa looked up from the hydrant, where he was washing his hands and face. "Ummmmp?" he said. His pa seldom said more than "ummmmp." It meant most everything. Now it meant did he catch any fish. "Nawsuh," Lemuel said.

His little sister, Ella, was setting the table. Lemuel washed his hands and sat down and his pa sat down and said the blessing while his ma stood bowed at the stove. It was very hot in the kitchen and the sun hadn't set. The reddish glow of the late sun came in through the windows, and they sat in the hot kitchen and ate greens and side meat and rice and baked sweet potatoes and drank the potliquor with the corn bread and had molasses and corn bread for dessert. Afterward Lemuel helped with the dishes, and they went and sat on the porch in the late evening while the people passed and said hello.

Nothing was said about the quarter. Next day Lemuel took four dimes, three nickels, and two half dollars. He went and found Burrhead. "What you got beat 'bout yesdiddy?"

"Nutton. Ma said I sassed her."

"I got some money." Lemuel took the coins from his pocket and showed them.

"Where you git it?" Burrhead's eyes were big as saucers.

"Ne you mind. I got it. Les go tuh the show."

"*Gangster Guns* at the Bijou."

"I been there. Les go downtown tuh the Grand."

On the way they stopped in front of Zeke's Grill. It was too early for the show. Zeke was in his window turning flapjacks on the grill. They were big, round flapjacks, golden brown on both sides, and he'd serve 'em up with butter gobbed between. Lemuel never had no flapjacks like that at home. Burrhead neither. They looked like the best tasting flapjacks in the world.

They went inside and had an order, then they stopped at Missus Harris' and each got double ice-cream cones and a bag of peanut brittle. Now they were ready for the show. It was boiling hot way up in the balcony next to the projection room, but what'd they care. They crunched happily away at their brittle and laughed and carried on.... "Watch out, man, he slippin' up 'hind you."

Time to go home, Lemuel had a quarter, two nickels, and a dime left. He gave Burrhead the nickels and dime and kept the quarter. That night after supper his ma let him go over to the lot and play catch with Sonny, Bluebelly, and Burrhead. They kept on playing until it was so dark they couldn't see and they lost the ball over in the weeds by the bayou.

Next day Lemuel slipped up to his ma's dresser and went into the magic black pocketbook again. He took enough to buy a real big-league ball and enough for him and Burrhead to get some more flap-jacks and ice cream too. His ma hadn't said nothing yet.

As the hot summer days went by and didn't nobody say nothing at all, he kept taking a little more each day. He and Burrhead ate flap-jacks every day. He set up all the boys in the neighborhood to peanut brittle and ice cream and rock candy and took them to the show. Sundays, after he'd put his nickel in the pan, he had coins left to jin-gle in his pocket, although he didn't let his ma or pa hear him jingling them. All his gang knew he was stealing the money from somewhere. But nobody tattled on him and they made up lies at home so their parents wouldn't get suspicious. Lemuel bought gloves and balls and bats for the team and now they could play regular ball out on the lot all day.

His ma noticed the new mitt he brought home and asked him where he got it. He said they'd all been saving their money all summer and had bought the mitt and some balls. She looked at him suspi-ciously. "Doan you dast let me catch you stealin' nothin', boy."

About this time he noticed the magic black bag was getting flat and empty. The money was going. He began getting scared. He wondered how long it was going to be before his ma found out. But he had gone this far, so he wouldn't stop. He wouldn't think about what was going to happen when it was all gone. He was the king of the neighborhood. He had to keep on being king.

One night after supper he and his pa were sitting on the porch. Ella was playing with the cat 'round the side. He was sitting on the bottom step, wiggling his toes in the dust. He heard his ma come downstairs. He could tell something was wrong by the way she walked. She came out on the porch.

"Isaiah, somebody's tuk all my missionary money," she said. "Who you reckin it was?"

Lemuel held his breath. "Ummmmmp!" his pa said.

"You reckin it were James?" He was her younger brother who came around sometimes.

"Ummmmp! Now doan you worry, Lu'belle. We find it."

Lemuel was too scared to look around. His pa didn't move. Nobody didn't say anything to him. After a while he got up. "I'm goin' tuh bed, ma," he said.

"Ummmmp!" his pa noticed.

Lemuel crawled into bed in the little room he had off the kitchen downstairs. But he couldn't sleep. Later he heard Doris Mae crying from way down the street. He just could barely hear her but he knew it was Doris Mae. Her ma was beating her. He thought Doris Mae's ma was always beating her. Later on he heard his ma and pa go up to bed. All that night he lay half awake, waiting for his pa to come down. He was so scared he just lay there and trembled.

Old rooster crowed. The sun was just rising. Clump-clump-clump. He heard his pa's footsteps on the stairs. Clump-clump-clump. It was like the sound of doom. He wriggled down in the bed and pulled the sheet up over his head. He made like he was sleeping. Clump-clump-clump. He heard his pa come into the room. He held his breath. He felt his pa reach down and pull the sheet off him. He didn't wear no bottoms in the summer. His rear was like a bare tight knot. He screwed his eyes 'round and saw his pa standing tall in mudstained overalls beside the bed, with the cord to his razor strop doubled over his wrist and the strop hanging poised at his side. His pa had on his reformer's look, like he got on when he passed the dance hall over on Elm Street.

"Lem-u-well, I give you uh chance tuh tell the truth. What you do with you' ma's missionary money?"

"I didn't take it, pa. I swear I didn', pa."

Whack! The strap came down. Lemuel jumped off the bed and tried to crawl underneath it. His pa caught him by the arm. Whack! Whack! Whack! Went the strap. The sound hurt Lemuel as much as the licks. "Owwwww-owwwwwwwwwWWWW!" he began to bawl. All over the neighborhood folks knew that Lemuel was getting a beating. His buddies knew that Lemuel was getting a beating. His buddies knew what for. The old folks didn't know yet but they'd know before the day was over.

"God doan lak thieves," his pa said, beating him across the back and legs.

Lemuel darted toward the door. His pa headed him off. He crawled between his pa's legs, getting whacked as he went through. He ran out into the kitchen. His ma was waiting for him with a switch. He tried to crawl underneath the table. His head got caught in the legs of a chair. His ma started working on his rear with the switch.

"MURDER!" he yelled at the top of his voice. "HELP! POLICE! Please, ma, I ain't never gonna steal nothin' else, ma. If you jes let me off this time, ma. I swear, ma."

He pulled out from underneath the table and danced up and down on the floor, trying to dodge the licks aimed at his leg.

"He gone, ma! Oh, he gone!" he yelled, dancing up and down. "Dat ol' devil gone, ma! I done tuk Christ Jesus to my heart!"

Well, being as he done seen the light, she sighed and let him off. Her missionary money wasn't gone clean to waste nohow if it'd make him mend his stealin' ways. She guessed them heathens would just have to wait another year; as Isaiah always say, they done waited this long 'n it ain't kilt 'em.

The way Lemuel's backsides stung and burned he figured them ol' heathens was better off than they knew 'bout.

Exercise Honesty:

- Although children may complain when we "fuss" over them and make it a point of knowing how they are spending their time, they actually welcome limits. Often, bad behavior is a cry for attention. It's when his mother leaves Lemuel unsupervised at home that he gets into trouble. The third time Lemuel steals, he knows that he is in rocky territory and wonders when he will be caught. As the bag gets emptier and emptier, he gets more and more scared, but his actions have gone unnoticed for so long that he feels compelled to keep stealing. Read Luke 16:10: "He that is faithful in that which is least is faithful also in much: and he that is unjust in the least is also unjust in much." Consider the meaning of this passage.

- "Mama's Missionary Money" is a wonderful story to share with your children. Ask your children to point out examples of why honesty is a virtue. Then read Proverbs 12:17 together: "He that speaketh truth sheweth forth righteousness: but a false witness deceit." How does Lemuel give false evidence when he is asked about the money?

- Are you involved in your child's life to the point where you know where he or she is after school? Do you regularly ask your children about their lives and their interests? Are they comfortable talking with you about important issues in their lives? Exercise honesty by creating a loving relationship in which they have a clear understanding of their limits and are aware that you are in their corner at all times.

- Mama realizes that her missionary money, though spent, has been put to a good cause. Ask your children to explain why she feels this way. Do they agree? Do you?

Buchi Offodile

This story from Buchi Offodile's collection The Orphan Girl and Other
Stories: West African Folktales *is one of many used by the Kpèlle people
of Liberia to teach virtues to their children.*

The River Demon

Once, in a remote village, there lived a woman and her two daughters. The sisters took turns preparing the meals for the family.
When their mother went to the farm, one of the girls prepared the
meal. She saved it in a calabash and kept it on the earthen mound.
There the food stayed. Then, the girls went out and played until their
mother came home, so they could all eat the meal together.

This village was an island, surrounded by waters so wide that you
could not see the end of them. Now, in this water, there lived a
demon who fed only on people who have done wrong. When someone was accused of any wrongdoing, he was taken to the center of the
river to swear by it. If he was innocent, the river left him alone. But if
he was guilty, the River Demon opened his wide mouth and swallowed him.

It happened that whenever this woman left her food in the house,
one of the daughters ate it. When she asked them about it, they denied
it. One day the woman came back from the farm with a rabbit she had
killed. She singed the rabbit and cut it up. Then she gave some of it to
the first daughter to make soup. The rest of the meat she dried over
her fireplace. That night, they ate like they never had before. They were
full and happy. The next day, the mother went back to the farm, leaving the girls at home.

When their mother came back later that day, she found the rest of
the meat was missing. She was furious.

"Food I can understand they ate because they were hungry," she thought. "But meat! That's outright greed and any child who grows up with such lofty taste buds will never amount to anything. She is likely to end up a rogue in order to satisfy her tastes for meat and such."

With that analysis she decided to confront the girls.

"Who ate the rabbit meat?" she asked them.

They each denied knowledge of the meat. "I didn't even know that it was out there on the fire," said the first daughter.

"Neither did I," denied the second daughter. "I thought we ate it all up last night."

Their mother was not happy with the situation. She begged them to tell the truth.

"I am not going to punish you," she begged them. "Just tell the truth. You know how much I hate people who steal. I hate people who lie even more. You must ask permission before you take anything. But, should you take it without permission, you must admit that you did."

"I didn't touch the meat, mother," denied the first daughter, "honest!"

"I was out playing," denied the second daughter. "I didn't even know we had any rabbit meat."

Poor woman. "And I thought I was raising very good children," she said to them. "Now, not only am I raising thieves, I am also raising liars."

For several days she weighed her options. She thought, "Should I get the truth out of them? Should I deny them food?" But she concluded that none of the options was viable, for she could be punishing the innocent girl as well. "Could they have colluded and eaten the meat together?" she wondered. After much debate with herself, she called the daughters together and announced her plan.

"Since I cannot get the truth out of you," she told them, "I will take you to the River Demon. But I will give you one last chance to confess. To make it easier for you, you can come and tell me privately and I will not let the other know you did. But if I do not hear from either of you by daybreak, we will let the River Demon have you for dinner."

With that she went to bed and her daughters went to their room.

There, they both lay on their backs. Each stared at the wall geckos stalking the night moths on the ceiling of their thatched house. They couldn't get any sleep.

"Why don't you admit it," said the first daughter. "Why do you want to shame everybody tomorrow?"

"What about you?" retorted her sister, "Why don't *you* admit it?"

They went at each other for most of the night until they finally fell asleep. When they woke up the next morning, their mother had already left for the farm. The girls were relieved that at least they would survive that day. "Before she comes back," thought the second daughter, "it'll be too late to go to the river."

Later that day, before the sun was barely past overhead, they saw their mother coming back in the distance. Their jaws dropped. Their hearts began to race and beat monotonously against their ribs. They were so beside themselves that they didn't know their mother had reached them.

"Won't you welcome me?" she asked them.

"Welcome, ma," they responded nervously.

They helped their mother put down her load. They served her food and after she ate, she asked whether they were ready to confess. But they said nothing. So she took the girls to the river. When they got there, she put the second girl in a big calabash bowl and pushed her to the center of the river.

"Serenade the River Demon," she instructed her. "If you are innocent, he will let you be; if you are not, then good-bye, my daughter, for this is the last I will see of you."

When the calabash flowed to the center of the river the girl began to sing:

> *River Demon! River Demon!*
> *If it was I that ate the rabbit meat*
> *Then here I come I am yours*

Open your mouth that you I may entreat
But if the meat was eaten by someone else
Then forever keep your mouth shut that I may retreat. . . .

After two to three verses of the song, nothing happened to her. The river reversed its course and the girl was washed ashore to her mother. Then her mother removed her from the calabash and put her sister, the first daughter, in it. She pushed her to the center of the river, telling her to serenade the River Demon.

River Demon! River Demon!
If it was I that ate the rabbit meat
Then here I come I am yours
Open your mouth. . . .

When the number one daughter started to sing to the River Demon, the river began to swirl. It carried her into the whirlpool and began to swallow her. Her mother pleaded with her to confess. But she still would not confess. Soon the water was up to her neck. Her mother pleaded with her again to confess. But she denied it and continued to sing until the river covered her completely.

After that, the woman cried for her daughter. When she could not cry anymore, she took her second daughter and went back home. There the two of them lived for a very long time. Whenever they went to the river, they'd remember the girl and cry again.

Exercise Honesty:

- A child's natural proclivity is to recoil when confronted with the truth about some dishonest deed. The fear of punishment causes many to shun the truth. This inability to face the truth keeps them in bondage and makes it difficult to develop trusting relationships. Our freedom is connected to our willingness to be truthful by confessing rather than lying; as John 8:32 tells us, "And ye shall know the truth, and the truth shall make you free." Are you teaching your children to be honest? What example are you setting for them? How honest are you with your time card, your spouse, or your tithes?

- Telling the truth is an important lesson for all of us, and especially for children. But try to instill in your children the idea that simply telling the truth is not exercising honesty to its fullest. The goal is to actually *live* the truth.

Love

*A willingness to sacrifice for someone else's happiness
or well-being, LOVE arises from a deep, tender compassion
and sense of underlying oneness with others.*

It seems that these days, hatred has become fashionable. Whether it's one person hating another, a group hating other groups, or even countries hating one another, the word "hate" is constantly ringing in our ears. Love, on the other hand, has become laughable. Love stories are all said to be contrived. Those who express love are mocked as disingenuous.

We, as a people, must reclaim love. Love fills our poetry and our songs; it must also fill our hearts, for love is the very fabric of our families, our churches, and our communities. Too many of our neighborhoods are torn by hatred. Too many of our homes are broken by a lack of love.

And why, why, don't we realize that when we hate others, we hurt ourselves? When we long to destroy our enemies, we succeed only in destroying ourselves. Hatred wounds our hearts and cripples our souls. Like a disease, it spreads its evil through our bodies until we lose control of our own minds. We must fight our impulse to hate, for if we allow our hatred to live, it may soon consume us.

I [Floyd] grew up in Houston, Texas, the deep, segregated South. I was one of thirteen children. My parents, who in their youth had been forbidden from attending school during the cotton-harvesting season, worked tirelessly to support our family. Needless to say, we were not rich. But one thing poverty helps you realize is that even when there is hardly enough food on the table, there can always be enough love to go around.

Black slaves knew this all too well. Though they suffered from deprivation and degradation, they knew that even the most wicked master could never take away what was in their heart. Love was often their most valuable possession. Slaves, who had nothing to give away, gave love, and they gave plenty of it. When their stomachs were empty, they had the fortitude to survive on the fullness of their hearts.

Take Ben and Betty Dodson, two slaves who were separated for twenty years after begging their master to sell them together. Two decades later, shortly after being emancipated, the Dodsons reunited in a refugee camp, at which point Ben shouted, "Glory! Glory! Hallelujah!"

Love, our ancestors knew, is not just kind words and sentiments. And it is not passion. It is compassion. Love is a dedication to ensuring the welfare and happiness of others. To love is to experience a caring so intense that it fosters a spirit of sacrifice. It is love that makes a mother who cannot swim jump into the water to save her drowning child. It is love that makes a father work an extra job to provide for his family. Love is a powerful thing.

Sometimes, I turn on the news at night and think that love is dead. Murder follows murder; misery begets misery. But I know that beneath the hatred, there is a flame of love waiting to be rekindled. We have all suffered, and there is sadness yet to come. Throughout our lives, love must be our anchor and our lighthouse, keeping us strong while guiding us through the night.

James Baldwin

Originally published as an essay in The Progressive *in 1962 and republished as part of* The Fire Next Time *in 1963, "My Dungeon Shook" is one of the most eloquent expressions of hope for the African American people in our literature. James Baldwin's anger at the iniquities of racism is palpable beneath the surface, but the overarching expression is one of love for family and fellow man.*

My Dungeon Shook

Letter to My Nephew on the One Hundredth Anniversary of the Emancipation

Dear James:

I have begun this letter five times and torn it up five times. I keep seeing your face, which is also the face of your father and my brother. Like him, you are tough, dark, vulnerable, moody—with a very definite tendency to sound truculent because you want no one to think you are soft. You may be like your grandfather in this, I don't know, but certainly both you and your father resemble him very much physically. Well, he is dead, he never saw you, and he had a terrible life; he was defeated long before he died because, at the bottom of his heart, he really believed what white people said about him. This is one of the reasons that he became so holy. I am sure that your father has told you something about all that. Neither you nor your father exhibit any tendency toward holiness: You really are of another era, part of what happened when the Negro left the land and came into what the late E. Franklin Frazier called "the cities of destruction." You can only be destroyed by believing that you really are what the white world calls a nigger. *I tell you this because I love you, and please don't you ever forget it.*

I have known both of you all your lives, have carried your daddy in my arms and on my shoulders, kissed and spanked him and watched him learn to walk. I don't know if you've known anybody from that far back; if you've loved anybody that long, first as an infant, then as a child, then as a man, you gain a strange perspective on time and human pain and effort. Other people cannot see what I see whenever I look into your father's face, for behind your father's face as it is today are all those other faces which were his. Let him laugh and I see a cellar your father does not remember and a house he does not remember and I hear in his present laughter his laughter as a child. Let him curse and I remember him falling down the cellar steps, and howling, and I remember, with pain, his tears, which my hand or your grandmother's so easily wiped away. But no one's hand can wipe away those tears he sheds invisibly today, which one hears in his laughter and in his speech and in his songs. I know what the world has done to my brother and how narrowly he has survived it. And I know, which is much worse, and this is the crime of which I accuse my country and my countrymen, and for which neither I nor time nor history will ever forgive them, that they have destroyed and are destroying hundreds of thousands of lives and do not know it and do not want to know it. One can be, indeed one must strive to become, tough and philosophical concerning destruction and death, for this is what most of mankind has been best at since we have heard of man. (But remember: most of mankind is not all of mankind.) But it is not permissible that the authors of devastation should also be innocent. It is the innocence which constitutes the crime.

Now, my dear namesake, these innocent and well-meaning people, your countrymen, have caused you to be born under conditions not very far removed from those described for us by Charles Dickens in the London of more than a hundred years ago. (I hear the chorus of the innocents screaming, "No! This is not true! How bitter you are!"—but I am writing this letter to you, to try to tell you something about how to handle them, for most of them do not yet really know that you exist. I know the conditions under which you were born, for I was there. Your countrymen were not there, and haven't made it yet. Your grandmother was also there, and no one has ever accused her of being bitter. I suggest that the innocents check with her. She isn't hard to find. Your countrymen don't know that she exists, either, though she has been working for them all their lives.)

Well, you were born, here you came, something like fourteen years ago; and though your father and mother and grandmother, looking about the streets through which they were carrying you, staring at the walls into which they brought you, had every reason to be heavyhearted, yet they were not. For here you were, Big James, named for me— you were a big baby, I was not—here you were: to be loved. To be loved, baby, hard, at once, and forever, to strengthen you against the loveless world. Remember that I know how black it looks today, for you. It looked bad that day, too, yes, we were trembling. We have not stopped trembling yet, but if we had not loved each other none of us would have survived. And now you must survive because we love you, and for the sake of your children and your children's children.

This innocent country set you down in a ghetto in which, in fact, it intended that you should perish. Let me spell out precisely what I mean by that, for the heart of the matter is here, and the root of my dispute with my country. You were born where you were born and faced the future that you faced because you were black and for no other reason. The limits of your ambition were, thus, expected to be set forever. You were born into a society which spelled out with brutal clarity, and in as many ways as possible, that you were a worthless human being. You were not expected to aspire to excellence: You were expected to make peace with mediocrity. Wherever you have turned, James, in your short time on this earth, you have been told where you could go and what you could do (and how you could do it) and where you could live and whom you could marry. I know your countrymen do not agree with me about this, and I hear them saying, "You exaggerate." They do not know Harlem, and I do. So do you. Take no one's word for anything, including mine—but trust your experience. Know whence you came. If you know whence you came, there is really no limit to where you can go. The details and symbols of your life have been deliberately constructed to make you believe what white people say about you. Please try to remember that what they believe, as well as what they do and cause you to endure, does not testify to your inferiority but to their inhumanity and fear. Please try to be clear, dear James, through the storm which rages about your youthful head today, about the reality which lies behind the words "acceptance" and "integration." There is no reason for you to try to become like white people and there is no basis whatever for their impertinent assumption that they must accept you. The really terrible thing, old buddy, is that you must accept them. *And I mean that very seriously. You must accept them and accept them with love. For these innocent people have no other hope. They are, in effect, still trapped in a history which they do not understand; and until they understand it, they cannot be released from it. They have had to believe for many years, and for innumerable reasons, that black men are inferior to white men. Many of them, indeed, know better, but, as you will discover, people find it very difficult to act on what they know. To act is to be committed, and to be committed is to be in danger. In this case, the danger, in the minds of most white Americans, is the loss of their identity. Try to imagine how you would feel if you woke up one morning to find the sun shining and all the stars aflame. You would be frightened because it is out of the order of nature. Any upheaval in the universe is terrifying because it so profoundly attacks one's sense of one's own reality. Well, the black man has functioned in the white man's world as a fixed star, as an immovable pillar, and as he moves out of his place, heaven and earth are shaken to their foundations. You, don't be afraid. I said that it was intended that you should perish in the ghetto, perish by never being allowed to go behind the white man's definitions, by never being allowed to spell your proper name. You have, and many of us have, defeated this intention; and, by a terrible law, a terrible paradox, those innocents who believed that your imprisonment made them safe are losing their grasp of reality. But these men are your brothers—your lost, younger brothers. And if the word "integration" means anything, this is what it means: that we, with love, shall force our brothers to see themselves as they are, to cease fleeing from reality and begin to change it. For this is your home, my friend, do not be driven from it; great men have done great things here, and will again, and we can make America what America must become. It will be hard, James, but you come from sturdy, peasant stock, men who picked cotton and dammed rivers and built railroads, and, in the teeth of the most terrifying odds, achieved an unassailable and monumental dignity. You come from a long line of great poets, some of the greatest poets since Homer. One of them said,* The very time I thought I was lost, My dungeon shook and my chains fell off.

You know, and I know, that the country is celebrating one hundred years of freedom one hundred years too soon. We cannot be free until they are free. God bless you, James, and Godspeed.

Your uncle,
James

Exercise Love:

- The picture Baldwin paints of the world is not sugarcoated, but in the end he tells his nephew that good values and morals have already advanced a "monumental dignity" in the African-American people, and will cultivate the same dignity in any individual who puts love before hatred. Talk about these ideas with your family. What "terrifying odds" have your own family or community members been able to overcome? How has love played a part?

- The title of this essay comes from lyrics in an old spiritual: "The very time I thought I was los', The dungeon shook an' the chain fell off. You may hinder me here. But you cannot there. 'Cause God in his heaven. Goin' to answer prayer." Baldwin's use of these lyrics is interesting, given the very real-world grounding of his essay. Explore with your family the ideas of spiritual release as well as Baldwin's "don't you forget it" advice to live life loving and accepting others, even your oppressors.

- We often wrote letters to our own children when they were growing up—letters to chastise them for failure to perform at expected levels in school, to encourage them to continue in their pursuit of success, to support them in a project, and simply to express love and pride. One tradition that emerged was writing letters to them just before or after they went away to college. We expressed our hopes, our fears, and our commitment to them and their growth. Write a letter of this kind to a young person in your life.

- Take the opportunity to tell your own child or grandchild that he was born "To be loved, baby, hard, at once, and forever. . . ." Say it every day in words, either spoken or written. Make it an annual ritual, perhaps on each birthday.

William J. Faulkner

COLLECTED FROM SIMON BROWN

William J. Faulkner was for many years university minister and dean of men at Fisk University in Nashville. A devoted folklorist, Faulkner collected many stories from Simon Brown, a former slave who worked for Faulkner's mother on a farm in Virginia. Faulkner recorded the stories he enjoyed hearing as a boy in his collection The Days When the Animals Talked. "How the Slaves Helped Each Other" is the poignant tale of how the slaves on a plantation honor the passing of one of their beloved, Sister Dicey, and her return to the heavenly Father.

How the Slaves Helped Each Other

Sister Dicey was as good a soul as ever lived. She was the friend of all the folks, black and white. One day Sister Dicey passed away in her sleep. Now, the slaves had no undertakers, so the womenfolk came in and prepared her body for burial, which had to be done in twenty-four hours. After bathing her, they put on her the best dress they could find and laid her out in a homemade coffin, resting on two chairs. Somebody pinned a flower on her bosom.

Later that night slaves from all about came to the cabin and sat around while they sang and prayed. People kept coming and going all night long. The singing was mostly sad songs with happy endings, because the folks felt that now Sister Dicey was freed from all the trials and tribulations of slavery and was safe in Heaven, at rest and at peace forevermore. She wouldn't be a barefoot slave dressed in rags anymore. In God's Heaven, she'd have everything she needed to make her happy. The mourners at Sister Dicey's sitting up knew that and sang:

I got shoes, you got shoes—
All God's children got shoes.
When I get to Heaven
I'm going to put on my shoes
And walk all over God's Heaven.
I got a robe, you got a robe—
All God's children got a robe.
When I get to Heaven
I'm going to put on my robe
And shout all over God's Heaven.

I got wings, you got wings—
All God's children got wings.
When I get to Heaven
I'm going to put on my wings
And fly all over God's Heaven.

I got a crown, you got a crown—
All God's children got a crown.
When I get to Heaven
I'm going to put on my crown
And wear it all over God's Heaven.

I got a harp, you got a harp—
All God's children got a harp.
When I get to Heaven
I'm going to play on my harp
And play all over God's Heaven.

So, with this picture of Heaven in mind, the mourners weren't too sad at Sister Dicey's going away. They knew she was better off with a loving heavenly Father than she had ever been in this wicked world of slavery. Some of the people got so happy thinking about Heaven that they burst out crying and shouting for joy. And so the sitting up went on all night.

The next morning old Master John Brown came over to the cabin to pay his last respects to Sister Dicey, his faithful servant, and to tell the people that he would let them off from work to go to the funeral. They could use a pair of mules and his best farm wagon to carry the coffin through the woods to the graveyard.

The coffin was a plain pine box built by a good slave carpenter on the plantation who could make them to fit any size body—man, woman, or child. I didn't walk with the coffin and the mourners out to the graveyard because I was about thirteen years old and had been sent to help some of the men dig the grave. It was six feet long, three feet wide, and six feet deep. But I didn't help with the last of the digging. I was too scared to stay in the grave when it got down past my head.

When the family and mourners reached the burying grounds, six men carried the coffin to the grave and rested it on two long-handled shovels. Then they put plowlines under each end and let it down easy-like into the hole. A box lid was let down with the same ropes and fitted in place, and then a man climbed into the grave and screwed the lid on.

When this was done, the slave preacher said words of comfort over the body—something like this: "Sister Dicey, since God in his mercy has taken your soul from earth to Heaven and out of your misery, I commit your body to the ground, earth to earth, ashes to ashes, dust to dust, where it will rest in peace. But on that Great Getting Up Morning, when the trumpet of God shall sound to wake up all the dead, we will meet you in the skies and join the hosts of saints who will go marching in. Yes, we want to be in that number, Sister Dicey, when the saints go marching in."

Before the preacher could finish his benediction, some of the women got so happy that they drowned him out with their songs and handclapping and shouting. Then some men and boys began to fill up the grave. When it was full, they rounded it up real pretty-like and put one wood shingle at the head and another at the foot of the grave. The womenfolk laid some flowers and ribbon grass on top and put colored bottles, broken glass, and seashells all around the grave of Sister Dicey.

In that way, they showed their love for her. It was the best that slaves could do in those days, when everybody was poor and owned by their masters. But no man could own their souls or keep them from loving one another. These gifts came only from God.

Exercise Love:

- Love for our brothers and sisters—and for God—helped us to survive slavery. In this story, the slaves on the plantation take special care to ensure that Sister Dicey's funeral is one that truly honors what she meant to them. They also believe that her physical death is cause for celebration: "They knew she was better off with a loving heavenly Father than she had ever been in this wicked world of slavery." Read Revelation 7:13–17 in connection with this story: "And one of the elders answered, saying unto me, What are these which are arrayed in white robes? and whence came they? And I said unto him, Sir, thou knowest. And he said to me, These are they which came out of great tribulation, and have washed their robes, and made them white in the blood of the Lamb. Therefore are they before the throne of God, and serve him day and night in his temple: and he that sitteth on the throne shall dwell among them. They shall hunger no more, neither thirst any more; neither shall the sun light on them, nor any heat. For the Lamb which is in the midst of the throne shall feed them, and shall lead them unto living fountains of waters: and God shall wipe away all tears from their eyes."
- "But no man could own their souls or keep them from loving one another. These gifts came only from God." Given the fact that many of our people are incarcerated, think about this sentence and how it might apply to the lives of these brothers and sisters today.

- This story provides a wonderful way to introduce your children to our unique legacy of folktales, spirituals, and love for community. In the context of this story, ask your children to identify the ways that the slaves demonstrated love for Sister Dicey, love for God, and love for community. Ask family members to make a list of the ways in which you help each other every day. Do these ways of helping each other add up to love?

- Helping others is one way we demonstrate love, but it's also important to do new and unexpected things just to demonstrate we care. Think of five unexpected things you can do just to show someone you love them. Then make a point of doing at least one of those things every day.

Philippe Wamba

*I*n this moving passage from his autobiography, twenty-four-year-old Philippe *Wamba finally meets the grandmother he has known only through aging photographs. Raised in the United States by his African father and African-American mother, Wamba expects his grandmother from Zaire to radiate the strength and pride of a woman who has worked tirelessly to raise nine children—the image reflected in the familiar black-and-white photographs that he studied in his youth. When Wamba is finally able to visit his grandmother, he is struck by the toll that time has taken on the woman's body. Wamba realizes, however, that although his grandmother's physical strength may have withered in her old age, her pride has swelled, for she has experienced the joy of a growing family.*

from Kinship

*T*he ancient woman crawled through the doorway on her hands and knees, moving with the slow and painful determination of a tortoise. She made her way across the porch and around the side of the house to the outhouse, concrete blocks and flimsy sheets of corrugated zinc that shielded the family's simple toilet from view. None of the adults sitting around the courtyard chatting offered to help her; no one really seemed to even see her.

My father, sitting next to me, sighed and stared at the floor. The little kids playing in the dust a few feet away continued with their game, chattering softly to each other and occasionally laughing or shouting. The chickens in the yard scratched at the dirt, pecking at insects, pebbles, and bits of bright plastic. Some young women with colorfully patterned cloths tied around their waists sat together talking in the sunshine that filtered through the leaves of the large tree in front of the house; one of them was braiding the hair of a restless young girl seated in front of her. And my father, my great-uncle, my cousin, and I sat in the porch's wooden white chairs, saying nothing.

We had already exchanged our greetings, and my father and I, who were visiting various relatives in Kinshasa, Zaire, on this Christmas vacation in 1994, had already shaken hands with most of the cousins, aunts, uncles, and in-laws who lived in this particular house, and had already received the drinks a cousin had been dispatched to bring for us. My deeply evangelical uncle had made a sound of disapproval in his throat when I chose beer from the beverages my aunt offered. So now we just sat, nursing our drinks, and seemed to wait. My father was silent. And I, born and partially raised in the United States, and equipped with only halting French and no Kikongo or Lingala to speak of, smiled at my cousin seated across from me, and said nothing.

I had been quiet for much of the four days we had so far spent in Kinshasa, having difficulty making myself understood, and getting slightly lost in the parade of relatives we visited in homes all over the huge city; sometimes I wasn't really sure who lived in what house, whom we had come to see, or how they were related to me, facts that my father, in his typically absentminded manner, often forgot to supply me with. Most of the relatives I met on that trip had me at a disadvantage when they happily embraced me; they always knew exactly who I was, calling me by name, and had been eagerly expecting me, while I would feel awkwardly ashamed that I didn't know their names or who they were in relation to me unless they or my father told me. It was all quite overwhelming, but also very moving, being greeted so warmly by my family, these strangers.

The old woman emerged from the outhouse and made her slow, deliberate journey back to the porch, once again on all fours, once again unassisted by anyone present. She got to the porch and stopped, sitting down on the concrete floor and leaning against the house, catching her breath. She was painfully small and thin, her face etched with deep wrinkles, her small shorn head covered by a head scarf, a once-colorful *pagne* tied around her waist, and a faded blouse hanging loosely on her wilted frame. She gazed at us, seemingly expectant.

I looked at my father.

He looked back at me, seeming in that moment to return from very far away. His voice attempted nervous cheer. "That's your grandmother," he said softly.

Though his words only confirmed what I had already suspected, I was struck with disbelief. I had seen old black-and-white pictures of my father's mother: She was a tall, stern-faced woman, strong-looking, with an unsmiling dignity that reminded me of the poker-faced Native American chiefs who stared unflinchingly from nineteenth-century portraits in the American history books I had studied in grade school. I had heard of my grandmother's failing health, but I had trouble accepting that the woman whom I had known only as a proud and impressive figure in a photograph, a woman who had raised my father and his eight brothers and sisters, had been so severely betrayed by time, losing her strength, her vitality, and even the use of her legs. I wondered at how difficult it must be for my father to see her like this. And I felt guilty; I was twenty-four years old, but this was my first time ever meeting her, ever speaking to her. I felt as if I were hopelessly late—if only I could have seen her in her prime, heard her tell the stories and sing the songs that our father had repeated for us when my

brothers and I were younger, and watched her effortlessly hoist a basket of cassava onto her head or a plump child onto her back. If only I
could have experienced her during her life, had been able to know and
learn from her. But all my life we had been separated by distance and
circumstance, bound by blood but living worlds apart.

My father got up from his chair and walked over to his mother. He
extended his hand, taking her spindly palm in his, and bowed, she gazing at him happily and fondly, his eyes filled with the greatest love and
respect. I followed suit, and he introduced me in Kikongo. "This is
Philippe Kiatuntu," he said, using the Kikongo name by which I was
known only to my relatives in Zaire.

She stared at me with deep, dark eyes that were bright and amused.
She spoke, in a soft, high, and warm voice that wheezed slightly with
age, and my father translated: "She says finally you've come to see her."
I felt tears prickling the corners of my eyes as I smiled down at her, my
heart full, frustrated by my inability to communicate.

After the initial greetings, my grandmother made her way slowly
into the house, and after a while we followed her to the little room
where she lived with my father's oldest sister, who had been helping to
take care of her since my grandfather died and my grandmother
moved to Kinshasa from the village where my father grew up. When
we entered the room she was perched next to my aunt on the bed,
which occupied more than half of the small space; she looked digni-
fied and regal, and indeed I felt like a humble subject in the hushed
presence of royalty as I crouched on a stool at the foot of the bed. She
stared at me again, smiling slightly. She gestured at her chin, jokingly
referring to my goatee, and said something to my father.

He laughed. "She says your father doesn't even have a beard, but you
have one." I presented her with the bolt of African fabric and the scarf
that I had bought for her in Boston before we left. She clapped her
hands in gratitude, immediately yanking her own head scarf off her
head, revealing a crown of close-cropped white hair. She asked my aunt
to help her put the new scarf on, and when it was in place, she spoke.

"Praise God that you have come," my father translated. "I'm so happy right now, if I weren't so old I would be dancing." My grandmother clapped and wriggled in a little seated jig to illustrate her point. I said that I was also very happy to meet her finally, after having heard so much about her from my father. She continued speaking, and my father said that she was complaining, as she apparently often did, that whenever he made one of his infrequent trips home to Zaire she always asked for us, her grandchildren in foreign lands, but that my father always said that we were unable to come. Now, at last, I, at least, had made it.

"Now you have seen your grandmother, and when you go home you will tell the others about me," my father interpreted. "I am happy now because I have children, and they are here." She gestured to my father. "And they also have children, and they are also here, so I am very happy." She addressed me earnestly. "You must also find a good wife and have many children, too, so that our"—my father's translation faltered for a moment, as he groped for the right word—"so that our species will spread."

I felt a sudden unmistakable rush of love for this small, wizened old woman, a love that eclipsed the regret I felt at not being able to speak her language and the guilt I felt about having taken so long to meet her. None of that seemed to matter. When I was little, my mother had told me that if you handle a baby bird that has fallen out of its nest, its mother will reject it as a strange-smelling impostor because she no longer recognizes it as part of herself. When I visited my grandmother, I know I looked, smelled, and acted like an alien, mute in my inability to speak her language. But she recognized me. She embraced me as her own; and with all that separated us—language, culture, nationality, generations, gender, and our very worlds of experience—we were still inextricably bound and could still reach each other across the divide. Though she, like most of my relatives in Zaire, saw me as a foreigner, I felt that I could never be foreign to her. And I realized that I wasn't too late. Maybe I was just in time.

Exercise Love:

- This story reminds me of the ways that we communicated our love to our children when they were infants. Although Philippe and his grandmother cannot communicate with each other verbally, they converse through gestures and with their eyes. Think about the power of nonverbal communication to express love. What are some ways that you and the people in your life communicate love without speaking a word?

- Respect for and appreciation of elderly members of our society has eroded in recent generations. Visit with senior members of your church or neighborhood. Bring children with you. Play checkers with an older relative or friend of the family. Sing for them. Read to them. Ask them about their lives and tape-record these conversations for precious posterity.

- Read Proverbs 20:11–12 in the context of this story: "Even a child is known by his doings, whether his work be pure, and whether it be right. The hearing ear, and the seeing eye, the Lord hath made even both of them."

Joseph Seamon Cotter, Jr.

Although poet, journalist, and playwright Joseph Seamon Cotter, Jr., lived only twenty-three brief years, his contribution to the world of literature lives on to this day. Carefully crafted and powerfully beautiful, Cotter's writing often addresses such compelling topics as racism's effect on society and African-American involvement in World War I. In this moving poem, Cotter illustrates that neither poverty nor racism can withstand the strength of a mother's love. "Black Baby" was first published in Opportunity Journal in February 1929.

Black Baby

The baby I hold in my arms is a black baby.
    Today I set him in the sun and
    Sunbeams danced on his head.
The baby I hold in my arms is a black baby,
    I toil, and I cannot always cuddle him.
    I place him on the ground at my feet.
    He presses the warm earth with his hands,
    He lifts the sand and laughs to see
    It flow through his chubby fingers.
    I watch to discern which are his hands,
    Which is the sand. . . .
Lo . . . the rich loam is black like his hands.

The baby I hold in my arms is a black baby.
    Today the coal-man brought me coal.
    Sixteen dollars a ton is the price I pay for coal—
    Costly fuel . . . though they say:
Men must sweat and toil to dig it from the ground.
Costly fuel . . . 'Tis said:
If it is buried deep enough and lies hidden long enough
'Twill be no longer coal but diamonds. . . .
My black baby looks at me.
His eyes are like coals,
They shine like diamonds.

Exercise Love:

- Read this poem aloud to your own children, adult or small.
- This poem illustrates the power of love from a mother to a child—
  the black child who is viewed by many as nothing more than

another statistic, another helpless black child in a helpless world. But through the lens of the mother's heart, he is a priceless creation with endless possibilities. He is like a piece of coal, a diamond in the rough whose potential, now hidden from the world, will one day shine. It is a mother's love that nurtures a child's potential and possibility into reality. What are some aspirations you have for your children?

Bible

Learning how to love appropriately is a necessary but difficult goal for all of us. Sexual desire, emotional need, and intellectual compatibility often masquerade as love; guilt, insensitivity, and codependency often taint love. Popular culture has distorted pictures of love, and sadly, many spouses, parents, and children have not learned the truths of love. Unmarried couples, family members and friends alike, are struggling under the weight of inaccurate media portrayals while trying to find the solid ground upon which to build healthy relationships.

When my younger son was in kindergarten his class went on a love-letter rampage. At age five these boys and girls were writing and exchanging notes with alarming content. They read something like this:

Dear Jean,
I love you. I want to sex you. Love Joe.

Of course, when I began to talk to my son about his note writing, it was clear to me that he did not have a clue about love or sex. In his mind love was friendship and having sex was kissing, so "sex" was a necessary ingredient for love. Unfortunately, his youthful misunderstanding about love is prevalent among many teens and adults. In many minds attraction is love and love is sex.

There's also a frequent assumption that giving gifts and buying "things" is love. Some months ago, I had to replace my son's cellular phone. When I got to the store, there was a less-than-half-price special on a certain designer phone that was normally

$300. When I returned home with the phone and a few other articles of clothing, my son's response to me was: "You must really love me!" I assured him that I did love him, but I tried to help him see that these purchases could in no way represent the depth and breadth of my love for him, and that even if I had returned home with a cheap phone and no new clothes, my love was certain and had little to do with the amount of money I'd spent.

One of the most beneficial things that we can do for ourselves and others is to learn how to recognize and show love. Love is at its best when it is most authentic. When we discover the beauty and expanse of real love, we will not settle for less. Perhaps one of the best definitions of love is found in Paul's first letter to the Corinthians.

1 Corinthians 13[*]

Though I speak with the tongues of men and of angels, but have not love, I am become as sounding brass or a tinkling cymbal.

And though I have the gift of prophecy, and understand all mysteries and all knowledge, and though I have all faith, so that I could remove mountains, but have not love, I am nothing. And though I bestow all my goods to feed the poor, and though I give my body to be burned, but have not love, it profiteth me nothing.

Love suffereth long and is kind; love envieth not; love vaunteth not itself, is not puffed up; doth not behave itself unseemly, seeketh not her own, is not easily provoked, thinketh no evil, Rejoiceth not in iniquity, but rejoiceth in the truth; Beareth all things, believeth all things, hopeth all things, endureth all things.

Love never faileth. But whether there be prophecies, they shall fail; whether there be tongues, they shall cease; whether there be knowledge, it shall vanish away.

For we know in part, and we prophesy in part.

---

[*]*We have quoted from the King James Version of the Bible throughout this book. In this passage we have substituted the word love where the King James Version uses* charity.

But when that which is perfect is come, then that which is in part shall be done away.

When I was a child, I spake as a child, I understood as a child, I thought as a child; but when I became a man, I put away childish things.

For now we see through a glass, darkly, but then face to face: Now I know in part, but then I shall know even as also I am known.

And now abideth faith, hope, love, these three; but the greatest of these is love.

Exercise Love:

- I have a friend whose eleven-year-old daughter copied these verses on a sheet of paper and then taped the paper above her bed. When my friend asked her daughter about it, the young girl answered that she'd just found the verses in her Bible, liked them, and wanted to write them down. My friend had recently had an argument with the child and immediately felt guilty, assuming that the act of copying and displaying the verses was—consciously or not—the child's plea for patience. No more mention was made of the fight or the sudden appearance of the Bible verses on the wall. But my friend has never forgotten the power the words must have had on her child and the influence they now have on her relationship with her budding teenager. Read other Bible versions of this passage, from the New International Version or the New King James Version. Make your own copy of I Corinthians 13. Put it on the refrigerator door or in a frame by your bedside. Let it penetrate your heart. Read it when there are quarrels, when you are irritable, when love is not the first thing on your mind.
- Discuss ways in which love might "parade itself" or be "puffed up."
- One of the biggest problems that arises in marriage is competition and jealousy between spouses. When a wife earns more than her husband or a husband gets a promotion that demands more of his time, it can create tension in a marriage. We remind couples that

"love does not envy," and the truth is that when two are one, there can be no competition. Love demands that we celebrate the accomplishments and successes of the ones we love. Pray that you are purged of all jealousy, especially jealousy of a spouse.

• In our family, our children view me [Elaine] as "law" and their father [Floyd] as "grace." I am the strict, demanding one who asks too many questions, and he is the "cool" one who gives them their space. I had to make a conscious decision not to try to compete with him for the children's approval. Our different techniques did not have to create conflict, but actually created balance. We complement each other. And that's what love is.

James Weldon Johnson

Writer, professor, and statesman James W. Johnson, an important part of the Harlem Renaissance, was the executive director of the National Association for the Advancement of Colored People from 1920 through 1931. The first African American admitted to the Florida bar, he also composed with his brother the song that would become known as the Negro National Anthem: "Lift Every Voice and Sing." His autobiography, Along This Way, is still in print after sixty years.

from Along This Way

I got acquainted with my father by being taken to the hotel to see him. As soon as Rosamond was big enough, he was taken too. My mother never went; one of the waiters fetched us until we were old enough to go alone. These visiting days were great days for us: the wide steps, the crowded verandas, the music, the soft, deep carpets of the lobby; this was a world of enchantment. My first definite thought about the hotel was that it belonged to my father. True, there was always around in the office a Mr. Campbell, a rather stooped man with a short reddish beard, who habitually gave me a friendly pat on the shoulder, and who evidently had something to do with the place. But just to the right, at the entrance to the big dining room, stands my father, peerless and imposing in full-dress clothes; he opens the door and takes me in; countless waiters, it seems, are standing around in groups; my father strikes a gong and the waiters spring to their stations and stand like soldiers at attention; I am struck with wonder at the endless rows of tables now revealed, the glitter of silver, china, and glass, and the array of napkins folded so that they look like many miniature white pyramids. Another gong, and the waiters relax; but one of them tucks a napkin under my chin and serves me as though I were a princeling. Then, with desires of heart and stomach satisfied and a quantity of reserves tied in a napkin, I am tucked away in a corner. Again the gong, the doors are thrown open, the guests stream in. My father snaps his fingers, waiters jump to carry out his orders, and guests smile him their thanks. He lords it over everything that falls within my ken. He is, quite obviously, the most important man in the St. James Hotel.

This childish portrait needs, of course, some rectification. No boy can make a fair estimate of his father. I was thirty years old before I was able to do it. The average boy all along thinks highly of his mother. In manhood he is likely even to sentimentalize her faults into tender virtues. With his male parent it is not so; his opinion goes through a range of changes and tends to be critical rather than sentimental. Up to ten a boy thinks his father knows everything; at twenty he indulgently looks upon the "old man" as a back number or, maybe, something less complimentary; at thirty, if the boy himself has any sense, he recognizes all of his father's qualities pretty fairly.

My father was a quiet, unpretentious man. He was naturally conservative and cautious, and generally displayed common sense in what he said and did. He never went to school; such education as he had was self-acquired. Later in life, I appreciated the fact that his self-development was little less than remarkable. He had a knowledge of general affairs and was familiar with many of the chief events and characters in the history of the world. I have the old sheepskin-bound volume of *Plutarch's Lives* which he owned before I was born. He had gained by study a working knowledge of the Spanish language; this he had done to increase his value as a hotel employee. When he was a young man in New York, he attended the theater a good deal, and, before I was aware of where the lines came from or of what they meant, I used to go around the house parroting after him certain snatches from the Shakespearean plays. I particularly recall: "To be or not to be; that is the question" and "A horse! My kingdom for a horse!"

The quality in my father that impressed me most was his high and rigid sense of honesty. I simply could not conceive of him as a party to any monetary transaction that was questionable in the least. I think he got his greatest satisfaction in life out of the reputation he had built up as a man of probity, and took his greatest pride in the consequent credit standing that he enjoyed. This element in his character was a source of gratification to my pride and also, more than once, to my needs. One instance of double gratification was when I was at home in Jacksonville in 1910, just a few weeks before I was to be married. My father and mother discussed an appropriate gift to me and, finally, to my undisguised joy, decided upon a check for a thousand dollars. My father, excusably, did not have a thousand dollars in cash; but he said to me, "My boy, we'll go downtown tomorrow and see if we can get the money." We went the next morning to one of the principal banks and my father spoke with John C. L'Engle, the president. The transaction was put through without any delay; he got the money on his note, without collateral security, without even an endorser. I was as proud to see him able to do such a thing as I was glad to have the money.

In the narrow sense, he was an unsociable man. My mother liked company; and when I was a boy we frequently had company at the house; occasionally there was a party. I, too, liked the company and the extra nice things to eat that were always a concomitant—especially ice cream, of which in my whole life I have never had too much. My father took practically no part in these affairs. In his opinion the entertaining of company as "company" was a waste of time and money.

Yet he was not devoid of graces. He played the guitar well as a solo instrument, a use seldom made of it now. He possessed a vein of eloquence and had a good ear for the well-turned phrase. He liked to get off pithy aphorisms. He keenly enjoyed witticisms, particularly his own. Some of the latter, through repetition, became fixed in my mind. On a hot afternoon he would say to me, "Bubs, draw a fresh bucket of water from the well, and be sure to get it from the north side." Or on a still hotter afternoon, "Son, suppose while you're resting you take the ax and chop a little wood." Not infrequently he would achieve a penetrating truth. It was not until he was in his middle forties that he became a church member; when he was past fifty he became a preacher; one day, after he had been a preacher for some years, he said to me, "My boy, do you know I was never compelled to associate with bad people until I joined the church?"

He was a jolly companion for a boy, and I loved to be with him and go about with him. He made my first kites. He was adept at folding paper, and he made me windmills and fashioned little boats to be sailed in a tub. He made shadow-figures on the wall at night. He took me and my brother to places along the river where we could paddle about and learn to swim. After we were big enough to trot around with him, he played with us a good deal in this way during the times between hotel seasons. Before I was able to hold the instrument on my knees he began to teach me the guitar. I had to stand up to it in the same manner in which a player stands up to a bass viol. By the time I was ten years old I was, for a child, a remarkable performer—I judge; for I remember people, sometimes guests from the hotel, coming to our house to hear me play.

My father was a man of medium size, but constitutionally strong. One of the traditions of the home was that he was never sick. His color was light bronze, and so, a number of shades darker than that of my mother. She at fifty bore more than a slight resemblance to the later portraits of Queen Victoria; so much so that the family doctor christened her "Queen," a name to which she afterward answered among her intimate friends.

The years as they pass keep revealing how the impressions made upon me as a child by my parents are constantly strengthening controls over my forms of habit, behavior, and conduct as a man. It appeared to me, starting into manhood, that I was to grow into something different from them; into something on a so much larger plan, a so much grander scale. As life tapers off I can see that in the deep and fundamental qualities I am each day more and more like them.

Exercise Love:

- Think about the impressions you make upon your children. They may never understand as Johnson did the sway your opinions and teachings can have over a lifetime, but with this in mind, make sure you teach them from a place of love and care.

- Which of your parents' sayings or witticisms do you remember fondly from your childhood? Be sure to pass these along to younger generations. Do you have a signature saying your children will remember with a groan or a laugh when you are gone? Consider embroidering it or having it printed and framed for them.

- Be a "jolly companion" for a son, daughter, grandchild, or other youngster in your neighborhood. Build and fly a kite. Go for walks along the river. Make boats for the tub or paper windmills or airplanes. Teach your daughter to swim or read or play the harmonica. Make a memory today.

Bishop Richard Allen

Bishop Richard Allen was born a slave in Philadelphia in 1760. In 1777, he began attending Methodist meetings and eventually joined the Methodist Society. He later purchased his freedom and traveled before settling down in Philadelphia. Licensed to preach in 1784, he joined the white congregation at St. George's Methodist Episcopal Church and began leading early-morning services. As the number of African American congregants increased, white church members began displaying a hostility that inspired Allen and his congregants to create their own worship space. In 1787, Allen became the first bishop of the African Methodist Episcopal Church. (Our own church in Queens is an Allen AME Church.) The lot in Philadelphia where the church was built is the oldest piece of real estate continuously owned by African Americans. In the following prayer, Bishop Richard Allen asks God to help him remain diligent in his love for him and to give him the strength to avoid the temptations of the secular world.

from The Life Experience and Gospel Labors of the Rt. Rev. Richard Allen

O Infinite amiableness! When shall I love thee without bounds? Without coldness or interruption, which, alas! So often seize me here below? Let me never suffer any creature to be thy rival, or to share my heart with thee; let me have no other God, no other love, but only thee.

Whoever loves, desires to please the beloved object; and according to the degree of love is the greatness of desire; make me, O God! Diligent and earnest in pleasing thee; let me cheerfully discharge the most painful and costly duties; and forsake friends, riches, ease, and life itself, rather than disobey thee.

Whoever loves, desires the welfare and happiness of the beloved object; but thou, O dear Jesus, canst receive no addition from my imperfect services; what shall I do to express my affection toward thee? I will relieve the necessities of my poor brethren, who are members of thy body; for he that loveth not his brother who he has seen, how can he love God whom he hath not seen?

O, Crucified Jesus! In whom I live, and without whom I die: mortify in me all sensual desires; inflame my heart with thy holy love, that I may no longer esteem the vanities of this world, but place my affections entirely on thee.

Let my last breath, when my soul shall leave my body, breathe forth love to thee, my God; I entered into life without acknowledging thee, my God; I entered into life without acknowledging thee, let me therefore finish it in loving thee; O let the last act of life be love, remembering that God is love.

Exercise Love:

- Bishop Richard Allen entreats God to "make me, O God! diligent and earnest in pleasing thee. . . ." Serving God, especially in a world that entices us with "riches, ease, and life itself," can make it difficult for us to remain faithful in our service to the Lord. Can you relate to the challenges Bishop Allen faces in his desire to be "diligent and earnest" in his love for God?

- Do the words "Love thy neighbor as thyself" take on a deeper meaning after reading Bishop Allen's conviction that he will express his affection for God by relieving "the necessities of my poor brethren"?

- Spend one night this week reading Bishop Allen's prayer at the dinner table. Have family members take turns reading the prayer aloud.

- Although Reverend Allen was a bishop, he still prayed for guidance and clarity and the ability to ". . . love thee without bounds. . . . Without coldness or interruption, which, alas! So often seize me here below . . ." How might you express love of God in your own faith practice? Are there "vanities" of this world that you esteem more than you should? What are some practical ways you can express more rightly your love of God in daily living?

Ruby Dee

Actress and writer Ruby Dee grew up in Harlem and graduated from Hunter College in New York. Inducted into the Theater Hall of Fame in 1989, she acted in classics such as A Raisin in the Sun *and* South Pacific *and appeared in Spike Lee's* Do the Right Thing *and the adaptation of Alex Haley's* Roots. *Married for more than fifty years to actor Ossie Davis, Dee has been a human rights advocate for nearly as long. The excerpt below is from* My One Good Nerve, *a book based on her one-woman show, which she has performed all over the country.*

Aunt Zurletha

Aunt Zurletha had pretty red hair, gray eyes, and blue-black skin. A circle of rouge was on each cheek. The shiny red lipstick on her full mouth matched the fingernail polish, which matched the toenail polish. Usually, she wore earrings that looked like diamonds that matched the three rings she always wore.

My brother William said she looked like a witch, which made me wonder when and where he had ever seen a witch. My other brother Curtis said she looked pathetic. "Pathetic" was his new word that year. Everything was "pathetic." My father Hosea said she looked like a hustler. Zurletha the Zero, he used to say. I thought she was pretty, especially when she smiled. Her teeth were even and so white.

Mama used to say, "You can just quit so much talk about Zurletha. She's the only roomer that pays her rent in advance."

I heard her say to Hosea one night, "Who could we turn to when we had that fire in the shop and folks suing you for their clothes and the insurance company practically blaming you for starting your own fire and all the fires in Harlem for the last ten years? Who in the world could we turn to? Tell me. We would have starved to death but for Zurletha. No, I will not let you put her out."

"Now hold on, Mat. Gratitude is a thing you have got to understand. I am grateful—grateful to God who made it possible for me not to go under. That woman was just God's instrument. God's way of showing me—"

"You just mad because you can't get her to that church of yours."

"Mat, the woman needs a church home. She needs something more in her life besides those white folks she works for. She needs to find God."

"Not in that raggedy little broken-down storefront, Hosea. You know how she likes pretty things."

"That is precisely what worries me, Mat. That is precisely why I want her out of here. Take Baby—she practically worships her. And if I catch her one more time messing around in that woman's room—"

"Zurletha doesn't mind. She told me Baby's just having a little fun," Mama said.

"A little fun can leave you dragging a lifetime load. I've seen too much, Mat. I know what I'm talking about."

"All right, Hosea—that's how you feel we can keep Baby out of there."

"Playing with them beads and that glass junk she calls jewelry. Rubbing up against those rabbits she's got hanging up on the door—"

"They are not rabbits, and you know it. Mink, that's what it is. A mink coat, and she's also got a fox stole."

"Don't care if it's dog. I want Baby's mind steady on her books and her grades and on what she is going to do with her life."

"All right, all right, Hosea. Stop preaching at me. Put that light out now. Go on to sleep."

"Keep that door locked when Zurletha's not in there, y'hear."

I didn't understand my father sometimes. Aunt Zurletha—and he made us call her "aunt"—had been living with us on her days off for as long as I can remember. She didn't want us to call her Miss Battles. And Hosea wouldn't let us say just "Zurletha." The people she worked for just called her "Zurlie." I think that's the only thing she didn't like—"Zurlie" this and "Zurlie" that for forty years.

She was always giving us something. Gave Curtis his own radio. Gave William a microscope. My last birthday, last August, she gave me a guitar. You should've heard her play the guitar. We'd come home from Sunday school and hear her singing and stomping her foot. Made us want to dance. Soon after, though, she'd stop—especially if Hosea came home to eat before going back to church. Then she'd open her door, and we'd all go in, me first.

She had so many beautiful things. Real crystal glasses that she could tap with her fingernail and make sounds like music. There wasn't too much room to walk, so mostly I sat on her big brass bed. And she'd let me play with the silver candlesticks or try on the jewelry and hats. She had such pretty suitcases, too. Since the guitar, though, whenever she came home, she'd show me how to play different chords. We'd practice very quietly.

One time she took us to the beach on the subway. Hosea was in Washington, and Mama had promised us we could go. It was still dark when I heard her in the kitchen. I got up and she let me help her pack this big straw basket with all kinds of food she had brought with her the night before. William and Curtis carried the blankets. She carried the basket. I had Curtis' radio. It was a beautiful day, and we had such a good time, too, even Curtis with his smart-alecky self.

Aunt Zurletha had on a silky blue and green bathing suit and some kind of rubber sandals that had lots of straps and curved heels with big holes through them and her pretty red hair was tied in a ponytail, and as always, she had on her jewelry. William and Curtis were whispering behind her back and making fun, saying she looked like a cow-pig. I think she must have heard them talking about her bunion sticking out of her strappy shoes, even though she was laughing and shaking her shoulders to the music on Curtis' radio as she set up the umbrella and opened the blankets. Later, when me and Curtis and William came out of the water, she had the lunch all set out and was stretched out reading *True Love* magazine. The sun was bouncing off her bracelet as I reached over and started twisting it around her arm. She took it off and said, "Here, you can wear it for a while." I put it on my arm and ran out from under the umbrella and started pretending I was a rich lady. William said, "You think you something, huh? She probably stole it." This time I know she heard because just before we started to eat, she took the bracelet off my arm.

"You always have such pretty things, Aunt Zurletha," I said.

And she said, "Ought to. I've been working mighty hard for a lotta years. Then, too, my people buy me—or give me—a lot of stuff. Especially when the children were small. We traveled all over then."

"They must be some rich people, man," Curtis said.

"Rich? They got money's mama," Aunt Zurletha said.

"What does money's mama look like, and who's the daddy?" William asked.

Zurletha laughed and took a dainty little bite of one of the sandwiches.

"They probably stole all that money," William said. "Hosea says that rich folks are thieves."

"Not my people," said Zurletha. "My people are just plain smart. And white, too, you know?"

I thought William sounded jealous and mean too.

"And how come they didn't give you some of that money instead of all that other junk?"

Aunt Zurletha didn't even seem mad.

"It's not junk, William. They give me expensive things. Years ago, too, when I wanted to bake pies to sell, they were going to set me up a place."

"What happened, Aunt Zurletha?" I asked.

Then she told us how her lady got pregnant again and didn't want her to leave, and how they kept promising to set up the pie place but never did what with all the traveling and more babies coming; then, being in charge of opening all the different houses; and with her people getting sick and dying one right after the other; and how the children not wanting her to leave, she just finally got out of the notion of a pie place.

"Why you never got married, Aunt Zurletha?" Curtis asked.

"One time I was gonna get married—this was before you children were even thought of. But again, something came up with my people, and we stayed in Europe. I should say we stayed all over Europe for a year. And when I came back, lo and behold he had married somebody else. Never will forget. Said it came to him that I was already married—married to a damn job was the way he put it."

"O-o-o, you should have quit that job, Aunt Zurletha, and married what's-his-name."

"Frank. His name was Frank." Aunt Zurletha looked sad for a second. The she leaned over and started cutting the cake. "Then I wouldn't have you for my kids," she said.

Curtis nudged William and pointed at the kinky gray hair sticking out from under the red wig. Aunt Zurletha must have eyes all around her head, just like Mama. She fixed the wig so the gray didn't show. And I thought it was strange—just at that moment that song "Darling I Am Growing Old" came on the radio. Then Aunt Zurletha started singing and doing a little dance on her tiptoes as she passed out the cake.

I wish I could remember more about Aunt Zurletha, but she was never really home that much. I think often about that last summer, though. Our for-real Aunt Marie was a nurse, and she had arranged for us to go to a summer camp for two weeks. Hosea and Mama just had to get our clothes ready—that's all. We didn't have to pay. We didn't even think about Aunt Zurletha we were having such a good time. And Mama and Hosea didn't tell us in their letter that she had been in the hospital. We didn't find out until they picked us up at the bus terminal on the way home. I was so ashamed that we hadn't thought about her. I could have drawn her a funny get-well card.

After camp, first thing. I knocked on her door and went in before she said come in. Even though she had the biggest of the three rented rooms, it looked so small and crowded. All her beautiful stuff was packed in boxes and piled on top of the radiator, and beside the window, under the bed—everywhere. It looked like she was planning to move. Everything looked gray, except for the afternoon sun against the window shade. A sweet-smelling spray mingled with the odor of— something like when Hosea found a dead mouse that had gotten caught in the little space between the stove and the sink. I had never seen Aunt Zurletha without the wig and without the red lipstick and the beautiful earrings. Her black, black face was lying on the white, white pillow. It looked smooth like wax. Her hair was cornrowed, end-ing in two thin braids, and almost gone in the front and on the sides where the wig used to be. It seemed like she stayed that way for the rest of the summer.

She didn't want us children to come into her room, so I would sit on the little rug outside her door and play some of the things she had showed me on the guitar. Mama would bring food. Hosea used to say, "It's a shame. Why didn't she tell somebody she was so sick?"

Mama said, "Guess she didn't want to worry us. She complained one or two times, but she told me she just didn't have the time to go sit in some doctor's office."

That fall they took her away to the hospital again. And one day while I was in school, Aunt Zurletha died. When I came home, the room was empty. All the boxes, the brass bed, the furs, the lamps, and the glasses, the china ornaments—everything, gone.

"It just so happened, Baby," Mama said, "the people she sold all her things to came today to pick them up."

A bottle of fingernail polish was on the windowsill. It was hard to open. I don't know why, but I started painting my thumbnail. Then I found myself kneeling on the floor, with my head on the windowsill, crying. Crying like I couldn't stop. And the polish spilled all over my middyblouse. Luckily I didn't spill it all. There was a little left, and I promised myself not to ever use it, because it was all I had to remember Aunt Zurletha by.

"Nail polish? That's not what she left you, Baby," Mama said. "She left us all her cash money. She left a will. Enough for each of you to go one year in college."

"I'm hoping they will get scholarships," Hosea said.

"Well, we can see to that when the time comes." Mama started crying.

"Aw, come on now, Mat, sweetheart," Hosea said. "You know Zurletha wanted to go. See how she planned everything. Too bad, though, she never planned time to get with God."

What Hosea said made me scream at him, "Yeah, but she will. And when she does, I hope she'll have on her red wig and her rouge and her fingernail polish with toes to match and all her jewelry, and kiss God with her greasy lipstick on. I bet he'll just hug and kiss her back, and tell her how beautiful she is."

Daddy just looked at me a long time after that. Then he walked across the room and put his arms around me. I couldn't remember the last time he did that. He said, "Come on now. Crying won't bring her back, Baby. If crying would bring her back, maybe I'd cry along with you. Won't find another roomer who—" He went over to Mama, took her by the shoulders, and shook her a little bit before he hugged her and said, "She got to be part of this family, Mat. She really did. We're going to miss her all right. All of us."

That day I felt something that I'd been afraid of all my life tumble down inside my father, and he became a gentler man. From that day whenever I think about Aunt Zurletha I hear the music of crystal glasses as they touch tingling around me and I feel happy.

Exercise Love

- Think about the people who come in and out of our lives, like roomers. If we're lucky we have folks in our lives who become part of the family even though they are not really related. The love we feel for the ones who touch our hearts is something we don't always recognize until after they are no longer part of our life. Make a point of recognizing and expressing your love for the Aunt Zurlethas in your own life.

- Ruby Dee hears the "music of crystal glasses" when she thinks about Aunt Zurletha. Make a list of images or sounds that come to mind when you think about certain people you love. Share the list with those loved ones.

Robert Hayden

"Those Winter Sundays" *celebrates the love that African Americans, with little material wealth, have shown for their families. Many of these acts of love have been so subtle that it is only in adulthood that we realize the sacrifices that our parents made to ensure our comfort. Robert Hayden, whose poetry gained international acclaim in the 1960s, was born in Detroit in 1913. In 1976 he became the first African American to be appointed consulate in poetry to the Library of Congress (later called poet laureate).*

Those Winter Sundays

Sundays too my father got up early
And put his clothes on in the blueblack cold,
Then with cracked hands that ached
From labor in the weekday weather made
Banked fires blaze. No one ever thanked him.

I'd wake and hear the cold splintering, breaking.
When the rooms were warm, he'd call,
And slowly I would rise and dress,
Fearing the chronic angers of that house.

Speaking indifferently to him,
Who had driven out the cold
And polished my good shoes as well.
What did I know, what did I know
Of love's austere and lonely offices?

Exercise Love:

• The narrator writes of a father who rises early every day of the week—even on the Sabbath—to make sure that his family is warm and that his son's shoes are polished. "No one ever thanked him." Are there people in your life who make sacrifices for your comfort? Have you thanked them?

• In what ways do you express your gratitude to those who have gone out of their way to help you? Think about how you might show those who have made sacrifices for you that you appreciate their generosity and love.

• The child in the poem fears the anger in the house. Consider the ways in which, as a pressured parent, you may be instilling fear in your children with anger or impatience. Perhaps you are overwhelmed by the stresses of parenthood, or of managing your family's budget, and have little time for yourself. Acknowledge your hard work and show your children, through words and actions, that they are a joy and not a burden. Get ready to bask in their love and affection.

• Every day try to do one loving thing for someone else—without him or her knowing who was responsible.

Loyalty

A steadfast allegiance, affection, or devotion to others,
LOYALTY strengthens our families and
holds our communities together.

Those of us who are married have spoken a vow of loyalty to our spouses. We have pledged to stand up for and stay connected to our wives and husbands through frustration and difficulty, sadness and misfortune. But even when vows are not spoken, they are still made, and they are not to be taken lightly. As mothers and fathers, sons and daughters, friends and neighbors, we must always be there for one another. Loyalty is tending to the welfare and happiness of others as much as you tend to your own. As the eloquent Gwendolyn Brooks once wrote, "We are each other's harvest; we are each other's business; we are each other's magnitude and bond."

While we cannot live for others, we have a responsibility to live with regard for others. Our obligation to support, defend, and assist those closest to us is a God-given duty that we must never forsake. As we are told in Proverbs 17:17, "A friend loveth at all times, and a brother is born for adversity." If we refuse to fulfill our responsibilities, we will find ourselves forever running away from our lives and forever disappointing those in our paths.

When I was elected to Congress in 1986, my family was living in New York. Every day, I would need to be in Washington, D.C., for work, but as a father and husband, I had responsibilities and obligations at home. I also had commitments to my church that I could not and would not forsake. For eleven years, I served in the United States House of Representatives, and for eleven years, I commuted daily from New York to Washington. Sometimes I spent the plane ride writing the sermons that I preached to my congregation each Sunday. I could have moved to Washington and abandoned my family and congregation in pursuit of my career, but I knew where my loyalties lay.

Even when the ones you love the most disappoint you, cause you stress, or bring sorrow into your life, you must not abandon them. It is too easy to walk away. When others lose hope in times of crisis, we must not forsake them. For it is then that our compassion is tested and then that our love must remain strongest. Loyalty carries us through the misfortunes that we all must face.

We persevere through our difficulties because we know there are many who love us, and we must lend our support to our loved ones so that they too can bear their burdens. Our friend Vernon Jordan had been invited to speak at our Sunday morning worship service when he heard of my indictment (see Forgiveness, p. 141). He called to inform us that he would honor the commitment he had made, although many had suggested he renege; we were his friends, and he came to lend his support. He gave the first donation to the legal defense fund that helped throw out the case and remains a loyal friend today.

The heroes of our history knew that their people needed them. They knew that they were working not only for themselves but also for their fellow blacks, their fellow countrymen, and their fellow human beings. We remember them because they dedicated themselves not to enjoying the world but to changing it for our benefit.

But as the famed civil rights activist, singer, actor, athlete, and law school graduate Paul Robeson explained long ago, "Negro history cannot rest with the recital of personal victories." Our heritage must be one of united movements rather than individual efforts. The greatest accomplishments are a product of the strongest teamwork. To change our nation's laws or remedy our world's injustices, we must unite. And we must live lives of loyalty, never forgetting the men and women we love.

Frankie and Doug Quimby

AS TOLD TO MARIAN BARNES

T*he story of Ibo Landing is told here by Marian Barnes and is based on an interview she conducted with Georgia Sea Islands storytellers Frankie and Doug Quimby.*

The Ibo Landing Story

D*uring* the time of slavery they would load and unload slaves at Dunbar Creek, on the north end of St. Simon's Island on the east coast of Georgia. On one particular trip a ship went to Africa to get more people to bring them here to America to sell them for slaves.

While the slave traders were in Africa, they went by the Ibo tribe, and they found eighteen grown people. They fooled them. They told them, "We want you to go to America to work."

When these people got to St. Simon's Island, they found out that they had been tricked and they were going to be sold as slaves. Then all eighteen of these people agreed together. They all said, "No! Rather than be a slave here in America, we would rather be dead."

They linked themselves together with chains and they said a prayer. They said, "Water brought us here, and water is going to carry us away." Then they backed themselves out into Dunbar Creek and drowned themselves.

As they were going down, they were singing a song in their African language. We continue to sing that same song today using English words.

Today, Dunbar Creek on St. Simon's Island is a historical spot visited by throngs of people who have heard the story. Some visitors who have gone to Dunbar Creek on nights when the moon shines a certain way say they have heard the muffled sounds of voices talking, people wailing, and chains clinking.

THE IBO LANDING SONG

Oh freedom, oh freedom, oh freedom over me
And before I'd be a slave I'll be buried in my grave
And go home to my Lord and be free.

No more crying, no more crying, no more crying will there be
And before I'd be a slave I'll be buried in my grave
And go home to my Lord and be free.
No more groaning, no more dying will there be
And before I'd be a slave I'll be buried in my grave
And go home to my Lord and be free.
Oh freedom, oh freedom, oh freedom over me
And before I'd be a slave I'll be buried in my grave
And go home to my Lord and be free.

Exercise Loyalty:

- When the Ibo tribe members learn that they have been tricked into slavery, they link themselves together with chains, say a prayer, and drown themselves. Talk about this action with your family. Think about how the story and the spiritual are also illustrative of the loyalty our ancestors expressed as a people—for each other and for the cause of freedom.

- The story of Ibo Landing has attracted thousands of visitors to Dunbar Creek. Why do you think this tale has impacted so many Americans, black and white? Consider the ways in which this tale of loyalty has given strength to black and white men and women who have struggled against injustice in this country.

- As a storyteller and historian, Marian Barnes is passionate about our knowing the history behind our hymns. The song that appears in the Quimbys' retelling of Ibo Landing is a spiritual that has been used both as a message song about escaping slavery and as a song about spiritual liberation. Known to many of us from our hymnbooks as "Oh, Freedom," this song—and others like it—was a mechanism used by our ancestors to survive, to rise above their circumstances. Think about the loyalty expressed in the actions of the Ibo Landing tribesmen. Can loyalty also be a mechanism for survival?

- As an expression of your loyalty to each other, make up your own new verse or verses to "Oh, Freedom" with your family members.

Colin L. Powell

*S*ecretary of State Colin L. Powell, a professional soldier for thirty-five years, held many command and staff positions and rose to the rank of four-star general. From 1989 to 1993, Powell served as the twelfth chairman of the Joint Chiefs of Staff, the highest military position in the Department of Defense. In his autobiography, My American Journey, written with Joseph E. Persico, Secretary Powell recalls coming of age in the South Bronx and attending City College, where he received a bachelor's degree in geology. An active participant in his college's ROTC, Powell found in the program the loyalty and sense of brotherhood that brought out the best in him and cultivated his leadership abilities.

from My American Journey

The Bronx can be a cold, harsh place in February, and it was frigid the day I set out for college. After two bus rides, I was finally deposited, shivering, at the corner of 156th Street and Convent Avenue in Harlem. I got out and craned my neck like a bumpkin in from the sticks, gazing at handsome brownstones and apartment houses. This was the best of Harlem, where blacks with educations and good jobs lived, the Gold Coast.

I stopped at the corner of Convent and 141st and looked into the campus of the City College of New York. I was about to enter a college established in the previous century "to provide higher education for the children of the working class." Ever since then, New York's poorest and brightest have seized that opportunity. Those who preceded me at CCNY include the polio vaccine discoverer Dr. Jonas Salk, Supreme Court Justice Felix Frankfurter, the muckraker novelist Upton Sinclair, the actor Edward G. Robinson, the playwright Paddy Chayefsky, the *New York Times* editor Abe Rosenthal, the novelist Bernard Malamud, the labor leader A. Philip Randolph, New York City mayors Abraham Beame and Edward Koch, U.S. Senator Robert Wagner, and eight Nobel Prize winners. As I took in the grand Gothic structures, a C-average student out of middling Morris High School, I felt over-whelmed. And then I heard a friendly voice: "Hey, kid, you new?"

He was a short, red-faced, weather-beaten man with gnarled hands, and he stood behind a steaming cart of those giant pretzels that New Yorkers are addicted to. I had met a CCNY fixture called, for some unaccountable reason, "Raymond the Bagel Man," though he sold pretzels. I bought a warm, salty pretzel from Raymond, and we shot the breeze for a few minutes. That broke the ice for me. CCNY was somehow less intimidating. I was to become a regular of Raymond's over the next four and a half years. And it either speaks well of his character or poorly of my scholarship that while my memory of most of my professors has faded, the memory of Raymond the Bagel Man remains undimmed.

As I headed toward the main building, Sheppard Hall, towering like a prop out of a horror movie, I passed by an undistinguished old building. I do not remember paying any attention to it at the time. It was, however, to become the focus of my life for the next four years, the ROTC drill hall.

My first semester as an engineering major went surprisingly well, mainly because I had not yet taken any engineering courses. I decided to prepare myself that summer with a course in mechanical drawing. One hot afternoon, the instructor asked us to draw "a cone intersecting a plane in space." The other students went at it; I just sat there. After a while, the instructor came to my desk and looked over my shoulder at a blank page. For the life of me, I could not visualize a cone intersecting a plane in space. If this was engineering, the game was over.

My parents were disappointed when I told them that I was changing my major. There goes Colin again, nice boy, but no direction. When I announced my new major, a hurried family council was held. Phone calls flew between aunts and uncles. Had anybody ever heard of anyone studying geology? What did you do with geology? Where did you go with it? Prospecting for oil? A novel pursuit for a black kid from the South Bronx. And, most critical to these security-haunted people, could geology lead to a pension? That was the magic word in our world. I remember coming home after I had been in the Army for five years and visiting my well-meaning, occasionally meddling Aunt Laurice. What kind of career was this Army? she asked, like a crossexaminer. What was I doing with my life? Snatching at the nearest defense, I mentioned that after twenty years I would get a half-pay pension. And I would only be forty-one. Her eyes widened. A pension? At forty-one? The discussion was over. I had made it.

During my first semester at CCNY, something had caught my eye—young guys on campus in uniforms. CCNY was a hotbed of liberalism, radicalism, even some leftover communism from the thirties; it was not a place where you would expect much of a military presence. When I returned to school in the fall of 1954, I inquired about the Reserve Officers' Training Corps, and I enrolled in ROTC. I am not sure why. Maybe it was growing up in World War II and coming of age during the Korean conflict: the little banners in windows with a blue star, meaning someone from the family was in the service, or a gold star, meaning someone was not coming back. *Back to Bataan, Thirty Seconds over Tokyo, Guadalcanal Diary,* Colin Kelly, Audie Murphy, the five Sullivan brothers who went down with the cruiser U.S.S. *Juneau, Pork Chop Hill,* and *The Bridges at Toko-Ri.* All these images were burned into my consciousness during my most impressionable years. Or maybe it was the common refrain of that era—you are going to be drafted anyway, you might as well go in as an officer. I was not alone. CCNY might not have been West Point, but during the fifties it had the largest voluntary ROTC contingent in America, fifteen hundred cadets at the height of the Korean War.

There came a day when I stood in line in the drill hall to be issued olive-drab pants and jacket, brown shirt, brown tie, brown shoes, a belt with a brass buckle, and an overseas cap. As soon as I got home, I put the uniform on and looked in the mirror. I liked what I saw. At this point, not a single Kelly Street friend of mine was going to college. I was seventeen. I felt cut off and lonely. The uniform gave me a sense of belonging, and something I had never experienced all the while I was growing up: I felt distinctive.

In class, I stumbled through math, fumbled through physics, and did reasonably well in, and even enjoyed, geology. All I ever looked forward to was ROTC. Colonel Harold C. Brookhart, professor of military science and tactics, was our commanding officer. The colonel

was a West Pointer and regular Army to his fingertips. He was about
fifty years old, with thinning hair, of only medium height, yet he
seemed imposing because of his bearing, impeccable dress, and no-
nonsense manner. His assignment could not have been a coveted one
for a career officer. I am sure he would have preferred commanding a
regiment to teaching ROTC to a bunch of smart-aleck city kids on a
liberal New York campus. But the Korean War had ended the year
before. The Army was overloaded with officers, and Brookhart was
probably grateful to land anywhere. Whatever he felt, he never let us
sense that what we were doing was anything less than deadly serious.

That fall, I experienced the novel pleasure of being courted by the
three military societies on campus, the Webb Patrol, Scabbard and
Blade, and the Pershing Rifles, ROTC counterparts of fraternities.
Rushing consisted mostly of inviting potential pledges to smokers
where we drank beer and watched pornographic movies. The movies,
in the sexually repressed fifties, were supposed to be a draw. I hooted
and hollered with the rest of the college boys through these grainy
8-millimeter films, in which the male star usually wore socks. But they
were not what drew me to the Pershing Rifles. I pledged the PRs
because they were the elite of the three groups.

The pledge period involved typical ritualistic bowing and scraping
before upperclassmen, and some hazing that aped West Point traditions. A junior would stand you at attention and demand the definition of certain words. To this day I can parrot the response for milk:
"She walks, she talks, she's made of chalk, the lactile fluid extracted
from the female of the bovine species . . ." And on and on. I can spout
half a dozen similar daffy definitions. When we finished the pledge
period, we were allowed to wear distinctive blue-and-white shoulder
cords and enamel crests on our uniforms. I found that I was much
attracted by forms and symbols.

One Pershing Rifles member impressed me from the start. Ronald
Brooks was a young black man, tall, trim, handsome, the son of a
Harlem Baptist preacher and possessed of a maturity beyond most col-

lege students. Ronnie was only two years older than I, but something in him commanded deference. And unlike me, Ronnie, a chemistry major, was a brilliant student. He was a cadet leader in the ROTC and an officer in the Pershing Rifles. He could drill men so that they moved like parts of a watch. Ronnie was sharp, quick, disciplined, organized, qualities then invisible in Colin Powell. I had found a model and a mentor. I set out to remake myself in the Ronnie Brooks mold.

My experience in high school, on basketball and track teams, and briefly in Boy Scouting had never produced a sense of belonging or many permanent friends. The Pershing Rifles did. For the first time in my life I was a member of a brotherhood. The PRs were in the CCNY tradition only in that we were ethnically diverse and so many of us were the sons of immigrants. Otherwise, we were out of sync with both the student radicals and the conservative engineering majors, the latter easy to spot by the slide rules hanging from their belts. PRs drilled together. We partied together. We cut classes together. We chased girls together. We had a fraternity office on campus from which we occasionally sortied out to class or, just as often, to the student lounge, where we tried to master the mambo. I served as an unlikely academic advisor, steering other Pershing Rifles into geology as an easy yet respectable route to a degree.

The discipline, the structure, the camaraderie, the sense of belonging were what I craved. I became a leader almost immediately. I found a selflessness within my family. Race, color, background, income meant nothing. The PRs would go the limit for each other and for the group. If this was what soldiering was all about, then maybe I wanted to be a soldier.

Exercise Loyalty:

- Before joining ROTC, young Powell felt adrift and never managed to achieve much in his life. The ROTC program taught Powell the meaning of brotherhood, cooperation, and the value of working toward a common goal. More important, Powell gained self-esteem and realized that his actions could make a difference, inspiring him to become a professional soldier. How has your loyalty to your faith, church, and the members of your community rewarded you? Has this loyalty provided your life with a sense of meaning?

• In I Chronicles 12, the men gather together to help David become King of Israel. Their loyalty to David will result in a greater good for all. How have Powell's leadership abilities and loyalty to his country benefited both him and our nation?

• Loyalty to traditional values is a legacy that has not been passed down to many of our young people. Many adolescents do not see the value in loyalty to church, family, and organizations that make up the fabric of American society. In many cases, these feelings are due to the fact that there are so few African Americans, particularly men, who lead our organizations. Share with your children the biographies of great African American leaders who fought for their country and fought to make a place in American history. Their inspiring stories will teach your children the value of persistence and loyalty.

Andrea Lee

*A*ndrea Lee's Sarah Phillipps *is one of the first post–civil rights novels about the black middle class. Sarah's father is a minister and a prestigious member of a black, affluent suburban Philadelphia community. In this excerpt, Sarah and her mother have learned that a local neighbor has committed suicide, leaving behind a wife and daughter.*

from Sarah Phillipps

On summer evenings, after the dinner dishes had been washed and as the remains of the iced tea stood growing tepid in the pitcher, my mother, dreamy and disheveled, finally would emerge from the kitchen. "Look at me," she'd murmur, wandering into the living room and patting her hair in the mirror over the piano. "I look like a Wild Man of Borneo."

She would change into a pair of oxfords and take a walk with me, or with a neighbor. At that time of day June bugs hurled themselves against the screens of the house, and my father, covered with mosquito repellent and smoking cigarette after cigarette, sat reading under the maple tree. In the diffuse light after sunset, the shadows around the perfectly ordinary houses up and down the street made the unambiguous details of their designs—turrets round Victorian towers, vague half-timbering—seem for once dramatic. All the backyards of the town seemed to have melted into one darkening common where packs of kids yelled faintly and fought their last battles before bedtime. Cars pulled out of driveways and headed for movie theaters or the shopping centers along the Pike, and the air smelled like honeysuckle and onion grass. When Mama and I walked together, we would wander up and down the long blocks until the streetlights came on.

One evening during the summer that I was six years old, we stopped to visit a neighboring family in which something sad and shocking had happened the previous winter. The father, a district judge named Roland Barber, had driven one gray afternoon to the marshland outside the airport and there had shot himself. Judge Barber, a short, grave, brown-skinned man with a curiously muted voice, had been a member of my father's congregation and had served with him on the board of the NAACP. His suicide, with hints of further-reaching scandal, sent a tremendous shock through the staid circles of my parents' friends, a shock that reached down even into the deep waters that normally insulated Matthew and me from adult life. For a few weeks after the suicide we held long grisly discussions on arcane, even acrobatic ways to do away with oneself.

The house in which Mrs. Barber continued to live with her teenage daughter was little different from our house, or any other in our neighborhood: a brick Colonial with myrtle and ivy planted around it instead of grass, and a long backyard that sloped down to a vegetable garden. I knew the Barbers' yard well, because there was an oak tree near the vegetable garden, with a swing in it that neighborhood kids were allowed to use. On the evening my mother and I came to visit, the daylight was fading, and the windows of the house were dark. It seemed that no one was home, but in the summers in our town, people often waited a long time in the evening before turning on lamps. It occurred to me as we walked up the driveway that the house itself seemed to be in mourning, with its melancholy row of blue spruces by the fence; I gave way, with a feeling that was almost like ecstasy, to a sudden shudder. Mama rubbed my goosepimply arms. "We'll just stay a minute," she said.

My mother was carrying a recipe for peach cobbler. It was intended for Mrs. Barber, a bony woman who had fascinated me even before her husband's death, because she wore very thick pairs of elasticized stockings. However, after we'd knocked and waited for a while, the front door was finally opened by Phyllis, the Barbers' sixteen-year-old daughter. Mama, who had taught Phyllis, sometimes referred to her as "the fair and brainless"; I had seen her plenty of times at the swim club, pretty and somewhat fat-faced, drawing the stares of the men to her plump legs in Bermuda shorts. That night, though it was only about eight o'clock, she opened the door in a light summer bathrobe and peered out at us without turning on the porch lights.

"Hello, Mrs. Phillipps. Hi, Sarah," she said in a low, hesitant voice. She came out onto the dark steps as she spoke, and let the screen door bang behind her. She explained that her mother wasn't there, and that she had been taking a shower when the bell rang; she radiated a fresh scent of soap and shampoo. When my mother asked her how she was feeling, she answered in the same hesitant tone, "All right."

I looked at her with a kind of awe. It was the first time I had seen her since I had heard the news about Judge Barber, and the first time I had ever stood right in front of anyone associated with an event that had caused such a convulsion in the adult world. In the light-colored robe, with her wet hair—which normally she wore flipped up at the ends and pulled back with a band, like other high school girls in the neighborhood—combed back from her forehead, she had a mysterious, imposing look that I never would have suspected of her. I immediately ascribed it—as I was ascribing the ordinary shadow of the summer twilight around the doorway—to the extraordinary thing that had happened to her. Her face seemed indefinably swollen, whether with tears or temper, and she kept her top lip tightly clenched as she talked to my mother. She looked beautiful to me, like a dream or an illustration from a book, and as I stared at her, I felt intensely interested and agitated.

In a few minutes Phyllis went back inside. My mother and I, as we had done many times before, walked quietly up the Barbers' driveway and through the backyard to the swing in the oak tree. Mama stopped to pick a few tomatoes from the overloaded plants in the Barbers' vegetable garden, and I helped her, though my second tomato was a rotten one that squashed in my fingers.

It was completely dark by then. Lightning bugs flashed their cold green semaphores across the backyards of the neighborhood, and a near-tropical din of rasping, creaking, buzzing night insects had broken out in the trees around us. I walked over and sat down in the oak-tree swing, and Mama, pausing occasionally to slap at mosquitoes, gave me a few good pushes, so that I flew high out of the leaves, toward the night sky.

I couldn't see her, but I felt her hands against my back; that was enough. There are moments when the sympathy between mother and child becomes again almost what it was at the very first. At that instant

I could discern in my mother, as clearly as if she had told me of it, the same almost romantic agitation that I felt. It was an excitement rooted in her fascination with grotesque anecdotes, but it went beyond that. While my mother pushed me in the swing, it seemed as if we were conducting, without words, a troubling yet oddly exhilarating dialogue about pain and loss.

In a few minutes I dragged my sneakered feet in a patch of dust to stop the swing. The light of a television had gone on inside the Barber house, and I imagined fat, pretty Phyllis Barber carefully rolling her hair on curlers, alone in front of the screen. I grabbed my mother's hand and said, "It's very sad, isn't it?"

"It certainly is," said Mama.

We took a shortcut home, and by the time we got there, it was time for me to scrub my grimy arms and legs and go to bed. Mama went immediately to the refrigerator and got out an uncooked roast of pork, which she stood contemplating as if it were the clue to something. She smelled of sage and dried mustard when she came upstairs to kiss Matthew and me good night.

Exercise Loyalty:

- While many members of the community shun the man's widow and her daughter, Sarah and her mother pay a visit to the house to make sure everything is all right. This simple act speaks of the loyalty necessary to bind a community together and the ways in which loyalty is an act of love. The act also speaks to the message in Ecclesiastes 7:2: "It is better to go to the house of mourning, than to go to the house of feasting: for that is the end of all men; and the living will lay it to his heart."

- By bringing Sarah along, Mrs. Phillipps demonstrates her duties as the wife of a minister: charity and the importance of maintaining a tight-knit community when the foundation has been ruptured by the suicide of one of its members. Loyalty is more than a duty, however. Is Mrs. Phillipps consciously teaching her daughter values that she wants her daughter to live by? Are Mrs. Phillipps's actions perhaps an act of atonement for a community that has not acknowledged the sickness of one of its members?

- The death of a community member brings Sarah and her mother closer together. Why do you think this is so? Ask your children what loyalty to family means to them. Loyalty to community? Loyalty to each other as human beings?

Bible

The story of *Ruth and Naomi*, from *Ruth 1:1–17*, is a call to humanity to stay connected to those who have loved, nurtured, and helped us. In a time when people so quickly forget those who have made a difference in their lives, we are reminded that loyalty is a desirable and admirable quality. Naomi was not just a mother-in-law to Ruth—she was a participant in her religious transformation. When this Moabite woman married Naomi's son, upon her integration into her new family, she was introduced to the God of Israel. So when Naomi, in her grief, suggested that the two of them separate, Ruth was clear that she would not leave the woman who had made such a major contribution to her life. She would remain devoted to Naomi, and together they would discover the blessings and mercies of God.

Ruth and Naomi

A terrible famine struck Bethlehem in Judah in the days when the judges ruled. A certain man and woman who dwelled there set out for the country of Moab with their two sons. The man's name was Elimelech, his wife's name Naomi, and their sons' names Mahlon and Chilion. Ephrathites of Bethlehem in Judah, they settled into the country of Moab.

Elimelech died, leaving his wife Naomi with their two sons.

Mahlon and Chilion married Moabite women; one was named Orpah, the other Ruth. They resided in the country of Moab about ten years. Mahlon and Chilion both died, and Naomi was left without her husband and two sons.

Upon learning in Moab that the Lord had supported his people by providing them with food, Naomi and her daughters-in-law prepared to return home. With Orpah and Ruth, Naomi left the land where she had been dwelling and embarked on the road that led back to the land of Judah.

And Naomi urged her two daughters-in-law, "Return, each of you, to your mother's home. May the Lord treat you kindly, as you have dealt with the dead and with me. May the Lord will it that each of you find sanctuary and shelter in the home of another husband."

She kissed them, and they wept aloud and told her, "We shall return with you to your people."

But Naomi cried, "Turn back, my daughters; why should you come with me? Are there still sons in my womb that may become your husbands? Return home, my daughters, for I am too old to have a husband. Even if there were still hope for me—even if I had a husband tonight and bore sons—would you wait until they were grown? Would you remain unwed for them? No, my daughters. I have tasted bitterness far worse than you have, for the hand of the Lord has turned against me."

And the women wept again; Orpah kissed her mother-in-law, but Ruth clung tightly to her.

Naomi said, "See, your sister-in-law is returning to her people and to her gods. Turn back with her."

But Ruth answered, "Do not urge me to leave your side, or to return from following you. Where you go, I shall go; where you dwell, I shall dwell. Your people will be my people, and your God my God. Where you die, I shall die, and I shall be buried there. May the Lord deal with me, no matter how severely, if anything but death separates me from you."

Exercise Loyalty:

- In the midst of famine and after the death of her husband, it certainly would have been easier for Ruth to go back to her own people. But she remains loyal to Naomi and stays with her. Her expression of loyalty is one of the Bible's most beautiful passages. Read the declaration aloud and think about Ruth's decision. Do you have similar commitments in your life? To your spouse? Your children? A friend?

- To stay with Naomi, Ruth was forced to let go of things that were familiar and easy. Are there attachments in your own life that you might let go of in favor of a greater loyalty?

- Read the Book of Ruth in its entirety to see how Ruth's loyalty is ultimately rewarded.

- Many of us have been in situations when loyalty makes an untenable demand on our lives. A family member who helped you years before has depleted you by his recurring requests for assistance and bailouts. Your mentor asks for an unethical favor after reminding you about all she has done for you. What are the boundaries? What is your moral obligation in this instance? Obviously, we cannot allow loyalty to compromise our integrity and responsible living. We must pray for appropriate guidelines: "Dear Lord, I am grateful for the friends and family that you have put in my life to bless me. I understand that I must now help those who have helped me. My desire is to be available to enhance the lives of those who have been my mentors, nurturers, and prayer partners, but I pray for the wisdom to know how to be appropriately loyal to them and to you. Help me to remember that because you are my creator, my Lord and my Redeemer, my first loyalty is to you. Amen."

Mary McLeod Bethune

Born in South Carolina in 1875, Mary McLeod Bethune was an educator and college president. She also founded the Southeastern Federation of Colored Women and the National Council of Colored Women, and served as president of the National Association of Colored Women, earning her the Southern Conference for Human Welfare's Thomas Jefferson Award. This excerpt from one of her speeches, which also includes a segment from one of her syndicated newspaper columns, still speaks vividly to our times long after Bethune's death. Loyalty takes on a whole new meaning when we consider it from within the context of tolerance, as Bethune does in this essay.

from The Lesson of Tolerance

The essence of Democracy is the concept that no one group or individual is all-wise or has a monopoly of all the virtues.

"Training ourselves and our children to have both tolerance and respect for opinions diverging from our own is one of the best possible ways to promote brotherhood—among the peoples of the world, and among our neighbors in our block! They who admit righteousness, sincerity, good intentions, understanding—*and loyalty*—in no one but themselves [, and] who can brook no opposition to their personal or group opinions, are unprepared for democratic living.

"Tyranny of opinion must never be our goal, for it is not the goal of Democracy or of Christianity. We must learn to *differ without denouncing; to listen without distrust; to reserve judgment.* 'Judge not that ye be not judged. For with what judgment ye judge ye shall be judged. And with what measure ye mete, it shall be measured unto you again.' You know the words, my friends.

"But listening to the 'other side' is a lesson in which we need training. Too often, in crisis, we 'panic.' We lose our sense of values—of fairness. We scoff at each other; we make sarcastic remarks and 'go righteous' as an alternative to thinking through our situations, calmly, with those who agree and those who do not agree.

"A little poise—a little tranquility of spirit—a little meditation and *maturing of the mind*, and we shall be able *to listen*, to learn, and *to go forward with those of other views*, of other races, and nations, and of other faiths, knowing that in every group that is worthwhile we shall find, and should encourage, a robust opposition—to whet our minds, strengthen our souls, and keep us on our toes."

Today, all of us are living in even graver days than were those when the words that I just read were written. I said then, and I say now, we need to strengthen our democratic principles—and to apply them more forthrightly and effectively. *For this task we need the aid and loyalty of all citizens devoted to their country and the good for which it stands.*

"*We cannot instill loyalty into the hearts of men by coercion and fear. Loyalty is a child of the spirit—and not a child of fear.* No one should know better than we Americans who are also Negroes, how *sterile and stultifying are the fruits of fear*, and, conversely, how loyalty grows joyfully and brings forth solid fruit, under the warming sunshine of confidence and opportunity for full development. In the late years of a life devoted to strengthening our faith in Democracy as a way of life, the sight of a generation of fearful conformists, in this, *my country*, would make me heartsick, indeed. The true practice of Brotherhood can save us from such a spectacle. Belief in and respect for others will produce, without panic, or repression, or injustice to any man, the loyalty we seek."

I had no way of knowing, when I wrote those words, how soon they might apply to *me*—to Mary McLeod Bethune! But what was evident to all who were concerned about the freedoms of our country, and who were taking time to think, calmly, was that the hue and cry of "subversive" hysteria was sweeping the country, twisting, rending, demolishing, and engulfing everything in its path, like some savage tornado. Some gave it one name, and some another. I do not call names nor use clichés. Since I do not like them applied to me, I do not use them in relation to others. *I merely describe what I see.*

Fifty-two weeks a year for more than three years—for 170 weeks—without interruption, my opinions have been on record in the press. My column, published each week on the editorial page of one of our largest weeklies, has addressed itself, repeatedly, to the sickness of communism *and of totalitarianism in all its forms*—and to the need for an articulate, loyal leadership that will stand, unafraid, as I am standing here, tonight, and dispute any point of view—any action—that gives evidence of being detrimental to the best interests of our common country, or to any part of its body politic.

In whole or in part, my story has been told in literally dozens of books and periodicals. Nothing could be more open than my thoughts on all phases of human relations. Yet the great question was raised with regard to me, as heedlessly as a smoldering match or cigarette is dropped from careless hands among the dry leaves of the woodland—starting a great conflagration whose scars may remain for generations in a wasted forest.

The world, today, is ablaze with the fires of hate and suspicion. The hands of too many men today are raised against their brothers. In these trying days the reputation of no man—no woman—is safe from suspicion and attack. The enemy has come among us! What then, my friends, must we do to be saved? We must cast out the devils of suspicion when they lay hold upon us, so that they may no longer make mockery of decent human relationships.

I wonder if people, inherently decent and honest—*people who think that they are being good citizens*—know what they are doing to their country when they permit themselves to take part in or be influenced, not only by outright, deliberate smears, but by such uninformed challenges of the actions and philosophy of an individual as those which were directed toward me in this city of Englewood?

I wonder if people in little cities and towns all over America realize that the enemy technique of "divide and conquer" is fast being replaced with the technique of "confuse and control"?

From time to time, in recent months, the Department of State has been issuing some most interesting pamphlets on Soviet techniques used to control East Germany. The first pamphlet of this series, called "confuse and control," State Department publication No. 4107, is well worth reading by those who cherish their freedoms, because it shows so clearly how the Soviets work to divide a house against itself; how they work to divide a nation against itself; how it teaches the peoples it would control to kill their leaders. Freedom-loving Americans should be ashamed to use these very tactics against their own fellow citizens.

We should be fully aware, by now, that what the enemies of Democracy cannot gain by a frontal attack on democratic institutions, they will attempt to gain by the more subtle techniques of question and innuendo, directed toward responsible leadership. Once a leader is subjected to suspicion, all the thousands who look to that leadership for direction become affected. If they stand fast with the leader, they become a part of the environment of suspicion which has been created—they are marked with the same question mark. If they desert, through fear, the effect is the same. The enemy has done his work.

Let us not work for the enemy. Let us not destroy with the virus of hysteria, the work which through the years the enemy has not himself been able to destroy. Let us rather, even in these days of hysteria, strive to preserve the basic principles of freedom of speech, freedom of the press, and freedom of assembly.

Think it over, my friends, when next you ask a fellow citizen to appear before you. If it is worth your time to listen to a speaker, you have a right to know who he is and what he stands for. But for the sake of your community and your country, decide for yourselves whether you want to hear him. Do not let others decide this for you. Do not let ignorance of the facts lead you into the position of joining hands with the enemy who seeks to divide and conquer—*to confuse and control.*

I am glad that I have been able to return to Englewood and that those who were responsible for questioning my loyalty have not only learned how mistaken they were, but have publicly acknowledged it. It is always a pleasing experience to be cleared of any suspicion—no matter how baseless was the origin of the suspicion. However, I was first cleared by my own conscience. I have always been cleared by the American people, who know where I have always stood and where I now stand—as one who loves her country dearly—but who likewise will not bow down before those whose actions tend to destroy the basic freedoms of our people by the process of fear and confusion.

The immortal words of our great leader Franklin D. Roosevelt are as true today as they were when he uttered them: "We have nothing to fear but fear itself."

Exercise Loyalty:

- "We cannot instill loyalty into the hearts of men by coercion and fear. Loyalty is a child of the spirit." What do you think Bethune means by this? How can you foster brotherhood or kinship with your spirit?

- "The world today is ablaze with the fires of hate and suspicion. The hands of too many men today are raised against their brothers." After the September 11 terrorist attacks, Bethune's call for brotherhood has special resonance. Examine your own personal loyalties and allegiances. Does your loyalty stem from a place of tolerance or fear?

- "A little poise—a little tranquility of spirit—a little meditation and *maturing of the mind,* and we shall be able *to listen,* to learn, and *to go forward with those of other views,* of other races, and nations, and of other faiths, knowing that in every group that is worthwhile we shall find, and should encourage, a robust opposition—to whet our minds, strengthen our souls, and keep us on our toes." True loyalty must stem from a place that accommodates differences. How might you be more accommodating in your dealings with others?

Ernest J. Gaines

Ernest J. Gaines was born in 1933 on the River Lake plantation in Pointe Coupee Parish, Louisiana. The fields he worked as a child and the black community he grew up in form much of the setting for his 1993 novel, A Lesson Before Dying. He is the recipient of numerous awards, including a MacArthur Foundation grant and the National Book Critics Circle Award for fiction for A Lesson Before Dying.

from A Lesson Before Dying

After church, the minister came back to the house with my aunt, Miss Eloise, Miss Emma, and Inez for coffee and cake. I lay across the bed in my room, looking out the window at the stack of beanpoles in the garden. As far back as I could remember, my aunt would pull up the rows of poles at the end of each season and stack them in that same corner of the garden, until a new crop of beans was ready to be poled. Beyond the poles, on the other side of the road, I could see the tops of the pecan trees in Farrell Jarreau's backyard. The trees had begun to bud again. The buds looked black from this distance. I could see above the trees how heavy, low, and gray the sky was. I had intended to go for a drive, but I was afraid it might rain while I was gone, making the road too muddy for me to drive back down the quarter. Anyway, I had work to do. But as usual, I ended up doing only a little, because of the singing and praying up at the church. After Tante Lou and her company had been at the house a while, she came into my room.

"You 'sleep?" she asked.

"I'm awake."

"Reverend Ambrose like to talk to you."

"What about?"

I lay on my back, gazing up at the ceiling, my hands clasped behind my head so that my arms stuck out, forming a cross.

"I done told you that's bad luck," my aunt said.

Without shifting my eyes from the ceiling, I unclasped my hands from behind my head and clasped them on my chest. Tante Lou stood there looking at me.

"He can come in?"

"Sure. He can come in."

"You go'n put on your shoes and tuck in that shirt?" she asked.

"I'll put on my shoes and tuck in my shirt," I said.

She stood there watching me a while, then she left the room. I sat up on the bed and passed my hands over my face. When the minister came into the room, I had tucked in my shirt and put on my shoes, and I was standing at the window looking out at the garden. My aunt had prepared a half-dozen rows about thirty feet long for spring planting. She would start her planting the week of Easter if the ground was dry enough.

The minister stood behind me, and I turned from the window to look at him.

"Care to sit down, Reverend?"

There were only two chairs in the room, the one at my desk and a rocker by the fireplace.

"You go'n sit down?" he asked me.

"I don't mind standing."

He looked at my desk.

"I see you been working."

"I tried to. Afraid I didn't get too much done."

He sat down in the chair and looked up at me.

"They learning anything?"

"I do my best, Reverend."

He nodded his baldhead. "I do the same. My best."

My back to the window, I waited to hear what he wanted to talk to me about. He looked down at his hands and rubbed them together.

For a man his size, he had really big hands. He rubbed them again before raising his eyes to me.

"There ain't much time."

"Jefferson?"

"Yes."

"Three weeks."

"Not quite."

"Minus couple days," I said.

He nodded his head, a small tired little man. He had preached a long sermon today, and it showed in his face.

"He ain't saved."

"I can't help you there, Reverend."

"That's where you wrong. He listen to you."

I turned my back on him and looked out on the garden.

"You ever think of anybody else but yourself?"

I didn't answer him.

"I ask you, 'You ever think of anybody but yourself?' "

"I have my work to do, Reverend, you have yours," I said, without looking around at him. "Mine is reading, writing, and arithmetic, yours is saving souls."

"He don't need no more reading, writing, and 'rithmetic."

"That's where you come in, Reverend."

I stared beyond the garden toward the budding pecan trees in Farrell Jarreau's backyard. The sky was so low the trees seemed nearly to touch it.

"When you going back?" Reverend Ambrose asked behind me.

"I don't know. One day next week, I suppose."

"And what you go'n talk about?"

"I don't know, Reverend."

"I'm going back with Sis' Emma tomorrow. I'm go'n talk about God."

"I'm sure he needs to hear that, Reverend."

"You sure you sure?"

"Maybe not. Maybe I'm not sure about anything."

"I know I'm sure," he said. "Yes, I know I'm sure."

I looked out at the newly turned rows of earth, and I wished I could just lie down between the rows and not hear and not be a part of any of this.

"This is a mean world. But there is a better one. I wish to prepare him for that better world. But I need your help."

"I don't believe in that other world, Reverend."

"Don't believe in God?"

"I believe in God, Reverend," I said, looking beyond the rows of turned-up earth, toward the budding pecan trees across the road. "I believe in God. Every day of my life I believe in God."

"Just not that other world?"

I didn't answer him.

"And how could they go on? You ever thought about that?"

I looked at the buds on the trees, and I did not answer him.

"Well?" he said to my back.

I turned from the window and looked at him where he sat at my desk. School papers, notebooks, textbooks, and pencils were spread out on the table behind him.

"She told me to help him walk to that chair like a man—not like a hog—and I'm doing the best I can, Reverend. The rest is up to you."

He got up from the chair and came toward me. He peered at me intently, his face showing pain and confusion. He stopped at arm's distance from me, and I could smell in his clothes the sweat from his preaching.

"You think you educated?"

"I went to college."

"But what did you learn?"

"To teach reading, writing, and arithmetic, Reverend."

"What did you learn about your own people? What did you learn about her—her 'round there?" he said, gesturing toward the other room and trying to keep his voice down.

I didn't answer him.

"No, you not educated, boy," he said, shaking his head. "You far from being educated. You learned your reading, writing, and 'rithmetic, but you don't know nothing. You don't even know yourself. Well?"

"You're doing the talking, Reverend."

"And educated, boy," he said, thumping his chest. "I'm the one that's educated. I know people like you look down on people like me, but"—he touched his chest again—"I'm the one that's educated."

He stared at me as if he could not make up his mind whether to hit me or scream.

"Grief, oh, grief." He muffled his cry. "When will you cease? Oh, when?" He drew a deep breath, then he began to speak faster. "When they had nothing else but grief, where was the release? None, none till he rose. And he said there's relief from grief across yon river, and she believed, and there was relief from grief. Do you know what I'm trying to say to you, boy?"

"I hear you talking, Reverend."

"You hear me talking. But are you listening? No, you ain't listening."

His eyes examined me, from the top of my head to my chest, and I could see the rage in his face, see his mouth trembling. He was doing all he could to control his voice so that the others, back in the kitchen, would not hear him.

"I won't let you send that boy's soul to hell," he said. "I'll fight you with all the strength I have left in this body, and I'll win."

"You don't have to fight me, Reverend," I told him. "You can have him all to yourself. I don't even have to go back up there, if that's all you want."

"You going back," he said, nodding his baldhead, and still trying hard to control his voice. "You owe her much as I owe her. And long as I can stand on my feet, I owe her and all the others every ounce of my being. And you do too."

"I don't owe anybody anything, Reverend," I said, and turned toward the window.

I felt his hand gripping my shoulder and pulling me around to face him.

"Don't you turn your back on me, boy."

"My name is Grant," I said.

"When you act educated, I'll call you Grant. I'll even call you Mr. Grant, when you act like a man." His hand still grasped my shoulder, and I needed all my willpower to keep from knocking it off. He could see what I was thinking, and he slowly released his grip and brought his hand to his side. "You think you the only one ever felt this way? You think she never felt this way? Every last one of them back there one time in they life wanted to give up. She want to give up now. You know that? You got any idea how sick she is? Soon after he go, she's going too. I won't give her another year. I want her to believe he'll be up there waiting for her. And you can help me do it. And you the only one."

"How?"

"Tell him to fall down on his knees 'fore he walk to that chair. Tell him to fall down on his knees 'fore her. You the only one he'll listen to. He won't listen to me."

"No," I said. "I won't tell him to kneel. I'll tell him to listen to you—but I won't tell him to kneel. I will try to help him stand."

"You think a man can't kneel and stand?"

"It hasn't helped me."

The minister drew back from me. His head was shining; so was his face. I could see his mouth working as though he wanted to say something but didn't know how to say it.

"You're just lost," he said. "That's all. You're just lost."

"Yes, sir, I'm lost. Like most men, I'm lost."

"Not all men," he said. "Me, I'm found."

"Then you're one of the lucky ones, Reverend."

"And I won't let you lose his soul in hell."

"I want him in heaven as much as you do, Reverend."

"A place you can't believe in?"

"No, I don't believe in it, Reverend."

"And how can you tell him to believe in it?"

"I'll never tell him not to believe in it."

"And suppose he ask you if it's there, then what? Suppose he write on that tablet you give him, is it there? Then what?"

"I'll tell him I don't know."

"You the teacher."

"Yes. But I was taught to teach reading, writing, and arithmetic. Not the Gospel. I'd tell him I heard it was there, but I don't know."

"And suppose he ask you if you believe in heaven? Then what?"

"I hope he doesn't, Reverend."

"Suppose he do?"

"I hope he doesn't."

"You couldn't say yes?"

"No, Reverend, I couldn't say yes. I couldn't lie to him at this moment. I will never tell him another lie, no matter what."

"Not for her sake?"

"No, sir."

The minister nodded his baldhead and grunted to himself. His dark brown eyes in that tired, weary face continued to stare back at me.

"You think you educated, but you not. You think you the only person ever had to lie? You think I never had to lie?"

"I don't know, Reverend."

"Yes, you know. You know, all right. That's why you look down on me, because you know I lie. At wakes, at funerals, at weddings—yes, I lie. I lie at wakes and funerals to relieve pain. 'Cause reading, writing, and 'rithmetic is not enough. You think that's all they sent you to school for? They sent you to school to relieve pain, to relieve hurt—and if you have to lie to do it, then you lie. You lie and you lie and you lie. When you tell yourself you feeling good when you sick, you lying. When you tell other people you feeling well when you feeling sick, you lying. You tell them that 'cause they have pain too, and you don't want to add yours—and you lie. She been lying every day of her life, your aunt in there. That's how you got through that university—cheating herself here, cheating herself there, but always telling you she's all right. I've seen her hands bleed from picking cotton. I've seen the blisters from the hoe and the cane knife. At that church, crying on her knees. You ever looked at the scabs on her knees, boy? Course you never. 'Cause she never wanted you to see it. And that's the difference between me and you, boy; that make me the educated one, and you the gump. I know my people. I know what they gone through. I know they done cheated themself, lied to themself—hoping that one they all love and trust can come back and help relieve the pain."

Exercise Loyalty:

- Grant seems oblivious to the sacrifices Tante Lou has made for him. Reverend Ambrose believes that hiding your pain from others because you do not want to add to their own pain is a form of loyalty. Do you think this is true?
- "I know my people. I know what they gone through. I know they done cheated themself, lied to themself—hoping that one they all love and trust can come back and help relieve the pain." Do you think Reverend Ambrose is suggesting that new generations should in some way be loyal to their ancestors because of the hardships their elders have gone through for them?
- "You owe her much as I owe her. And long as I can stand on my feet, I owe her and all the others every ounce of my being. And you do too." Reverend Ambrose's words cut deep. Grant's response that he doesn't owe anybody anything is a familiar refrain of young people today. The fact is, we don't want to have to enforce loyalty; it should arise naturally from our interactions with each other. Feeling like we "owe" someone is different from having an unquestioned and heartfelt loyalty.

- When you think about the many African-Americans upon whose shoulders you stand, you should feel obligated not only to give something back, but to keep the next generation in mind. I recently accepted the call to be president of my alma mater, Wilberforce University. When I was a young man, they accepted me and gave me a job when I had no money, allowing me to work my way through college. Have you given anything back to the people who helped you get where you are today? How do you show your loyalty to institutions?

Booker T. Washington

Booker T. Washington was asked by the president of the University of Chicago to give a speech as part of a weeklong celebration of peace in the city of Chicago following the end of the Spanish-American War. As noted by the editors of the Chicago Times-Herald, "Booker T. Washington's address at the Jubilee Thanksgiving services at the Auditorium contained one of the most eloquent tributes ever paid to the loyalty and valor of the colored race, and at the same time, was one of the most powerful appeals for justice to a race that has always chosen the better part." Here is that address, reprinted from the Times-Herald, October 18, 1898.

Jubilee Thanksgiving Address

Mr. Chairman, Ladies and Gentlemen:

On an important occasion in the life of the Master, when it fell to him to pronounce judgment on two courses of action, these memorable words fell from his lips: "And Mary hath chosen the better part." This was the supreme test in the case of an individual. It is the highest test in the case of a race or nation. Let us apply this test to the American Negro.

In the life of our Republic, when he has had the opportunity to choose, has it been the better or worse part? When in the childhood of this nation the Negro was asked to sub-

mit to slavery or choose death and extinction, as did the aborigines, he chose the better part, that which perpetuated the race.

When in 1776 the Negro was asked to decide between British oppression and American independence, we find him choosing the better part, and Crispus Attucks, a Negro, was the first to shed his blood on State Street, Boston, that the white American might enjoy liberty forever, though his race remained in slavery.

When in 1814 at New Orleans, the test of patriotism came again, we find the Negro choosing the better part, and General Andrew Jackson himself testifying that no heart was more loyal and no arm more strong and useful in righteousness.

When the long and memorable struggle came between union and separation, when he knew that victory on the one hand meant freedom, and defeat on the other his continued enslavement, with a full knowledge of the portentous meaning of it all, when the suggestion and the temptation came to burn the home and massacre wife and children during the absence of the master in battle, and thus ensure his liberty, we find him choosing the better part, and for four long years protecting and supporting the helpless, defenseless ones entrusted to his care.

When in 1863 the cause of the Union seemed to quiver in the balance, and there was doubt and distrust, the Negro was asked to come to the rescue in arms, and the valor displayed at Fort Wagner and Port Hudson and Fort Pillow, testify most eloquently again that the Negro choose the better part.

When a few months ago, the safety and honor of the Republic were threatened by a foreign foe, when the wail and anguish of the oppressed from a distant isle reached his ears, we find the Negro forgetting his own wrong, forgetting the laws and customs that discriminate against him in his own country, and again we find our black citizen choosing the better part. And if you would know how he deported himself in the field at Santiago, apply for answer to Shafter and Roosevelt and Wheeler. Let them tell how the Negro faced death and laid down his life in defense of honor and humanity, and when you have gotten the full story of the heroic conduct of the Negro in the Spanish-American War—heard it from the lips of Northern soldiers and Southern soldiers, from ex-abolitionist and ex-master—then decide within yourselves whether a race that is thus willing to die for its country should not be given the highest opportunity to live for its country.

In the midst of all the complaints of suffering in the camp and field, suffering from *fever and hunger, where is the official or citizen that has heard a word of complaint from the lips of a black soldier? The only request that has come from the Negro soldier has been that he might be permitted to replace the white soldier when heat and malaria began to decimate the ranks of the white regiment, and to occupy at the same time the post of greatest danger.*

This country has been most fortunate in her victories. She has twice measured arms with England and has won. She has met the spirit of rebellion within her borders and was victorious. She has met the proud Spaniard and he lays prostrate at her feet. All this is well, it is magnificent. But there remains one other victory for Americans to win— a victory as far-reaching and important as any that has occupied our army and navy. We have succeeded in every conflict, except the effort to conquer ourselves in the blotting out of racial prejudices. We can celebrate the era of peace in no more effectual way than by a firm resolve on the part of Northern men and Southern men, black men and white men, that the trenches which we together dug around Santiago, shall be the eternal burial place of all that which separates us in our business and civil relations. Let us be as generous in peace as we have been brave in battle. Until we thus conquer ourselves, I make no empty statement when I say that we shall have especially in the Southern part of our country, a cancer gnawing at the heart of the Republic, that shall one day prove as dangerous as an attack from an army without or within.

In this presence and on this auspicious occasion, I want to present the deep gratitude of nearly ten million of my people to our wise, patient, and brave Chief Executive for the generous manner in which my race has been recognized during this conflict. A recognition that has done more to blot out sectional and racial lines than any event since the dawn of our freedom.

I know how vain and impotent is all abstract talk on this subject. In your efforts to "rise on stepping stones of your dead selves," we of the black race shall not leave you unaided. We shall make the task easier for you by acquiring property, habits of thrift, economy, intelligence, and character, by each making himself of individual worth in his own community. We shall aid you in this as we did a few days ago at El Caney and Santiago, when we helped you to hasten the peace we here celebrate. You know us; you are not afraid of us. When the crucial test comes, you are not ashamed of us. We have never betrayed or deceived you. You know that as it has been, so it will be. Whether in

war or in peace, whether in slavery or in freedom, we have always been loyal to the
Stars and Stripes.

Exercise Loyalty:

- "By each making himself of individual worth in his own community" is as relevant a call to action today as it was then. Talk to your
  children about the value of building individual worth. Pray with
  your family as well for understanding of one another: "Dear Lord,
  Help us to be more understanding of one another; not threatened
  by the differences and diversity that has made America a great
  nation, but embracing it as the true definition of 'life, liberty, and
  the pursuit of happiness' for all people, regardless of race or gender.
  Amen."

- Some African-American scholars have referred to this address as
  Washington's "compromise speech," since in it he called for blacks
  to dedicate themselves to becoming self-reliant rather than calling
  for changes in the social system. What do you think Washington
  means by the words "until we conquer ourselves"?

Prudence

Cautious wisdom, careful foresight, and personal discretion,
PRUDENCE gives you the ability to exercise
good judgment in practical affairs.

Every day, we hear about how fast-paced the world is becoming. Everything around us is constantly accelerating. We have become obsessed with speed, and if there is one thing we cannot stand, it is waiting.

Now, I will not tell you to slow down, because I know the world will not slow down with you but will only pass you by. Indeed, we must be sure to keep up. Time is a precious commodity that we must not waste. But although we must never stop moving or lose hold of the reins, we must continue to make intelligent, carefully considered decisions. To think quickly is not to stop thinking altogether. As the Bible tells us, "The simple believeth every word: but the prudent man looketh well to his going" (Proverbs 14:15).

Our choices must always be based on reason rather than whim. As God's creations, we are all instilled with intelligence.

Prudence is about cultivating and exercising the powers God has given us. Wisdom is not obtaining information but using it. When our decisions are informed, they are more respected by others and we have more confidence in the paths we choose to follow.

Know that the best decision will not always be the most popular one. There will always be people who disagree with you. And although you must be receptive to criticism, you must also maintain confidence in the choices you make. If you are confident, even your opponents will respect you.

While in Congress, I came to realize that in order for me to bring resources to my community, it was imperative that I develop relationships with the Republican members on the other side of the aisle. My fellow Democrats frowned upon this type of bipartisan approach. After eleven years in Congress, I looked back on my accomplishments in terms of federal buildings, jobs, and programs and realized that I could not have been so successful without the help of my Democratic and Republican friends.

Confidence, we must never forget, is not the same as arrogance. To be prudent is to be adaptable. The strength of your convictions need not become rigidity, and faith in your good judgment does not eliminate the need for compromise. We must all train ourselves to roll with the punches and adapt to the different circumstances and environments we will face throughout our lives.

When Elaine and I married in 1975, we named the cities we would never live in, and New York headed the list. However, nine months later, we were invited to pastor in a church in Queens, New York. When we see now how blessed we have been in New York, we realize that our move to this city was God's will for us.

Discretion and restraint are essential to smart decision-making. Too often, we allow our actions to be controlled by our impulses. As human beings, we have an obligation to make important decisions through reason rather than instinct. We all know that sometimes what we want is not what is right, and we must dedicate ourselves to following our morals rather than our desires. Our passions, like our enemies, may provoke us to sin, but we must resist the provocation. It is prudence that must protect us from evil, wisdom that must guide our feet.

Ann Petry

*A*nn *Petry (1908–1997) was raised in a middle-class family in the predominantly white town of Old Saybrook, Connecticut. A writer since childhood, Petry followed in her father's footsteps and obtained a Ph.D. in pharmacy from Connecticut College. After getting married, Petry and her husband moved to Harlem, where she pursued a career as a reporter and writer for ten years. Her novel* The Street, *published in 1946, tells the story of a young single mother struggling to survive in 1946 Harlem. Sadly, many of the social conditions that Lutie faces in the novel still exist today.*

from The Street

*A*fter she came out of the subway, Lutie walked slowly up the street, thinking that having solved one problem there was always a new one cropping up to take its place. Now that she and Bub were living alone, there was no one to look out for him after school. She had thought he could eat lunch at school, for it didn't cost very much—only fifty cents a week.

But after three days of school lunches, Bub protested, "I can't eat that stuff. They give us soup every day. And I hate it."

As soon as she could afford to, she would take an afternoon off from work and visit the school so that she could find out for herself what the menus were like. But until then, Bub would have to eat lunch at home, and that wasn't anything to worry about. It was what happened to him after school that made her frown as she walked along, for he was either in the apartment by himself or playing in the street.

She didn't know which was worse—his being alone in those dreary little rooms or his playing in the street where the least of the dangers confronting him came from the stream of traffic which roared through 116th Street: crosstown buses, post office trucks, and newspaper delivery cars that swooped up and down the street, turning into the avenues without warning. The traffic was an obvious threat to his safety that he could see and dodge. He was too young to recognize and avoid other dangers in the street. There were, for instance, gangs of young boys who were always on the lookout for small fry Bub's age, because they found young kids useful in getting in through narrow fire-escape windows, in distracting a storekeeper's attention while the gang lightheartedly helped itself to his stock.

Then, in spite of the small, drab apartment and the dent that moving into it had made in her week's pay and the worry about Bub that crept into her thoughts, she started humming under her breath as she went along, increasing her stride so that she was walking faster and faster because the air was crisp and clear and her long legs felt strong and just the motion of walking sent blood bubbling all through her body so that she could feel it. She came to an abrupt halt in the middle of the block because she suddenly remembered that she had completely forgotten to shop for dinner.

The butcher shop that she entered on Eighth Avenue was crowded with customers, so that she had ample time to study the meat in the case in front of her before she was waited on. There wasn't, she saw, very much choice—ham hocks, lamb culls, bright-red beef. Someone had told Granny once that the butchers in Harlem used embalming fluid on the beef they sold in order to give it a nice fresh color. Lutie didn't believe it, but like a lot of things she didn't believe, it cropped up suddenly out of nowhere to leave her wondering and staring at the brilliant scarlet color of the meat. It made her examine the contents of the case with care in order to determine whether there was something else that would do for dinner. No, she decided. Hamburger would be the best thing to get. It cooked quickly, and a half-pound of it mixed with breadcrumbs would go a long way.

The butcher, a fat red-faced man with a filthy apron tied around his enormous stomach, joked with the women lined up at the counter while he waited on them. A yellow cat sitting high on a shelf in back of him blinked down at the customers. One of his paws almost touched the edge of a sign that said "No Credit." The sign was fly-specked and dusty; its edges curling back from heat.

"Kitty had her meat today?" a thin black woman asked as she smiled up at the cat.

"Sure thing," and the butcher roared with laughter, and the women laughed with him until the butcher shop was so full of merriment it sounded as though it were packed with happy, carefree people.

It wasn't even funny, Lutie thought. Yet the women rocked and roared with laughter as though they had heard some tremendous joke, went on laughing until finally there were only low chuckles and an occasional half-suppressed snort of laughter left in them. For all they knew, she thought resentfully, the yellow cat might yet end up in the meat-grinder to emerge as hamburger. Or perhaps during the cold winter months the butcher might round up all the lean, hungry cats that prowled through the streets, herding them into his back room to skin them and grind them up to make more and more hamburger that would be sold way over the ceiling price.

"A half-pound of hamburger" was all she said when the butcher indicated it was her turn to be waited on. A half-pound would take care of tonight's dinner and Bub could have a sandwich of it when he came home for lunch.

She watched the butcher slap the hamburger on a piece of waxed paper, fold the paper twice, and slip the package into a brown paper bag. Handing him a dollar bill, she tucked the paper bag under her arm and held her pocketbook in the other hand so that he would have to put the change down on the counter. She never accepted change out of his hand, and watching him put it on the counter, she wondered why. Because she didn't want to touch his chapped roughened hands? Because he was white and forcing him to make the small extra effort of putting the change on the counter gave her a feeling of power?

Holding the change loosely in her hand, she walked out of the shop and turned toward the grocery store next door, where she paused for a moment in the doorway to look back at 116th Street. The sun was going down in a blaze of brilliant color that bathed the street in a glow of light. It looked, she thought, like any other New York City street in a poor neighborhood. Perhaps a little more down-at-the-heels. The windows of the houses were dustier and there were more small stores on it than on streets in other parts of the city. There were also more children playing in the street and more people walking about aimlessly.

She stepped inside the grocery store, thinking that her apartment would do for the time being, but the next step she should take would be to move into a better neighborhood. As she had been able to get this far without help from anyone, why, all she had to do was plan each step and she could get wherever she wanted to go. A wave of self-confidence swept over her and she thought, I'm young and strong, there isn't anything I can't do.

Her arms were full of small packages when she left Eighth Avenue—the hamburger, a pound of potatoes, a can of peas, a piece of butter, besides six hard rolls that she bought instead of bread, big rolls with brown crusty outsides. They were good with coffee in the morning and Bub could have one for his lunch tomorrow with the hamburger left over from dinner.

She walked slowly, avoiding the moment when she must enter the apartment and start fixing dinner. She shifted the packages into a more comfortable position and feeling the hard-roundness of the rolls through the paper bag, she thought immediately of Ben Franklin and his loaf of bread. And grinned thinking, You and Ben Franklin. You ought to take one out and start eating it as you walk along 116th Street. Only you ought to remember while you eat that you're in Harlem and he was in Philadelphia a pretty long number of years ago. Yet she couldn't get rid of the feeling of self-confidence and she went on thinking that if Ben Franklin could live on a little bit of money and could prosper, then so could she. In spite of the cost of moving the furniture, if she and Bub were very careful they would have more than enough to last until her next pay-day; there might even be a couple of dollars over. If they were very careful.

Exercise Prudence:

- Lutie is raising her son in an environment in which desperation has destroyed the spirits and motivation of many of her community members. One thinks of Proverbs 1:20–22: "Wisdom crieth without; she uttereth her voice in the streets: She crieth in the chief place of concourse, in the openings of the gates: in the city she uttereth her words, saying, How long, ye simple ones, will ye love simplicity?" But Lutie is determined to make a way out of no way. My mother exercised prudence by stretching limited resources: She bought day-old bread and purchased clothing for her children before herself. How have the heroes or heroines in your own family demonstrated prudence?

- By evoking Benjamin Franklin and his teachings on thrift, Lutie is able to stick to her careful budget, plan for the future, and remain hopeful that if she keeps to a plan, her life will improve. Why do you think many of us have succumbed to "simple ways" rather than committing ourselves to improving our situations, no matter how difficult, one day at a time? Do you think it is possible to raise one-self out of poverty single-handedly? Think about the power that prudence could have in our communities.

- When buying the hamburger meat, Lutie must deal with a store owner who is rude and exploitative. As a young African-American woman, she has very little power in the situation; however, she displays dignity and self-respect and does not stoop to the base level of the storekeeper. Proverbs 12:16 teaches us, "A fool's wrath is presently known: but a prudent man covereth shame." How can you use prudence in your interactions with people who are disrespectful and inconsiderate?

Phillis Wheatley

In 1761, slave traders captured a little girl of only seven or eight and brought her to America. A prosperous tailor named John Wheatley purchased the girl and renamed her Phillis Wheatley. Although slaves were forbidden to read at that time, the Wheatley family taught Phillis to read and encouraged her writing skills. She published her first poem in 1773, becoming the first African American woman to be published. Wheatley was granted her freedom in her twenties and married a free black man. However, in her later life, she was forced to become a servant, and despite an illustrious writing career she died in poverty. In "An Hymn to the Evening," Wheatley writes a praise-song to the day's end and marvels at the beauty of God's majesty. She then thanks God for the ability to rest after a day of work and the opportunity to wake again refreshed and ready for a new day.

An Hymn to the Evening

Soon as the sun forsook the eastern main,
The pealing thunder shook the heavenly plain;

Majestic grandeur! From the zephyr's wing,
Exhales the incense of the blooming spring.
Soft purl the streams, the birds renew their notes,
And through the air their mingled music floats.

Through all the heavens what beauteous dyes are spread!
But the west glories in the deepest red:
So may our breasts with ev'ry virtue glow,
The living temples of our God below!

Filled with the praise of him who gives the light,
And draws the sable curtains of the night,
Let placid slumbers soothe each weary mind,
At morn to wake, more heavenly, more refined;
So shall the labors of the day begin
More pure, more guarded from the snares of sin.
Night's leaden sceptre seals my drowsy eyes;
Then cease, my song, till fair Aurora rise.

Exercise Prudence:

- Our lives are so busy that we sometimes forget the majesty of night and day and the gifts that God has given us. Do you and your family take the time to be thankful for the gift of day and night? For the beauty and bounty of nature and the earth? God has definitely taught by example: He exercises prudence on a daily basis by providing us with the gift of a beautiful planet that operates like clockwork.

- Phillis Wheatley is a shining example of someone who exercised prudence. Despite losing her family and culture, she retained a love for life and the desire to continue to learn and grow as a person. Although she was not rewarded with material riches for her talents, she continued to work and persevere. Her work was not in vain; Wheatley left an indelible mark on American culture and will be remembered forever. With your children, discuss other figures in our nation's past who practiced prudence in difficult times.

• The words "pure and guarded from the snares of sin" allude to the exercise of prudence and careful forethought as we go about our day-to-day life. This evening, pray for the wisdom that allows one to live with discretion and good judgment.

Gwendolyn Brooks

G wendolyn Brooks was born in Topeka, Kansas, but lived most of her life in Chicago. In her private life, she was known as Mrs. Henry Blakely and was the mother of two children. As a poet, she was the recipient of numerous awards and honors, including two Guggenheim Fellowships and the Pulitzer Prize, bestowed in 1950 on her second book of poetry, Annie Allen, published in 1949. "We Real Cool" has been widely anthologized and is one of Brooks' best-known works. No matter what your age or perspective, the poem is fertile ground for a discussion of prudence.

We Real Cool

THE POOL PLAYERS.
SEVEN AT THE GOLDEN SHOVEL.

We real cool. We
Left school. We

Lurk late. We
Strike straight. We

Sing sin. We
Thin gin. We

Jazz June. We
Die soon.

Exercise Prudence:

- Read literally, "We Real Cool" suggests what can happen to young people who do not learn anything about the virtue of prudence. Where's the cautious practical wisdom in leaving school? Lurking late? Singing sin? As parents, we should also be prudent when our children reach the age of testing and adolescent turmoil. Talk to your children about their lives. Know where they are and whom they are with. Let them know you care. Drive them crazy with your questions. They will appreciate it one day.

- Talk about the idea of good judgment with your family. Make a list of activities or decisions and discuss whether or not good judgment was exercised. Discuss how good judgment should come into play in even the smallest-seeming situations. To wear a raincoat or not? To buy lunch when brown-bagging it is healthier and more economical? What are some ways you and your family can find to be more prudent in daily life?

- Scholars might debate the poet's intentions: Are we to identify with the young men, become the "we" ourselves, and understand their lives as they live it? Does the free-form structure and casual language of the poem suggest some sort of approval of the youths' lifestyle? As ministers and parents we can't help but identify more as observant and even disapproving adults. With whom do you identify in this poem? Are there young people in your own life whose behavior worries you? If they are not being prudent, if they are not exercising forethought in their lives, can you be more prudent in your efforts to help them?

Anita Hill

*I*n Speaking Truth to Power, *an account of her rise from Oklahoma farm girl to prominent attorney, Anita Hill remembers the women who were the backbone of the church that her family attended. The church was one of the few havens for blacks, who made up only a fraction of Oklahoma's population. In this excerpt, Hill praises the quiet, practical consistency of the women who managed the books, planned programs, and made sure that their families always arrived at church on time.*

from Speaking Truth to Power

Every Sunday the family went to Sunday school at Lone Tree Missionary Baptist Church, the church my paternal grandfather had helped to establish. And on every first and third Sunday we went there to church. The alternating Sunday church service was a part of the rural tradition of the "circuit" minister who pastored two or more churches and visited them on a rotating basis. Our pastor's visit fell on these two Sundays. Presumably, he spent other Sundays at another church. This was typical of small rural communities and continues even today. The whitewashed wood-frame building now sits quietly during the week attracting little attention from passersby, as it awaits Sunday services.

In earlier days when my parents' family was young, the building rattled with activity daily. Prior to 1960 it was the home of the grammar school for the "colored" children in the rural neighborhood. At one point two teachers taught as many as sixty schoolchildren at a time within its walls. Before my memory, on occasion on Saturday nights when musicals were not held in the church, there was a different kind of bustle in the building. That week's farmwork completed, the members of the community dressed in close to their Sunday best and gathered at the "church house" for family movies. A man who traveled about with projector, film, and screen collected nickels from families and created a makeshift theater, thus compensating for the lack of entertainment available to rural blacks. My sisters Joyce and Doris recall watching the films *The Wolf Man* and *Dracula* in the church building and being afraid to walk the three miles home afterward. This was the 1950s. The family never went to the movie theater together, so it was not part of our experience. I saw my first movie in an actual theater in 1967, when my brother Ray took JoAnn and me to see *Bonnie and Clyde.*

On Wednesday night the school and social center became a place of worship as church deacons led parishioners in prayer meeting. Prayer meeting was my favorite church activity. I particularly enjoyed the traditional hymns as they were performed in the church. "I love the Lord, he heard my cry and pitied every moan," Deacon Jesse Barnett (my friend Pocahontas' father) would call out to the worshipers. "I love the Lord, he heard my cry," they would sing in response, almost moaning the words. "Long as I live, when troubles rise, I'll hasten to his throne," again Deacon Barnett called. As the song went on, the imagery was so strong, coupled with the words and singing, that I would see Jesus "bowing his head and chasing my griefs away." Perhaps childhood griefs were so limited that they vanished with ease.

On Friday night Lone Tree conducted business meetings. From appearance, the men mostly ran the church's business, but the women of Lone Tree firmly yet diplomatically let their opinions be known. On Saturday night Lone Tree might offer a musical, bringing in choirs, soloists, and duos from Okmulgee and surrounding counties. My parents' friends S.L. and Red Reagor were among the most interesting with their a cappella selection of jubilees—a lively syncopated form of gospel song that evoked images of happy times or deliverance. Due to their years together, the Reagors as a duo had mastered the form of singing like no other couple had and were known throughout the rural churches because of it. During service it was the tradition that the women sat on the right side of the church and the men sat on the left. Couples who came in together separated at the door and walked separately down the church's two aisles to sit on one of the wooden pews. Young children sat with their mothers. When it came time for the Reagors to sing, they approached the front of the congregation from separate corners and returned separately when they concluded. It was our tradition and we never questioned or commented on it.

Lone Tree Missionary Baptist Church was the center of the family spiritual and social life. The women of Lone Tree were my role models. Most were farmers and homemakers who came out of the fields to clean their homes and the church building. The lessons they taught, both religious and social, are the most valuable to me. They were not "feminists," in the modern sense of the word. They worshiped in a service which prohibited women from preaching or leading. When women and men sat separately in church, it was most likely out of this denigration of women's roles. Yet they were essential to the operation of the church and voiced their opinions. Importantly, they expected just as much from the girls in the church as from the boys. Even more importantly, by example, they taught me about concern for the collective—the community. Some Sundays family members and friends assembled at our home around 2 P.M. for Sunday dinner. It was as though they just materialized. We had no telephones to communicate an invitation or to announce an event. Miraculously, or so I always felt, whether there were ten or thirty extra mouths to feed, my mother always seemed to have enough food. Each of those days seemed like a mini-reunion that gave me a sense of being in touch with people outside of the farmwork and my everyday school life.

Exercise Prudence:

- As Hill writes, the women in her church were fundamental to its operation. These church ladies never boasted about their work and did it so gracefully and effortlessly that it is only when Hill reaches adulthood that she realizes the business acumen they possessed. Like CEOs of a successful company, these women led with finesse. Like Deborah (Judges 4:1–22; 5:1–31), the church mothers led by example. How do you think the examples set by these women influenced Hill's decision to become a lawyer?

- The African American church has served as a place of worship, a community center, and a preparatory school for black children, many churches combining all of these things under one roof. Hill's church was a simple building that served the spiritual, social, and educational needs of its flock. Talk to your family about the church you grew up in and how it compares with the church your family attends today. Think about ways that you can contribute to the day-to-day operations of your church.

- Anita Hill is known for accusing Judge Clarence Thomas of sexual harassment during his Supreme Court confirmation hearings in 1991. Thomas was confirmed by a 52–48 vote in the Senate, a fact that the many people who believed Hill's accusations thought was a defeat. But the controversy and the media coverage surrounding it had repercussions beyond Thomas' appointment. As a nation we were all made more aware of issues like sexual harassment, women's unequal representation in national politics, the pros and cons of affirmative action, and the sensationalistic power of the media. In the end, was it prudent of Anita Hill to accuse Judge Clarence Thomas?

Asha Bandele

*A*sha Bandele, author of The Prisoner's Wife, *is an acclaimed journalist and poet—and the wife of a man serving a prison term. She met her husband while volunteering at the prison where he is doing time. In this excerpt, Bandele talks about how her love for her husband and child completely changed her life and taught her the* *value of living a thoughtful, conscientious life. Today she is a successful author, an editor-at-large for* Essence *magazine, a popular lecturer, and, most important, a loving wife and mother.*

from The Prisoner's Wife

Prison toys with time, teases its meaning, confuses those of us trapped and defined by the fourth dimension. During visits and phone calls, minutes and hours disappear within a single greedy swallow. Whatever else may need to be said—and there is always something else which needs to be said—must be postponed, put on the back burner, minimized, or forgotten.

Waiting for the court to rule, *just to rule,* on an appeal which could free Rashid is horrifically long, dragged out like his homecoming. The years stretched out, yawned, took their own sweet time to pass. They went on vacation, those years, and left me staring at calendars hoping that eventually they would indeed return and get the job of bringing Rashid home to me finally done.

Every time I looked up, there was always more time ahead of us than there was time behind us. As I write this, there are six more years left on Rashid's sentence, and that's just the time between today and the parole board where Rashid could get hit with more time. He's got life on the end of his bid, so there's no guarantee of anything.

I get lost when I think about what could happen in my life in the next six years, what has already happened in the past six years. I am not the same woman I was a half decade ago, not even close.

Six years ago, I was married to another man; the idea of falling in love with a man in prison had never even crossed my mind. Six years ago I spent weekends in clubs and bars. I smoked cigarettes and I drank alcohol regularly. Six years ago, the idea of getting my own book of poetry published by someone was a fantasy. I was barely willing to read my poems publicly. Six years ago I hadn't finished college, and didn't know if I was ever going to finish college. Six years ago the only emotions I could access regularly were anger and pain.

The woman I am today prefers to stay home, is still attracted to, but doesn't want to get caught up in, "the mix." Today I am a vegetarian who eats organic foods. Today I have finished my bachelor's degree and am nearly done with my master's. I am a published poet now, and have read my work before audiences in New York State prisons and before audiences in London. I don't go to clubs and rarely to parties. Today I set achievable goals, concentrate on them, and complete them in realistic time frames. Today I time-manage and write daily. I do affirmations. I meditate. I run. When people ask, How did you finish school finally, stop smoking, get published? I tell them, *Slowly.* I tell them about discipline and focus and isolating yourself into your own dreams and hopes. I tell them about struggling to never live in reaction to my fears.

In six years, I asked Rashid once, What will happen to me? I think about how I could have six new lives in that time. How am I supposed to stay here with you? How realistic is this relationship? How do other women do this time?

I looked to him for answers that I knew and he knew he would never have. Our relationship is strictly trial-and-error. Or trial by error. And I cannot imagine how I will make it. And I cannot imagine how I won't.

Exercise Prudence:

- Before her marriage, Bandele is a party girl who leads a frivolous and empty life. Today, Bandele's life is one in which motherhood, writing, and self-care are paramount. She writes, "Today I set achievable goals, concentrate on them, and complete them in realistic time frames." Have you experienced life-changing events, such as love or loss, which made you realize the importance of living prudently? How has your life changed as a result of your lifestyle changes? Share your story with family and friends.

- Are there ways in which your lifestyle choices make you a prisoner? Bandele realized that she was a prisoner of her desires. When she is asked how she overcame an empty, self-destructive lifestyle, she says, "I tell them about discipline and focus and isolating yourself into your own dreams and hopes." Is Bandele's advice useful to you? How can you exercise prudence in your own day-to-day life so that you, too, can realize your dreams and your potential?

J. California Cooper

A former playwright, J. California Cooper was discovered by Alice Walker, who approached her after seeing one of her plays. The author of several acclaimed novels, Cooper focuses her work on the struggle between right and wrong. The following is the prologue to In Search of Satisfaction, *published in 1994.*

from In Search of Satisfaction

Once upon any time, when a person is born, no matter what color of mankind you are, a body with a mind seeks for the truth of life. A way. A chest is opened for you, filled with many truths and things that pass as truths for you to find, pick, choose from, live your life with. Be the things you value.

Now, you may have a brain and still be a fool. Many people choose those things that pass as the truth but are false. Still others find real truths, then twist, bend, and misuse them, even bury them. Some, the lazy, don't search or dig deep for the truth but find a way and use it until they find it is not so good, then they pick up another way, often just as useless. They spend years and years, their lives, doing this. Very often to the detriment of themselves and others. Very often . . . just a nothing life.

It's a sad truth that many get all the way to the end of their lives, then stop and look closely at their way, their impostor truths; then they cry out to life, "Cheat! Empty!"

The mind is a mighty, mighty tool. A body just has to think and reason.

I think one of the main ingredients to reason your way to the truth is, first, love. If love is missing from your soul, your mind, you won't be able to find what you need. You may not recognize it.

It's a wise, wise person who looks into the Ten Commandments. Whether one is Christian or not, they are a universal, huge power. They are tools. They are good. They are the main wisdom, the main direction in the search for truth, peace, love, and ultimately happiness here on earth. Don't just wait for heaven. What you believe has no effect on what is the truth. One thing is sure, you will bump your head hard on the truth if you don't recognize it when you need to.

Almost everyone on earth believes there is a God. Some god. Some wise people believe there is a Satan or evil power. This Satan laughs at God because he, the devil, the evil power, has so many people following him. It's a hollow laughter. Because who can really be pleased and proud of fools? But another fool?

God waits for his own time. Time is passing. His time is coming. He has a plan. He need not be concerned with the laughter of fools.

Exercise Prudence:

• J. California Cooper's prologue reads like many of the proverbs in that it stresses the importance of tools for living. How has the Bible provided you with tools that you use in everyday life? Ask your family for examples of biblical proverbs and commandments that have greatly increased their ability to live a prudent life.

• Do you agree with Cooper when she says, "Many people choose those things that pass as the truth but are false"? Why do you think people choose a way that leads to a nothing life—especially when the teachings in the Bible provide the way? Proverbs 15:5 states, "A fool despiseth his father's instruction: but he that regardeth reproof is prudent." How does this proverb reflect what Cooper is trying to say in the prologue to *In Search of Satisfaction*?

- After reading this excerpt, what do you think Cooper believes is the true meaning of satisfaction? Read Ecclesiastes 2:24: "There is nothing better for a man, than that he should eat and drink, and that he should make his soul enjoy good in his labor. This also I saw, that it was from the hand of God." Discuss the meaning of satisfaction as defined in the Bible.

Rosemary L. Bray

Rosemary L. Bray is a writer and former editor of the New York Times Book Review. Unafraid of the Dark, *a coming-of-age memoir that vividly describes Bray's youth in poverty-stricken Chicago in the 1960s and 1970s, also eloquently details the extraordinary resourcefulness and prudence that Bray observed in her mother.*

from Unafraid of the Dark

What made our lives work as well as they did was my mother's genius at making do—worn into her by a childhood of rural poverty—along with her vivid imagination. She worked at home endlessly, shopped ruthlessly, bargained, cajoled, charmed. Her food store of choice was the one that stocked pork and beans, creamed corn, sardines, Vienna sausages, and potted meat, all at ten cents a can. Clothing was the stuff of rummage sales, trips to Goodwill, and bargain basements, where thin cotton and polyester reigned supreme. Our shoes came from a discount store that sold two pairs for five dollars.

It was an uphill climb, but there was no time for reflection; we were too busy with our everyday lives. Yet I remember how much it pained me to know that Mama, who recruited a neighbor to help her teach me how to read when I was three, found herself left behind by her eldest daughter, then by each of us in turn. Her biggest worry was that we would grow up uneducated, so Mama enrolled us in parochial school.

When one caseworker angrily questioned how she could afford to send four children to St. Ambrose School, my mother, who emphatically declared, "My kids need an education," told her it was none of her business. (In fact, the school had a volume discount of sorts; the price of tuition dropped with each child you sent. I still don't know quite how she managed it.) She organized our lives around church and school, including Mass every morning at 7:45. My brother was an altar boy; I laid out the vestments each afternoon for the next day's Mass. She volunteered as a chaperone for every class trip, sat with us as we did homework she did not understand herself. She and my father reminded us again and again that every book, every test, every page of homework was in fact a ticket out and away from the life we lived.

Exercise Prudence:

- Bray has written that she "never understood how [her mother] was able to do what she did for as long as she did." Why do you think her mother was able to endure the uphill climb of her life? Did she find the strength to persevere when she thought about the bright futures she desperately wanted for her children?
- Teach a child the simple lesson in prudence of laying out his clothes for the following day. Talk about what this kind of preparation and forethought does for him. How does it make life easier?
- A friend of our family would rather tie her tomato vines with panty hose than buy expensive twine or cages at the garden supply store. Tell prudence stories about people in your own family. How do they do it? What are some of their most creative solutions in daily life?

Private Bert B. Babero

Arican Americans turned out in record numbers to join the U.S. armed forces in World War II, but soon realized that the fight for democracy abroad had to begin at home. Segregated from their white counterparts and often assigned more menial tasks, America's black soldiers questioned why they were fighting for a country that treated them as second-class citizens. Writing letters as a means of protest, these courageous patriots intelligently and persuasively argued for the equal treatment they were entitled to as Americans. This letter, written by a private serving in Pennsylvania, eloquently captures the spirit of prudence.

from Taps for a Jim Crow Army

ATTY. TRUMAN K. GIBSON
CIVILIAN AIDE TO SECY OF WAR
WHITE HOUSE, WASHINGTON, D.C.

CO. C. GRP. 2, 1ST REG.
CAMP REYNOLDS, PA.
MAR. 13, 1944

Dear Mr. Gibson:

As you may recall I wrote you several times while at Camp Barkeley, Texas. I am at present in Pennsylvania, on the brink of embarkation for overseas duty. Leaving the South was like coming back to God's country.

You might readily understand my aversion when I discovered that as far north as Pennsylvania segregation and discrimination is practiced in the army camps. I sometimes wish I could be indifferent but I can't. Right is right and I realize there's no such thing as halfway right. Although in comparison with conditions at Camp Barkeley, these here are much more favorable but why are we segregated? Why aren't we allowed to attend but one theater out of four on the post and why can't we use any post exchange of our choice? I tried to answer these questions but I'm on the ebb of becoming neurotic.

I didn't start this war but I didn't hesitate to come when I believed I was needed.

When inducted, I honestly believed that as a negroe [sic], I comprised an important part of this nation and it was my patriotic duty to avail myself when my country was in danger of peril. My attitude now is greatly changed. I'm indifferent toward the whole affair.

I sincerely hope that through you, Mr. Gibson, and others like you, America will awaken unto the realization that we too are human and desire to be treated as such and also we want to readily do our part in the process of the nation.

I feel sure that while we are fighting on the battlefront, you will continually be fighting on the home front, for your fight is as great as ours. Good luck.

Yours truly,
Pvt. Bert B. Babero

Exercise Prudence:

- Think of an issue that affects your community and discuss potential solutions to the problem. Then write a letter to your congressman or representative requesting attention to the matter. Encourage members of your family and congregation to do the same.
- Letter-writing is just one of many nonviolent methods of problem-solving. What other peaceful, prudent tactics have our relatives, past and present, utilized in the fight against injustice?
- Our history as African Americans is tainted by mistreatment and abuse, tolerated and even encouraged by our government. In light of the many wrongs we have suffered, why do you think black Americans answered the call to serve our country?
- Read and compare Private Babero's Letter to the excerpt from Colin L. Powell on loyalty (page 249).

Responsibility

*An attentiveness to your obligations and an accountability
for your actions, RESPONSIBILITY defines you as an autonomous
individual and allows you control over your own life.*

According to the well-known aphorism, the first step to solving a problem is acknowledging its existence. However, even before we try to understand our problems, we must understand that we have the ability to solve any problems we may discover. This is responsibility—knowing that you are your own master and have control over your own life.

Our capacity for reasonable decision-making is the grounds on which our freedom stands. If we fail to exercise responsibility, we cannot demand autonomy. In claiming our rights, we must also fulfill our obligations. To be responsible is to answer for your actions, attitudes, words, or choices. It is to own up to the consequences and carry the weight for what you have thought, done, or said.

These days, we spend far too much time explaining our problems and far too little time solving them. Modern-day thinkers have gone to great lengths to relieve individuals of the burden of being held accountable for their personal behavior. We pay therapists to tell us that our irresponsible behavior is not our fault. We listen to social scientists who blame the sins we commit as adults on the lives we suffered through as children.

Yes, conditions in inner cities are reprehensible. We know too well that life is not easy for children growing up in neighborhoods where the streets are filled with drugs and guns. But if we are to succeed, we must stop portraying ourselves as victims.

By historical definition, I should not have graduated from college or been elected to Congress. According to sociologists, I should never have become the president of a multimillion-dollar corporation, built a congregation of over fifteen thousand, or become the president of a university. Statistics say that because I grew up in poverty, I should have failed in life.

But I did not listen to statistics. I did not sit around complaining about my misfortunes. I took responsibility for my life and worked to defy the stereotypes surrounding me.

Successful black men and women must not continue to be the exception—they must become the norm. We must be able to receive the help of others without becoming dependent on charity. We must create our own opportunities and depend on ourselves to defeat the oppressive systems around us.

As a parent of four children, I know that life is "unfair." I have heard it for years. Having to wash the dishes is unfair. Not being allowed to go out on weekends is unfair. Being punished for staying out too late or receiving bad grades is unfair. Making my son clean his dirty and disheveled room before he goes out on Saturday afternoon is unfair.

In our ministry, mothers and fathers we counsel are often angry and frustrated when they are forced to deal with the poor choices and mistakes of their children. "Why should I have to support my son's children?" How long do I allow my daughter to 'find herself' before I wash my hands of her?" The truth is, life is filled with unfair expectations and demands and sometimes we have to assume responsibility for the mistakes and folly of others. It may not be fair, but the need is there nonetheless.

And beyond the mundane, the world is filled with things that really are unfair. Poverty and starvation, oppression and murder, hatred and genocide are all realities. No, the world is not fair. But it is time we stop complaining and start acting to remedy this injustice. Only we can make a difference. History has taught us that injustice will not remedy itself. As basketball legend Shaquille O'Neal once said, "We must believe that the investments we make into our community today will yield successful returns for those who come after us."

It is time we realize that society's designated "power brokers" don't have all the power. We too are among God's creations and we too have the power to make a difference in our world. If we continue emphasizing our impotence, we will remain powerless. If we are to succeed, we must take responsibility for our lives and actions and dedicate ourselves to changing our futures rather than lamenting our pasts. When we seek to do the right thing, our responsibility is rewarded in the end.

Lorene Cary

*I*n 1972, Lorene Cary left her home in a predominantly black suburb of Philadelphia to attend St. Paul's preparatory school in New Hampshire on scholarship. In the wake of the civil rights movement, St. Paul's—an elite, formerly all-male prep school—was actively recruiting minority and female students. The first person in her family to have such an opportunity, Cary felt tremendous pressure to succeed and felt responsible to her family, her race, and the school. She was in good company, as her fellow students of color carried the same burden. These young people learned that shouldering this level of responsibility was a heavy load and that there was often an

*emotional price to pay. Cary suffered feelings of loneliness, racial alienation, and the fear
that her efforts were never good enough. Responsibility indeed carries quite a price, but
as Cary learns later in life, it is well worth it: Today, she is a professor at the University of Pennsylvania and the author of four novels and an autobiography,* Black Ice.

from Black Ice

Still barefoot, I ran into my house to cry. Even when I closed the
door to my room, however, I could hear girls. They were talking
and laughing. Who could cry? I washed my face and wandered upstairs
to Fumiko's room. It was empty. I took the long route back to my
room by making a circle down past the common room and peeked in.
Two black students, a boy and a girl, smiled back at me.

Jimmy Hill, one of the skinniest boys I had ever seen, had arrived
that morning from Brooklyn. He had extravagant brown eyes. His black
satin jacket, emblazoned on the back with a red-and-yellow dragon,
hung open to reveal a fishnet T-shirt that cast tiny shadows on his chest.

Annette Frazier was a ninth-grader (or "Third-Former," as I was
learning to say) whose theatrical mannerisms made her seem older
than she was. She had an appealing face, rounded, with regular features
that she used to great effect. When we met, she pantomimed our wari-
ness with a quick movement of her eyes. She caught precisely our
exposure and our collusion.

We shouted with laughter and touched hands. Had anyone told me
two hours before that I would be engaging in such high-decibel, bare-
naked black bonding, I would have rolled my eyes with scorn. We sat
in our small circle until Annette decided that it was time for her to get
back to unpacking her things. I wondered if she was as organized as
and as self-assured as she looked. Neither Jimmy nor I could face our
rooms, so we left together in search of a place to smoke.

We found one next to the squash courts. It was marked by a sand-
filled stone urn and a few butts. We liked the place, because we could

smoke there, and because we had a solid wall to lean on and buildings with which to swaddle ourselves against the open sky.

I was not afraid to go to St. Paul's School, although it was becoming clear to me from the solicitous white faces that people thought I was—or ought to be. I had no idea that wealth and privilege could confer real advantages beyond the obvious ones sprawled before us. Instead, I believed that rich white people were like poodles: overbred, inbred, degenerate. All the coddling and permissiveness would have a bad effect, I figured, now that they were up against those of us who'd lived a real life in the real world.

I knew that from a black perspective Yeadon had been plenty cushy, but after all, I had been a transplant. West Philly had spawned me, and I was loyal to it. Jimmy felt just as unafraid, just as certain as Darwin that we would overcome. Jimmy had grown up in the projects, the son of a steadfast father and a mother who was a doer, a mover who led tenant-action and community groups. Together, his parents had raised a boy who had a job to do.

"Listen to me, darling," he said. "We are going to turn this mother out!"

And why not? I, too, had been raised for it. My mother who had worked in a factory, and her mother, who had cleaned apartments in Manhattan, had been studying these people all their lives in preparation for this moment. And I had studied them. I had studied my mother as she turned out elementary schools and department stores.

I always saw it coming. Some white department-store manager would look at my mother and see no more than a modestly dressed young black woman making a tiresome complaint. He'd use that tone of voice they used when they had *important* work elsewhere. Uh-oh. Then he'd dismiss her with his eyes. I'd feel her body stiffen next to me, and I'd know that he'd set her off.

"Excuse me," she'd say. "I don't think you understand what I'm trying to say to you . . ."

And then it began in earnest, the turning out. She never moved back. It didn't matter how many people were in line. It didn't matter how many telephones were ringing. She never moved back, only forward, her body leaning over counters and desk tops, her fingers wrapped around the offending item or document, her face getting closer and closer. Sometimes she'd talk through her teeth, her lips moving double time to bite out the consonants. Then she'd get personal. "How dare you," would figure in. "How dare you sit there and tell me . . ." Finally, when she'd made the offense clear, clearer even than the original billing error or the shoddy seam, she'd screw up her eyes: "Do you hear me? Do you hear what I'm saying to you?"

They'd eventually, inevitably, take back the faulty item or credit her charge or offer her some higher-priced substitute ("Like they should've done in the first place," she'd say, and say to them). They would do it because she had made up her mind that they would. Turning out, I learned, was not a matter of style; cold indignation worked as well as hot fury. Turning out had to do with will. I came to regard my mother's will as a force of nature, an example of and a metaphor for black power and black duty. My duty was to compete in St. Paul's classrooms. I had no option but to succeed and no doubt that I could will my success.

Jimmy understood. He knew the desperate mandate, the uncompromising demands, and the wild, perfect, greedy hope of it. If we could succeed here—earn high marks, respect, awards; learn these people, study them, be in their world but not of it—we would fulfill the prayers of our ancestors. Jimmy knew as I did that we could give no rational answer to white schoolmates and parents who asked how we had managed to get to St. Paul's School. How we got there, how we found our way to their secret hideout, was not the point. The point was that we had been bred for it just as surely as they. The point was that we were there to turn it out.

Exercise Responsibility:

- Those of us who were the first to attend predominantly white high schools and universities can recognize ourselves in Cary's story. We may have felt as if all eyes were upon us and as if we were representing every black person in America. For many African Americans, these experiences helped them grow into successful, thoughtful, and mature citizens. Would you agree?

- Cary recalls that her mother never failed to address racial slights and speak out in the face of injustice. Watching her mother counter prejudice by making it her mission to do so instilled in Cary the belief that she could attain an education at a predominantly white school and succeed in areas in which the majority culture assumed she would fail. Seeing our elders exercise responsibility by standing up for their rights and by challenging injustice can give us the impetus to take responsibility for our lives and not succumb to despair and the status quo. Are you exercising responsibility in your life? Are you a role model for someone else? Do you set an example for others to follow?

- Cary says she came to understand that "turning out" had to do with will. It was "an example of and metaphor for black power and black duty." I like to think that it also means our responsibility to accomplish what our ancestors dreamed we'd accomplish. All of us have felt at one time the need to change someone's prejudiced opinion or negative expectation of us. Tell a story about a time in your life when you "turned out" for a successful end? How did you do it?

Robert Hayden

*P*rior to the publication of his first volume of poetry, Heart-Shape in the Dust, in 1940, Robert Hayden researched African American history for the Federal Writers' Project. His research there influenced his later writings, as the charac-

ters of our past often served as the subject of his poems. His poem "Frederick Douglass" not only celebrates a great man in African American history; it also asserts that our future hinges on our responsibility as African Americans to live out the ideals of freedom for which Douglass stood and which he championed throughout his life.

Frederick Douglass

When it is finally ours, this freedom, this liberty, this beautiful
and terrible thing, needful to man as air,
usable as earth; when it belongs at last to all,
when it is truly instinct, brain matter, diastole, systole, reflex
    action; when it is finally won;
when it is more than the gaudy mumbo of politicians:
this man, this Douglass, this former slave, this Negro
beaten to his knees, exiled, visioning a world
where none is lonely, none hunted, alien,
this man, superb in love and logic, this man
shall be remembered. Oh, not with statues' rhetoric,
not with legends and poems and wreaths of bronze alone,
but with the lives grown out of his life, the lives
fleshing his dream of the beautiful, needful thing.

Exercise Responsibility:

• For Robert Hayden, the life of Frederick Douglass is not just something to be remembered or paid tribute to, but is a force that continues to inspire and motivate us. Do one small thing this week—and do it consciously—in remembrance of Frederick Douglass, Harriet Tubman (about whom Hayden also wrote), or another courageous person in our history. You might do something as simple as speak to a visitor at church, invite a new neighbor for coffee, or be friendlier than usual to the cashier at your grocery store. No one needs to be aware of your silent tribute for it to be an effective reminder to you of your responsibility to live up to the dream of heroes like Frederick Douglass.

- Hayden suggests here that poems and statues are not enough to remember our heroes by. Rather, we have a responsibility to our forebears to grow out of their lives a more beautiful future. Make a list of the things you are responsible for every day, whether it's earning a living or meeting the school bus. Imagine yourself at a banquet table seated next to Frederick Douglass. Which of your "responsibilities" would you feel good talking about with him?

- If the "beautiful, needful thing" in this poem refers to freedom—about which Douglass dreamed and contributed to so mightily—what beautiful, needful things can you contribute to in your own community?

Hank Aaron

Born in Mobile, Alabama, in 1934, baseball legend Hank Aaron is the only player in history to hit at least twenty home runs for twenty consecutive seasons; in fact, he hit more home runs than anyone else ever has. He won the Most Valuable Player award in 1957 and was inducted into the Baseball Hall of Fame in 1982. Today he is an executive with the Atlanta Braves. Aaron has always felt the responsibility to do whatever he can to help his fellow African Americans. This stance has made him unpopular with the segment of the population that dislikes outspoken African Americans, but that has never stopped Aaron from remembering where he came from and the sacrifices that his people have made, past and present, which enabled him to become the man he is today. The following passage is taken from Aaron's autobiography, written with Lonnie Wheeler.

from If I Had a Hammer

The day I left Mobile, Alabama, to play ball with the Indianapolis Clowns, Mama was so upset she couldn't come to the train station to see me off. She just made me a couple of sandwiches, stuffed two dollars in my pocket, and stood in the yard crying as I rode off with my daddy, my older brother and sister, and Ed Scott, a former Negro League player who managed me with the Mobile Black Bears and scouted me for the Clowns. When we got to the station, Mr. Scott handed me an envelope with the name Bunny Downs on it. Downs was the business manager of the Clowns, and when I arrived at their camp in Winston-Salem, North Carolina, I was to hand him the envelope unopened.

My knees were banging together when I got on that train. I'd never ridden in anything bigger than a bus or faster than my daddy's old pickup truck. As we pulled out of the station and Daddy and Sarah and Herbert Junior and Mr. Scott kept getting smaller and smaller, I never felt so alone in my life. I just sat there clutching my sandwiches, speaking to nobody, staring out the window at towns I'd never heard of. It was the first time in my life that I had been around white people. After a while, I got up the courage to walk up and down the aisle a few times. I wanted to see what a dining car looked like, and I needed somebody to tell me where I wasn't allowed to go. Then I sat back down, listened to those wheels carrying me farther away from home, and tried to talk myself out of getting off at the next stop and going back.

I've never stopped wondering if I did the right thing that day. I was barely eighteen at the time, a raggedy kid who wore my sister's hand-me-down pants and had never been out of the black parts of Mobile. I didn't know anything about making a living or taking care of myself or about the white world I'd have to face sooner or later. I didn't know what I wanted to be doing when I was forty or any of the other things I needed to know to make a decision that would affect the rest of my life—except for one. I knew that I loved to play baseball. And I had a feeling that I might be pretty good at it.

I suppose that's reason enough for an eighteen-year-old boy to board a train and set off on his life's journey, and I suppose it's time I stopped second-guessing myself. But I'm not eighteen anymore, and two generations later I'm still living with a decision I made back when JFK was starting out as a senator. I live with the fact that I spent twenty-five of the best years of my life playing baseball. Don't get me wrong; I don't regret a day of it. I still love baseball—Lord knows, it's the greatest game in the world—and I treasure the experience. God, what an experience. But sometimes I have to wonder just how far I've really come since I took that envelope from Mr. Scott and walked onto the L&N. How far can a guy really go playing baseball? I guess that's what I wonder about. I can only thank God that I played the game well enough that maybe it meant something. Maybe in the end, I can do as much good, in my way, as, say, a teacher. That's what Mama wanted me to be.

With all of my wondering, I don't doubt for a minute what baseball has done for me. Let me put that another way: I don't doubt what my ability to play baseball has done for me. I realize that if I hadn't been able to hit the hell out of a baseball, I would have never been able to lay a finger on the good life that I've been fortunate to have. Playing baseball has given me all that a man could ask for—certainly a lot more than a timid little black kid like me ever dared to dream about. I've traveled the world, met Presidents, had my share of fortune and more fame than I ever wanted. I even have a place in history, if only for hitting home runs. The fact is, I have every reason to be content. My kids have all been to college. I don't know how I managed to stumble onto the great woman who is my wife. Everything is just about perfect. I don't even hear much about Babe Ruth anymore, thank goodness, and I haven't received a really nasty piece of hate mail in about fifteen years.

Believe me, I take none of this for granted, because there was a time when my life was very painful. One of my sons passed away as an infant. My first marriage was rough, and I was struggling to get over the divorce at the same time I was starting to close in on the home run record. The Ruth chase should have been the greatest period of my life, and it was the worst. I couldn't believe there was so much hatred in people. It's something I'm still trying to get over, and maybe I never will. I know I'll never forget it, and the fact is, I don't want to. I feel like if I forget about that and everything else I've been through in the last four decades, I'll be content. It would be so easy to be content. It would also be so unforgivably selfish that I can't let it happen. I used to have talks with Jackie Robinson not long before he died, and he impressed upon me that I should never allow myself to be satisfied with the way things are. I can't let Jackie down—or my people, or myself. The day I become content is the day I cease to be anything more than a man who hit home runs.

I might not feel this way if I weren't black. I'm sure this is a hard thing to understand for somebody who isn't black: But what kind of a man would I be if I cashed in my fame and retired to a comfortable life with my wife and my trophies and my tennis court? See, I'm one of the lucky ones. I could do something that white people would pay to see. Singers, dancers, boxers, ballplayers—sure, we can make it in the white world. White people love to have us entertain them. But what about all the black teachers and mechanics and carpenters and janitors and wait-resses? Am I supposed to say to them: Hey, folks, I know it's rough, but look at me, I made it? What am I supposed to do with my good for-tune? Am I just supposed to say, Thank you, Lord, and then get fat and sign autographs for fifteen bucks a shot? I don't believe that's the reason God gave me the gifts that he did. I think that if I were the kind of man to be satisfied with the way things are, he would have given my eyes and my hands and my mind to somebody who would put them to better use.

And so I make it my business not to be content. Of course, that rubs some people the wrong way. They say that I'm bitter. They say that I have a chip on my shoulder, that I read racism into every phrase and discrimination into every decision. But I don't think white people can understand that I have a moral responsibility to do whatever I can. With all of my worldly advantages, how can I look the other way? If I did that, how could I face the people I come from? How could I justify who I am?

Look, I don't have the vision or the voice of Martin Luther King or James Baldwin or Jesse Jackson or even of Jackie Robinson. I'm just an old ballplayer. But I learned a lot as a ballplayer. Among other things, I learned that if you manage to make a name for yourself—and if you're black, believe me, it has to be a big name—then people will start listening to what you have to say. That was why it was so important for me to break the home run record. Believe me, there were times during the chase when I was so angry and tired and sick of it all that I wished I could get on a plane and not get off until I was someplace where they never heard of Babe Ruth. But damn it all, I had to break that record. I had to do it for Jackie and my people and myself and for everybody who ever called me a nigger.

And when it was over, my real job was only starting. Once the record was mine, I had to use it like a Louisville Slugger. I believed, and still do, that there was a reason why I was chosen to break the record. I feel it's my task to carry on where Jackie Robinson left off, and I only know of one way to go about it. It's the only way I've ever had of dealing with things like fastballs and bigotry—keep swinging at them. As a ballplayer, I always figured that I had a bat and all the pitcher had was a little ball, and as long as I kept swinging that bat I'd be all right. It worked pretty well. People said I pounded the ball as if my bat was a hammer, and they called me Hammerin' Hank. Well, I can't pound a baseball anymore. I'm fifty-seven years old. My back aches, my knees are weak, and I need glasses to read. These days, I couldn't hit a good slider with a snow shovel. But I can do what I can do.

The way I see it, it's a great thing to be the man who hit the most home runs, but it's a greater thing to be the man who did the most with the home runs he hit. So as long as there's a chance that maybe I can hammer out a little justice now and then, or a little opportunity here and there, I intend to do as I always have—keep swinging. I'm taking my cuts as you read this. I'm telling my story, and when everything's said and done, maybe it'll mean more than a bunch of home runs. I can only hope and keep hammering.

Exercise Responsibility:

* Aaron writes, "The way I see it, it's a great thing to be the man who hit the most home runs, but it's a greater thing to be the man who did the most with the home runs he hit." The members of Aaron's generation, raised during and after the Depression, saw firsthand the struggles that their parents and grandparents endured just in order to place food on the table. His generation seems to have had more of a sense of communal responsibility than the last few generations of African Americans. What events have eroded our sense of responsibility to each other? Ask your family for examples.

* Although Hammerin' Hank has retired from baseball, he remains committed to bringing justice to the lives of "the black teachers and mechanics and carpenters and janitors and waitresses" who live much humbler lives—lives that are often touched by racism and lack of opportunity. Exercise your responsibility to your community by making it a point to give back in any way that you can. Many of our people fought and even lost their lives for the educational achievements and financial successes we enjoy today.

* Talk about role models with your family. Ask what singers or athletes they admire and then discuss what responsibility those figures have to model behavior or actions for the rest of us, and especially for children.

Debra Dickerson

*D*ebra Dickerson's life is an all-American success story. The daughter of South-
erners who migrated to St. Louis in search of a better life, Dickerson grew up
in a hardscrabble environment. She was highly intelligent and, despite some slips and
starts, took the road that many working-class sons and daughters have taken in pursuit
of a better life: She joined the military. Dickerson enjoyed a successful military career
but eventually decided she wanted something more. That something more led her to
Harvard Law School. Now a full-time writer and journalist, Dickerson looks back on
a life that she desperately wanted to escape and, in doing so, is surprised to learn that
her father, with whom she had a tumultuous relationship, had a far more positive than
negative influence on her life.

from An American Story

In the mid-1950s, with JoAnn and Dorothy born, my family was
still so new to the North that they had to give up raising pet rabbits
in the backyard because the neighbors ate them. The rabbits would
have had to go anyway eventually as my father's junk began to take over
more and more of the backyard.

He'd long since turned the basement into a dark catacomb filled
with long-forgotten crates that, even so, could not be parted with.
Ever the orphan required to survive by his wits, what seemed like trash
to other people looked like pennies from heaven to him. An irre-
deemable pack rat and independent trucker always operating on a
shoestring, he kept the yard filled with transmissions and dead batter-
ies, cannibalized trucks and cars teetering on bricks, piles of mismatched hubcaps and lots of unidentifiable, greasy gizmos, all of
which he was confident he would one day put to use. When *Sanford and
Son* aired in the 1970s, the other kids would torment us by humming
the theme as my father passed by. But when I was a child, his junk piles

were a paradise full of fun stuff to play with and cozy hiding places to curl up in with a book.

Driving anywhere with Daddy was an adventure when I was small. I loved the station wagons he created for us from the varied parts of many other sacrificial cars. We never knew what we'd be riding in, but there were some constants: multicolored bodies with mismatched tires and doors that almost fit. Missing windows replaced with cardboard we thought was there for us to draw on, missing floorboards we could drag our Keds out of when Mama wasn't looking. More often than not, we'd end up getting to play alongside the road while Daddy jogged up the highway to the nearest gas station for water to pour into a radiator on its last legs or ripped up old rags to secure a muffler. People honked and pointed at us as we passed; it felt special, like being part of a circus caravan.

He would pull the car over—whether we were on a side road or jam-packed Highway 70—and pick up any box, bag, or jug that looked likely. Whatever it contained, Daddy would bring it home with us. Whatever its condition, he made us use it. This included a box of key blanks; toilet paper rain-swollen to volleyball size and notebook paper consistency; a shampoo so tarlike and viscous we knew it had been dumped on purpose; an armchair with actual bloodstains and tire marks.

Daddy's finds went far beyond car parts and household goods to include fancy toys discarded by the rich. They kept us in demand as playmates and made Daddy famous as a master magician who could make something from nothing.

Exercise Responsibility:

- Debra Dickerson's father, despite being a poor migrant from the South, did everything in his limited power to provide for his family. And he did it with such style that his finds and the car that he culled together made his family feel special. Imagine if all low-income fathers in our communities adapted such an attitude in the face of the ongoing economic hardships many of us face. Are there low-income fathers in your community who display the sort of can-do responsibility that Debra Dickerson's father displayed? Consider ways that these men can be celebrated, especially in a society that promotes fast money, fast living, and as few responsibilities as possible.

- Debra Dickerson did not realize the legacy of responsibility that her father bestowed upon her until she became an adult. Who passed on the need to exercise responsibility, either by word or deed, to you? Have you continued to pass this legacy on to future generations?

Bible

The challenge that the African American community faces in light of the tremendous gaps between our people and White America—in education, home ownership, economics—is to use every resource in a responsible manner. Our gifts, talents, time, and energy must be invested wisely in order to realize the appropriate returns. We have a responsibility to use well all that God has given us, as the "Parable of the Talents," retold from Matthew 25:14–30, reminds.

Parable of the Talents

The kingdom of heaven may be likened to a man who journeyed to a faraway place, who called upon his servants and placed his possessions in their care. To one servant he presented five talents; to another, two talents; to a third servant, one talent, each amount determined by the servant's ability. He then embarked on his journey.

The servant who had been given five talents bartered with the others to earn five more. The servant who had received two talents also used his two talents to secure two talents more. But the man to whom the master had entrusted only one talent dug a hole and veiled his master's money within the earth.

After much time had passed, their lord returned and sought to settle his debts.

The servant who had received five talents brought with him the additional five. "Master," he declared, "you presented me with five talents; behold, I have gained five more." His lord replied, "Well done, good and loyal servant. You have proven yourself faithful with only a few things; I will now put in your charge many things. Share in your master's joy!"

Then the servant to whom the master had entrusted two talents entered. "Master," he proclaimed, "you presented me with two talents; see, I have gained two more." His master returned, "Well done, good and loyal servant. You have proven yourself faithful with only a few things; I will now put in your charge many things. Share in your master's joy!"

Finally, the man who had received only one talent came. "Master," he said, "I know that you are a hard man, reaping where you did not sow and gathering the fruits of seeds you did not plant. I was frightened and hid your talent in the earth. Here is what belongs to you."

His master answered, "You wicked and indolent servant! If you knew that I reaped where I had not sown and gathered where I planted no seeds, you ought to have brought my money to the bank so that upon my return I would have obtained it with interest.

"Take this talent away from him, and give it instead to the servant who possesses ten talents. Unto everyone who has shall be given more to assure a plentiful supply; from he who does not have, even what he does not possess shall be taken away. Cast this unfaithful servant out into the darkness, where there is weeping and grinding of teeth."

Exercise Responsibility:

- Life and the talents we've been given are precious resources. The message of this parable is that we must spend our time wisely and apply our talents responsibly. What common, everyday events drain our talents?
- Even if we are given fewer talents than others, we are expected to invest them wisely. Make a list of some of your abilities. Write down creative uses of each of those abilities and commit to carrying out at least three of them this week.
- If you had to open up your life's account book for a spiritual reckoning, would you be happy with what you find there? How might you spend your talent and time more wisely?

James Whitfield

J ames Whitfield was a preeminent antislavery poet. In order to exercise responsibility, we must be aware of what is within our power and what we must rely on from God. Whitfield suggests some things here that are certainly within our power.

Self-Reliance

I love the man whose lofty mind
　　On God and its own strength relies;
Who seeks the welfare of his kind,
　　And dare be honest though he dies;
Who cares not for the world's applause,
　　But, to his own fixed purpose true,
The path which God and nature's laws
　　Point out, doth earnestly pursue.

When adverse clouds around him lower,
    And stern oppression bars his way,
When friends desert in trial's hour,
    And hope sheds but a feeble ray;
When all the powers of earth and hell
    Combine to break his spirit down,
And strive, with their terrific yell,
    To crush his soul beneath their frown—
When numerous friends, whose cheerful tone
    In happier hours once cheered him on,
With visions that full brightly shone,
    But now, alas! Are dimmed and gone!
When love, which in his bosom burned
    With all the fire of ardent youth,
And which he fondly thought returned
    With equal purity and truth,
Mocking his hopes, falls to the ground,
    Like some false vision of the night,
Its vows a hollow, empty sound,
    Scathing his heart with deadly blight,
Choking that welling spring of love,
    Which lifts the soul to God above,
In bonds mysterious to unite
    The finite with the infinite;
And draw a blessing from above,
    Of infinite on finite love.
When hopes of better, fear of worse,
    Alike are fled, and naught remains
To stimulate him on his course:
    No hope of bliss, no fear of pains
Fiercer than what already rend,
    With tortures keen, his inmost heart,
Without a hope, without a friend,

With nothing to allay the smart
From blighted love, affections broken,
From blasted hopes and cankering care,
When every thought, each word that's spoken
Urges him onward to despair.
When through the opening vista round,
Shines on him no pellucid ray,
Like beam of early morning found,
The harbinger of perfect day;
But like the midnight's darkening frown,
When stormy tempests rear on high,
When pealing thunder shakes the ground,
And lurid lightning rends the sky!
When clothed in more than midnight gloom,
Like some foul specter from the tomb,
Despair, with stern and fell control,
Sits brooding o'er his inmost soul—
'Tis then the faithful mind is proved,
That, true alike to man and God,
By all the ills of life unmoved,
Pursues its straight and narrow road.
For such a man the siren song
Of pleasure hath no lasting charm;
Nor can the mighty and the strong
His spirit tame with powerful arm.
His pleasure is to wipe the tear
Of sorry from the mourner's cheek,
The languid, fainting heart to cheer,
To succor and protect the weak.
When the bright face of fortune smiles
Upon his path with cheering ray,
And pleasure, with alluring wiles,
Flatters, to lead his heart astray,

His soul in conscious virtue strong,
  And armed with innate rectitude,
Loving the right, detesting wrong,
  And seeking the eternal good
Of all alike, the high or low,
  His dearest friend, or direst foe,
Seeks out the brave and faithful few,
  Who, to themselves and Maker true,
Dare, in the name and fear of God,
  To spread the living truth abroad!
Armed with the same sustaining power,
  Against adversity's dark hour,
And from the deep deceitful guile
Which lurks in pleasure's hollow smile,
Or from the false and fitful beam
  That marks ambition's meteor fire,
Or from the dark and lurid gleam
  Revealing passion's deadly ire.
His steadfast soul fearing no harm,
  But trusting in the aid of heaven,
And wielding, with unfaltering arm,
  The utmost power which God has given—
Conscious that the Almighty power
  Will nerve the faithful soul with might,
Whatever storms may round him lower,
  Strikes boldly for the true and right.

Exercise Responsibility:

- For the strong man, "His pleasure is to wipe the tear / Of sorrow from the mourner's cheek, / The languid, fainting heart to cheer, / To succor and protect the weak." Do you feel a responsibility to help others?

- A favorite line in the context of this book would be "His soul in conscious virtue strong." How might you cultivate consciously the virtue of responsibility in your life?

- Whitfield also urges us as Christians to be conscious of the power that God has given us and of our responsibility to "Strike boldly for the true and right." As Luke 12:48 tells us, "For unto whomsoever much is given, of him shall be much required; and to whom men have committed much, of him they will ask the more."

- "Who cares not for the world's applause / But, to his own fixed purpose true" is a challenge for many of us in today's world. It is certainly within your power to adhere to a true purpose in life. What is the path that God points out for you? Are you earnestly and responsibly pursuing it? Talk with your family about our culture of celebrity. What is good and bad about it? Is seeking the world's applause something that can ever be a responsible act?

- Who is the most responsible person you know? List the ways he or she is responsible.

- Think about people whose sense of responsibility you often need to evaluate: employees, child care providers, teachers, car mechanics. How do you judge them?

Service

A voluntary act of generosity, assistance, or kindness,
Service *allows you to do your duty to God and*
fulfill your worldly purpose.

One thing even the most hardworking people know is that our work is never done. There are always tasks that need to be completed, jobs that we have yet to start. With all we have to do for ourselves, it can seem futile to even think about doing things for other people.

And yet our obligation to serve others must not be taken lightly. It is indeed an obligation, not something we may do but something we must do. As the prominent activist and children's rights advocate Marian Wright Edelman once put it, "Service is the rent we pay for living. It is the very purpose of life and not something you do in your spare time."

Too often I hear people say that they are so busy fighting for their own survival that they forget to fight on behalf of others. Too many people have yet to experience the supreme fulfillment of giving. We must all recognize that when our labor lacks a higher purpose it becomes drudgery but when our hard work is instilled with a greater ideal it is noble sacrifice.

One of the biggest challenges that many of us face is finding the time to help others. Between spousal and parental responsibilities, meetings, sermon preparation, and all of the responsibilities that pastoring demands, it is practically impossible for me to find the time to reach out to others. And while my job requires that I make time for hospital visits, funerals, and counseling, I also feel compelled to attend to service for those who don't know or expect anything from me. A few weeks ago, I had to take my son to the mall between meetings. As we were rushing to the department store, I noticed an older woman in the middle of the parking lot wearing a puzzled expression. As she struggled to take steps with her cane, I could see the pain written on her face. I surmised that she was walking around in search of her car. I looked at my watch and saw that I had only an hour and a half before my next meeting. While I really needed to move on, I knew that I had to help this lady. My son and I spent almost thirty minutes running from section to section trying to find her white Oldsmobile. It turned out that her car was not where she thought it was at all—she had come out of the wrong exit. When we finally found the car, she was too tired to walk to it, so my son had to drive the car to her. I believe that as we sent her on her way, we were as thankful as she was. She had provided my son and me with a wonderful opportunity to help another person. Our shopping trip was cut short and I was late for my meeting, but the woman was able to get home safely.

By helping others, you help yourself. As we lift others, so will we too be lifted. Service adds meaning and purpose to your life. "Everyone," Martin Luther King, Jr., said, "has the power for greatness, not for fame but for greatness, because greatness is determined by service."

Not only do good deeds nourish your soul and satisfy your spirit, but they also foster an environment of benevolence. If we hope for others to come to our aid whenever we need, we must come to the aid of others whenever we can. We are instructed by the Bible not to become weary of generosity, for in sowing the seeds of kindness, we will ultimately reap a harvest of prosperity.

If we have not started yet, we must start now. Rather than making excuses for not giving back, give back. There are billions of people who need help. Although our task may seem daunting, remember that even the longest journey begins with a single step.

Recall the courageous Arthur Ashe, whom we met in the Courage chapter. The only African American male ever to win the U.S. Open tennis tournament, Ashe was born in segregated Virginia, received a scholarship to attend the University of California at Los Angeles, and eventually rose to become the world's top-ranked singles player in tennis. He was a man who knew what overcoming obstacles meant. But Arthur Ashe also knew that obstacles must not simply be overcome, but destroyed. Dedicating himself to the causes he believed in, Ashe spent much of his time fighting discrimination around the world, promoting AIDS education, and teaching young people about the game of tennis.

Ashe knew that our success cannot be measured by dollars or trophies. In one speech, he said, "True heroism is remarkably sober, very undramatic. It is not the urge to surpass all others at whatever cost, but the urge to serve others at whatever cost." The legacy we leave to the future must be the good deeds we perform in the present. No, we cannot all change the world, but I assure you that we can indeed make a difference.

Sarah Louise Delany and
Annie Elizabeth Delany

Sadie and Bessie Delany, born in 1890 and 1891, respectively, lived through Jim Crow, the Depression, three wars, and the civil rights movement. Born to Henry Beard Delany, an emancipated slave who became the first elected African American bishop of the Episcopal Church in the United States, and Martha Logan Delany, a mixed-race free woman who was an educator, the sisters were well-equipped to weather the storms of the twenty-first century. In the following passage from Having Our Say, *their best-selling book written with Amy Hill Hearth, Sadie talks about the ways in which she and Bessie shared the little they had with their clients during the Depression.*

from Having Our Say

People think of the 1920s as the good old days, but of course there were many of the same problems we have now—except then, we didn't have this widespread drug problem, or this thing called AIDS. Still, there was terrible poverty, even in our own family, mostly among our relatives down South.

Bessie and I tried to help them, as much as we could. It was our little project. A lot of those folks did not have refrigeration and we worried they would get sick. So one of the things we did was to buy iceboxes for some of our relatives, especially Mama's folks in Virginia. I think those folks thought we were rich, Bessie and me. But nothing could be further from the truth. All the time we were buying new iceboxes for those folks, we had a broken-down old icebox ourselves.

Among my students in New York City there were plenty of children, white and colored, who had problems. There was one girl who comes to mind from P.S. 119. All the girls made fun of her because she had this mark, like a dark ring, around her neck. Well, it was obvious to me that it was just plain old dirt! When there were no other children around I asked her about it, and she said, "My mama says it's a birthmark."

So I said, "Child, I don't think it is. Would you like me to try and fix it?" So she stayed after school and I took her into the girls' room and took a towel and cleaned her neck. Soap and water didn't get it off, so I rubbed cold cream in it, and I rubbed and rubbed until I got it all off. The next day, she came in and said, "Miss Delany, my mama said to thank you so much for cleaning up my neck."

Now, I think that's kind of funny. Imagine not knowing that your child's neck is dirty. Well, there are a lot of people who weren't raised properly themselves, so how can they teach their children right? Sometimes it's neglect, sometimes it's just ignorance. And what people don't know will really hold them back. This is especially true of colored children once they try to succeed among white people in the job market. Being presentable and having good manners—don't underestimate the importance of this, especially if you're colored. It's amazing how many people don't know the basics about simple hand-washing, how to iron a shirt properly, things like that.

That's why you need home economics. Back in the twenties it was called "domestic science." It was nutrition, cooking and canning, sewing, hygiene—anything you can think of that makes a home a proper, healthy environment. Of course, home economics was for girls. Before I retired in 1960, I did have a few boys in my classes. I think it's good for boys to take it, especially now that men are expected to do more around the house.

It was domestic science that brought me the greatest accomplishment of my life: saving Cousin Daisy from dying. Cousin Daisy was Mama's cousin in Virginia. She was a granddaughter of Aunt Pat—the one who had her baby by the side of the road. Well, one day we got a letter that Cousin Daisy was sick. The white doctor in Danville said she had pellagra, and there was nothing could be done. Although she was still a fairly young woman, she was going to die.

Pellagra was a disease that you got from not eating enough vegetables and fresh fruit. First your hair would fall out; then you'd get weak and not be able to walk, and eventually—it might take several years—you had one foot in the grave.

Well, back then, people were just beginning to understand the importance of vitamins and minerals. As a teacher of domestic science, I kept up-to-date on the new developments in nutrition. One day, I saw in the newspaper that Dr. Carlton Fredericks, a scientist who worked with the man who had discovered Vitamin B_{12}, was going to be visiting New York City. So I invited him to my school to speak at an assembly.

After his talk, I took him aside and told him all about Cousin Daisy down in Virginia. I said, "Please, can you help me?" And he told me exactly what to do. So I went and bought these liquid vitamins at a store in New York. You couldn't buy them in Virginia, and I realized that Cousin Daisy and her husband, who was a farmer, would not be able to afford them. I shipped those vitamins to Daisy, along with a schedule for taking them. I also drew up menu plans for her of what I thought she should eat. She was eating too much fatback and cornbread, things like that.

Well, that old white doctor in Danville was wrong. There was something could be done for Cousin Daisy. With those vitamins and my meal plans, she started to get a little better. Then she got a lot better. And her hair even grew back!

Once we realized that Cousin Daisy was going to live after all, Bessie and I had a little talk. Bessie said, "Sadie, now that you've saved Cousin Daisy, you are responsible for her life." So I sent those vitamins, plus twenty dollars a month for food, until Cousin Daisy died. She lived to be an old woman. I think she was eighty-three years old when she passed on.

It's only now that I'm telling anyone about how I helped Cousin Daisy. I never told anyone at the time, except Bessie. The way we were brought up, it was only natural for Bessie and me to help other people. It wasn't something you did so that people thought well of you.

No, you did it because that was what was expected of you. It was the example that was set by the Good Lord, Jesus. It was also the example set by Mama and Papa.

Exercise Service:

- Although the Delany sisters did not have much extra money, they never hesitated to help those in need. Their acts of selfless giving were indeed rewarded: They lived long, fruitful, and healthy lives (Bessie died in 1995 at the age of 104, and Sadie passed away in 1999 at the ripe old age of 109). Read 2 Corinthians 9:6–11 and consider the ways in which the Delany sisters embodied the virtue of service.

- Remember stories in your own family that recall how people helped one another during the Depression years. Read the Delanys' story to your children and share a tale of ancestors who helped each other survive during the Depression or through a recent recession. Have a discussion with your family about the meaning of service and discuss how important this virtue has been in African American communities. Find a service project that you and your children can do together. Work on it for at least one month.

- Sadie writes, "It was only natural for Bessie and me to help other people." Indeed, service to others should be something that comes naturally. What are some of the things that have kept you from becoming more involved in service to others? How important are they?

- Sadie's interest in "domestic science" proved immensely helpful to Aunt Daisy. How might you use your own special knowledge or talents to help someone?

Alice Moore Dunbar-Nelson

orn Alice Ruth Moore in 1875 in New Orleans, Alice Moore Dunbar-Nelson was a women's and civil rights advocate. A journalist, public speaker, and activist, Dunbar-Nelson was the coeditor and publisher of the Wilmington Advocate, *a progressive African-American newspaper in the 1920s, and helped found the Industrial School. Dunbar-Nelson recognized that she could best pursue her political and social reform goals through the women's club movement in the first quarter of the twentieth century, and fought on behalf of women accordingly. One of Dunbar-Nelson's more popular poems, "I Sit and Sew," is a passionate protest against the cultural roles ascribed to women, especially during war. If we look beyond its literal meaning, the poem also beautifully captures the spirit of wanting to give back.*

I Sit and Sew

I sit and sew—a useless task it seems,
My hands grown tired, my head weighed down with dreams—
The panoply of war, the martial tread of men,
Grim-faced, stern-eyed, gazing beyond the ken
Of lesser souls, whose eyes have not seen Death,
Nor learned to hold their lives but as a breath—
But—I must sit and sew.

I sit and sew—my heart aches with desire—
That pageant terrible, that fiercely pouring fire
On wasted fields, and writing grotesque things
Once men. My soul in pity flings
Appealing cries, yearning only to go
There in that holocaust of hell, those fields of woe—
But—I must sit and sew.

The little useless seam, the idle patch;
Why dream I here beneath my homely thatch,
When there they lie in sodden mud and rain,
Pitifully calling me, the quick ones and the slain?
You need me, Christ! It is no roseate dream
That beckons me—this pretty futile seam,

It stifles me—God, must I sit and sew?

Exercise Service:

- This poem is a compelling illustration of one's impulse to care. Alice Dunbar-Nelson became heavily involved in the political and social causes she believed in. Recall some of the people and experiences that have inspired you to be a caring person.

- Dunbar-Nelson wrote about being stifled by the work in front of her, the result of society's restrictions on black women at the time. Your own work may be stifling on any given day—we've all had moments at our desks or our jobs when the task at hand seems futile or unimportant. Exercise service even in those moments by thinking of ways you can help others. Are there ways you can be of service to coworkers? Make a list of things you might do and keep the list on your desk. Refer to the list regularly and make a point to accomplish some of the things you write down.

- Do at least one thing at work today that is completely unexpected and service-oriented. You might involve yourself in a cleanup project, figure out where to donate the old office computers, or give a school group a tour of your workplace on Career Day.

Ella Baker

*T*he granddaughter of slaves, Ella Baker was an activist known for her work with the National Association for the Advancement of Colored People and the Southern Christian Leadership Conference, headed by Martin Luther King, Jr., among many other organizations. She devoted her life entirely to service; below, we get a sense of how and why she worked so hard to make a better way. Gerda Lerner interviewed Ella Baka in 1957. The following excerpt is taken from Lerner's anthology, Black Women in White America, published in 1972.

from Black Women in White America

*I*n my organizational work, I have never thought in terms of my "making a contribution." I just thought of myself as functioning where there was a need. And if I have made a contribution I think it may be that I had some influence on a large number of people.

As assistant field secretary of the branches of the NAACP, much of my work was in the South. At that time the NAACP was the leader on the cutting edge of social change. I remember when NAACP membership in the South was the basis for getting beaten up or even killed.

I used to leave New York about the 15th of February and travel through the South for four to five months. I would go to, say, Birmingham, Alabama, and help to organize membership campaigns. And in the process of helping to organize membership campaigns, there was opportunity for developing community reaction. You would go into areas where people were not yet organized in the NAACP and try to get them more involved. Maybe you would start with some simple thing like the fact that they had no street lights, or the fact that in the given area somebody had been arrested or had been jailed in a manner that was considered illegal and unfair, and the like. You would deal with whatever the local problem was, and on the basis of the needs of the people you would try to organize them in the NAACP.

Black people who were living in the South were constantly living with violence. Part of the job was to help them to understand what that violence was and how they in an organized fashion could help to stem it. The major job was getting people to understand that they had something within their power that they could use, and it could only be used if they understood what was happening and how group action could counter even when it was perpetrated by the police or, in some instances, the state. My basic sense of it has always been to get people to understand that in the long run they themselves are the only protection they have against violence or injustice. If they only had ten members in the NAACP at a given point, those ten members could be in touch with twenty-five members in the next little town, with fifty in the next and throughout the state as a result of the organization of state conferences, and they, of course, could be linked up with the national. People have to be made to understand that they cannot look for salvation anywhere but to themselves.

I left the NAACP and then worked at fund-raising with the national Urban League Service Fund and with several national health organizations. However, I continued my work with the NAACP on the local level. I became the advisor for the Youth Council. Then I served as president of the New York branch at a point where it had sunk to a low level in membership and otherwise. And in the process of serving as president we tried to bring the NAACP back, as I called it, to the people. We moved the branch out of an office building and located it where it would be more visible to the Harlem community. We started developing an active branch. It became one of the largest branches. I was president for a couple of years. It was strictly volunteer work which lasted until four o'clock in the morning, sometimes.

When the 1954 Supreme Court decision on school desegregation came, I was serving as chairman of the Educational Committee of the

New York branch. We began to deal with the problems of de facto segregation, and the results of the de facto segregation which were evidenced largely in the achievement levels of black children, going down instead of going up after they entered public school. We had called the first committee meeting and Kenneth Clark became the chairman of that committee. During that period, I served on the Mayor's Commission on School Integration, with the subdivision on zoning. In the summer of 1957, I gave time to organizing what we called Parents in Action for Quality Education.

I've never believed that the people who control things really were willing and able to pay the price of integration. From a practical standpoint, anyone who looked at the Harlem area knew that the potential for integration per se was basically impossible unless there were some radically innovative things done. And those innovative things would not be acceptable to those who ran the school system, nor to communities, nor even to the people who call themselves supporters of integration. But when you raised the question of whether they would permit or would welcome blacks to live in the same houses with them, which was the only practical way at that stage to achieve integration, they squirmed. Integration certainly had to be pushed concurrently with changing the quality of education that the black children were getting, and changing the attitudes of the educational establishment toward the black community.

I don't think we achieved too much with the committee except to pinpoint certain issues and to have survived some very sharp confrontations with the superintendent and others on the Board of Education. But out of it came increased fervor on the part of the black communities to make some changes. One of the gratifying things to me is the fact that even as late as this year I have met people who were in that group and who have been continuously active in the struggle for quality education in the black communities ever since.

There certainly has been progress in the direction of the capacity of people to face this issue. And to me, when people themselves know what they are looking for and recognize that they can exercise some influence by action, that's progress. . . .

There are those, some of the young people especially, who have said to me that if I had not been a woman I would have been well known in certain places, and perhaps held certain kinds of positions. . . .

For myself, circumstances frequently dictated what had to be done as I saw it. For example, I had no plans to go down and set up the office of SCLC [Southern Christian Leadership Conference]. But it seemed unless something were done whatever impetus had been gained would be lost, and nobody else was available who was willing or able to do it. So I went because to me it was more important to see what was a potential for all of us than it was to do what I might have done for myself. I knew from the beginning that as a woman, an older woman, in a group of ministers who are accustomed to having women largely as supporters, there was no place for me to have come into a leadership role. The competition wasn't worth it.

The movement of the '50s and '60s was carried largely by women, since it came out of church groups. It was sort of second nature to women to play a supportive role. How many made a conscious decision on the basis of the larger goals, how many on the basis of habit pattern, I don't know. But it's true that the number of women who carried the movement is much larger than that of men. Black women have had to carry this role, and I think the younger women are insisting on equal footing.

I don't advocate anybody's following the pattern I followed, unless they find themselves in a situation where they think that the larger goals will be shortchanged if they don't. From the standpoint of the historical pattern of the society, which seems to assume that this is the best role for women, I think that certainly the young people who are challenging this ought to be challenging it, and it ought to be changed. But I also think you have to have a certain sense of your own value, and a sense of security on your part, to be able to forgo the glamour of what the leadership role offers. From the standpoint of my work and my own self-concepts, I don't think I have thought of myself largely as a woman. I thought of myself as an individual with a certain amount of sense of the need of people to participate in the movement. I have always thought what is needed is the development of people who are interested not in being leaders as much as in developing leadership among other people. Every time I see a young person who has come through the system to a stage where he could profit from the system and identify with it, but who identifies more with the struggle of black people who have not had his chance, every time I find such a person I take new hope. I feel a new life as a result of it.

Exercise Service:

- Why do you think Ella Baker distinguished between "making a contribution" and "functioning where there was a need" in the first paragraph?

- Rent the movie *Fundi: The Life of Ella Baker* for a striking example of a life devoted to service, or read the biography *Ella Baker: Freedom Bound* by Joanne Grant. Arrange to have the movie shown to a local scout troop or at a school assembly.

- In the words of Baker biographer Joanne Grant, Ella Baker was a radical: "She came out of a family that rebelled against the status quo, and she carried on the family tradition. But she was not against; she was for. She was for the participation of people in whatever affected their lives. She was for the best in all of us." Service is the opportunity for us to find the best in ourselves and put it to use for others. What service activities have you participated in that bring out the best in you and your family?

- Ella Baker did much to serve the youth in Harlem. Choose a youth group in your area and volunteer your time at one of their meetings. Organize a service project with a local church or scout troop, read aloud to a community nursery school, or volunteer as a chaperon for an outing or field trip.

- Baker discusses the idea that being a leader is perhaps not as important as developing leadership roles in others. Perhaps we can't all be leaders, but certainly we can all be of service. List ten things you can do to be of service to people and organizations in your community. Then make good on the list.

Alma B. Androzzo

W e sing this hymn often at Allen AME Cathedral. It is one of the first songs that comes to mind when I think about service, perhaps the most practical virtue of all.

If I Can Help Somebody as I Pass Along

If I can help somebody as I pass along,
If I can cheer somebody with a word or song,
If I can show somebody he is traveling wrong,
Then my living shall not be in vain.
Then my living shall not be in vain.

If I can do duty as a good man ought,
If I can bring beauty to a world up-wrought,
If I can spread love's message that the Master taught,
Then my living shall not be in vain.
Then my living shall not be in vain.

Exercise Service:

- Dr. Martin Luther King, Jr. references this hymn in his "Drum Major Instinct" speech, delivered at Ebenezer Baptist Church, in Atlanta, on February 4, 1968: "Yes, if you want to say that I was a drum major. Say that I was a drum major for justice. Say that I was a drum major for peace. Say that I was a drum major for righteousness. And all of the other shallow things will not matter. I won't have any money to leave behind. I won't have the fine and luxurious things in life to leave behind. But I just want to leave a committed life behind. And that's all I want to say. If I can help somebody as I pass along..." Read Dr. King's "Drum Major Instinct" speech in its entirety with your family. It is available in *A Knock At Midnight: Inspiration from the Great Sermons of Reverend Martin Luther King, Jr.* Have everyone sign up to be drum majors for specific services—helping a neighbor, cleaning out a closet, making a certain family member smile—for one week.

- Think of the many ways you might perform the services suggested in the lyrics to this song. Are you living each day with service to others in mind? Are your cares more about helping somebody as you pass along or about making and spending money? Will you do something today that helps bring beauty to "a world up-wrought"?

- Think about the organizations or people to whom you give money and support. Why do you serve these particular organizations? What other organizations would you like to get involved with?

Roger D. Abrahams

I n this Hausa folktale, retold by Roger D. Abrahams from his collection, African Folktales, *six young girls compete for the hand of a young man. Before journeying to meet him, they turn themselves into beautiful maidens. One of the maidens, Drippings, is humiliated by the other girls, who do not allow her to follow them. She lags behind, but the tale turns when the girls encounter an old woman bathing in a stream.*

Salt, Sauce, and Spice, Onion Leaves, Pepper, and Drippings

This story is about Salt, and Sauce and Spice, and Onion Leaves, and Pepper and Drippings. A story, a story! Let it go, let it come, Salt and Sauce and Spice and Onion Leaves and Pepper and Drippings heard a report of a certain youth who was very handsome, but the son of the evil spirit. They all rose up, turned into beautiful maidens, and then set off.

As they were going along, Drippings lagged behind the others, who drove her still farther off, telling her she stank. But she crouched down and hid until they had gone on, and then she kept following them. When they had reached a certain stream, they came across an old woman who was bathing. Drippings thought they would rub down her back for her if she asked, but one said, "May Allah save me that I should lift my hand to touch an old woman's back." The old woman did not say anything more, and the five passed on.

Soon Drippings came along, encountered the old woman washing, and greeted her. She answered, and said, "Maiden, where are you going?" Drippings replied, "I am going to find a certain youth." And the old woman asked her, too, to rub her back, but unlike the others, Drippings agreed. After she had rubbed her back well for her, the old woman said, "May Allah bless you." And she said, too, "This young man to whom you are all going, do you know his name?" Drippings said, "No, we do not know his name." Then the old woman told her, "He is my son. His name is Daskandarini, but you must not tell the others." Then she fell silent.

Drippings continued to follow far behind the others till they got to the place where the young man dwelled. They were about to go in when he called out to them, "Go back, and enter one at a time." Which they did.

Salt came forward first and was about to enter when the voice asked, "Who is there?" "It is I," she replied. "I, Salt, who make the soup tasty." He said, "What is my name?" She said, "I do not know your name, little boy, I do not know your name." Then he told her, "Go back, young lady, go back," and she did.

Next Sauce came forward. When she was about to enter, she, too, was asked, "Who are you?" She answered, "My name is Sauce and I make the soup sweet." And he said, "What is my name?" But she did not know, either, and so he said, "Turn back, little girl, turn back."

Then Spice rose up and came forward, and she was about to enter when she was asked, "Who is this, young lady, who is this?" She said, "It is I who greet you, young man, it is I who greet you." "What is your name, young girl, what is your name?" "My name is Spice, who makes the soup savory." "I have heard your name, young woman, I have heard your name. Speak mine." She said, "I do not know your name, little boy, I do not know your name." "Turn back, young lady, turn back." So she turned back, and sat down.

Then Onion Leaves came and stuck her head into the room. "Who is this, young girl, who is this?" asked the voice. "It is I who salute you, young man, it is I who salute you." "What is your name, little girl, what is your name?" "My name is Onion Leaves, who makes the soup smell nice." He said, "I heard of your name, little girl. What is my name?" But she didn't know it and so she also had to turn back.

Now Pepper came along. She said, "Your pardon, young man, your pardon." She was asked who was there. She said, "It is I, Pepper, young man, it is I, Pepper, who make the soup hot." "I have heard your name, young lady. Tell me my name." "I do not know your name, young man, I do not know your name." He said, "Turn back, young maid, turn back."

Now only Drippings was left. When the others asked her if she was going in she said, "Can I enter the house where such good people as you have gone and been driven away? Would not they the sooner drive out one who stinks?" They said, "Rise up and go in," for they wanted Drippings, too, to fail.

So she got up and went in there. When the voice asked her who she was, she said, "My name is Drippings, little boy, my name is Batso, which makes the soup smell." He said, "I have heard your name. There remains my name to be told." She said, "Daskandarini, young man, Daskandarini." And he said, "Enter." A rug was spread for her; clothes were given to her, and slippers of gold. And then of Salt, Sauce, Spice, Onion Leaves, and Pepper, who before had despised her, one said, "I will always sweep for you," another, "I will pound for you," another, "I will draw water for you," another, "I will pound the ingredients of the soup for you," and another, "I will stir the food for you." They all became her handmaidens. And the moral of all this is that it is from such common things that our most blessed foods are made. So just as such common stuff may be transformed under the right circumstance, if you see a man is poor, do not despise him. You do not know but that someday he may be better than you. That is all.

Exercise Service:

- Drippings is rewarded for taking the time to rub the old woman's back. While service should be something we do selflessly, we are often rewarded in unexpected ways when we serve others. Read this story to your family and talk about the idea of service for service's sake, not for outcome or rewards. Ask members of your family to describe a rewarding act of service they have performed.

- Sacrifice is an important part of service. Time and money are usually the first things we offer when we think of doing something for someone else. Could you give up something other than time or money the next time you volunteer for a cause you really believe in? What might it be?

- Proverbs 21:13 tells us, "Whoso stoppeth his ears at the cry of the poor, he also shall cry himself, but shall not be heard." After a hard day at work or a particularly expensive purchase, you may feel as though you haven't the time or money to spend helping others. But remember that by serving others, you will be paid back by the knowledge that you have brought hope into the lives of disadvantaged people. Helping others is one of the best uses of our resources. We urge our congregants to tithe 10 percent of their income, no matter how small. If you can't afford 10 percent, figure out how much you can commit to charity.

Marian Wright Edelman

Marian Wright Edelman is the founder and president of the Children's Defense Fund (CDF), a Washington-based organization that speaks out on behalf of children and families. In this passage from The Measure of Our Success, *Edelman reflects on the hope and confidence her father instilled in her and her siblings despite the racism and inequality surrounding them every day. Not surprisingly, Edelman's Children's Defense Fund emphasizes the importance of a supportive family and a strong community in a child's life.*

from The Measure of Our Success

I was fourteen years old the night my daddy died. He had holes in his shoes but two children out of college, one in college, another in divinity school, and a vision he was able to convey to me as he lay dying in an ambulance that I, a young black girl, could be and do anything; that race and gender are shadows; and that character, self-discipline, determination, attitude, and service are the substance of life.

I have always believed that I could help change the world because I have been lucky to have adults around me who did—in small and large ways. Most were people of simple grace who understood what [the novelist] Walker Percy wrote: "You can get all As and still flunk life."

Life was not easy back in the 1940s and 1950s in rural South Carolina for many parents and grandparents. We buried children who died from poverty (and I can't stand it that we still do). Little Johnny Harrington, three houses down from my church parsonage, stepped on and died from a nail because his grandmother had no doctor to advise her, nor the money to pay for health care. (Half of all low-income urban children under two are still not fully immunized against preventable childhood diseases like tetanus and polio and measles.) My classmate, Henry Munnerlyn, broke his neck when we jumped off the bridge into the town creek because only white children were allowed in the public swimming pool. I later heard that the creek where blacks swam and fished was the hospital sewage outlet. (Today thousands of black children in our cities and rural areas are losing their lives to cocaine and heroin and alcohol and gang violence because they don't have enough constructive outlets.) The migrant family who collided with a truck on the highway near my home and the ambulance driver who refused to take them to the hospital because they were black still live in my mind every time I hear about babies who die or are handicapped from birth when they are turned away from hospitals in emergencies or their mothers are turned away in labor because they have no health insurance and cannot pay preadmission deposits to enter a hospital. I and my brothers and sister might have lost hope—as so many young people today have lost hope—except for the stable, caring, attentive adults in our family, school, congregation, civic, and political life who struggled with and for us against the obstacles we faced and provided us positive alternatives and the sense of possibility we needed.

Exercise Service:

- Talk about the idea of being able to "change the world" with your children. What can you do to model caring for others to your family?
- The mission of Marian Wright Edelman's Children's Defense Fund is: "To leave no child behind and to ensure every child in life a successful passage to adulthood with the help of caring families and communities." Visit the CDF website [www.childrensdefense.org] and follow the links to the Black Community Crusade for Children site to discover ways you, your family, or your church organization can get involved in programs that serve children.
- In John 21:15–16, when Jesus and Simon Peter have finished breakfast, Jesus asks, "Simon, son of Jonas, lovest thou me more than these?" He replies, "Yea, Lord; thou knowest that I Love thee." Jesus says to him, "Feed my lambs." A second time he asks him, "Simon, son of Jonas, lovest thou me?" He says to him, "Yea, Lord; thou knowest that I love thee." Jesus tells him, "Feed my sheep." Talk with your children about the idea of feeding lambs and sheep as a metaphor for service.

Frances E. W. Harper

P oet, novelist, lecturer, and rights advocate Frances E. W. Harper was a well-known leader in such service organizations as the American Association of Education of Colored Youth, the Women's Christian Temperance Union, and the American Woman's Suffrage Association. The following poem, originally published in 1895 and reprinted here from the 1900 edition of Harper's collection, Poems, is certainly representative of the religious and racial themes Harper explored in most of her writing. When it is read in a more modern context, we think it is a beautiful evocation of the idea of service, no matter your means or position in society.

Go Work in My Vineyard

Go work in my vineyard, said the Lord,
And gather the bruised grain;
But the reapers had left the stubble bare,
And I trod the soil in pain.

The fields of my Lord are wide and broad,
He has pastures fair and green,
And vineyards that drink the golden light
Which flows from the sun's bright sheen.

I heard the joy of the reapers' song,
As they gathered golden grain;
Then wearily turned unto my task,
With a lonely sense of pain.

Sadly I turned from the sun's fierce glare,
And sought the quiet shade,
And over my dim and weary eyes
Sleep's peaceful fingers strayed.

I dreamed I joined with a restless throng,
Eager for pleasure and gain;
But ever and anon a stumbler fell,
And uttered a cry of pain.

But the eager crowd still hurried on,
Too busy to pause or heed,
When a voice rang sadly through my soul,
You must staunch these wounds that bleed.

My hands were weak, but I reached them out
To feebler ones than mine,
And over the shadows of my life
Stole the light of a peace divine.

Oh! then my task was a sacred thing,
How precious it grew in my eyes!
'Twas mine to gather the bruised grain
For the "Lord of Paradise."

And when the reapers shall lay their grain
On the floors of golden light,
I feel that mine with its broken sheaves
Shall be precious in his sight.

Though thorns may often pierce my feet,
And the shadows still abide,
The mists will vanish before his smile,
There will be light at eventide.

Exercise Service:

- "My hands were weak, but I reached them out to feebler ones than mine." The message I take from this poem is that there is always someone for whom our extended hand is a welcome blessing. No matter what your circumstance, there is someone you can help today, even in a small way. This is what it means to serve in the Lord's vineyard.

- Are you caught up in the "restless throng, eager for pleasure and gain?" Are there "stumblers" around who need your help? Reach out to them. Drive an elderly neighbor to a doctor's appointment. Read to a sick child. Prepare a meal for a family in need. Take a walk with someone in your neighborhood who lives alone.

- What do you think Harper means by the idea of "gathering the bruised grain?" What might bruised grain symbolize in the context of service? Might it be interpreted to mean that there is as much if not more value in gleaning than in reaping?
- Compare this poem with Arna Bontemps' "A Black Man Talks of Reaping" on page 50.

Oseola McCarty

In 1995, Oseola McCarty donated $150,000 to the University of Southern Mississippi. This money comprised her life savings, money she'd put away over a lifetime of taking in washing and ironing and earning anywhere from a dollar to a dollar and a half in Hattiesburg, Mississippi. She endowed a scholarship at the university for students in need, with a preference for African Americans. McCarty planned carefully (and prudently) to give this money away, and she told many an interviewer just how proud she was to have been able to leave something positive behind. What follows is an excerpt from an interview she gave to historians at the university.

from An Oral History with Miss Oseola McCarty

Interviewer: Now, when you decided to leave as much money as you did to the university—

McCarty: To help the other children.

Interviewer: What did you want to accomplish? What did you want the university to do with that money?

McCarty: Take it and give the children an education with, you know, scholarships. I wanted a scholarship for children what couldn't. If I do—I didn't know how to do it, but I was just trying to know, because I hadn't never been to a college in my life and know nothing about their rules and nothing about it, but I was trying to do all I could. And Mr. Paul—we at first had a meeting, we met down there. They told me to come down there and they say, you have to get you a lawyer. So I got Mr. McKenzie, Mr. Jimmy Frank McKenzie. You know him?

Interviewer: Uh-hm.

McCarty: Well, I got him. I've been working for him for years and years. And he knowed about my situation and how they did me when my aunt, after my aunt died. So, after then I didn't have nobody else to help me. Then I decided I'd give it—

Interviewer: Right.

McCarty: I give three of my cousins—he's told me, said, "Now, Ola, you don't have to give all of your relatives." See, I had a gang of them. This girl, what I give her, she had—it was nine of them in their family, nine children. Well, I couldn't give all nine of them nothing. Then Annie Pearl and her boy, I felt like they needed more than she did, because she didn't have no husband and she had a child and then he was killed and her other child was killed. So all the work was on—of course, she was a teacher. She made a teacher out of herself. She finished in Alcorn; I think that's what they said.

Interviewer: So you left some to three cousins, right?

McCarty: I left three cousins—

Interviewer: And some to your church.

McCarty: And my church. And I wanted the university to have some to help with the black children and then I said *any* of them, any of the children, not the black and white, but all nations. If they want a scholarship, let them have it.

Interviewer: Anybody that deserves it, a youngster that deserves to have one.

McCarty: Right. I don't know the rules of—

Interviewer: Yeah.

McCarty: And so, that's the reason why I said it like that.

Interviewer: Right. Well, they set that up last year, as everybody knows now, and Stephanie Bullock was the first recipient of that scholarship. What do you think about Stephanie?

McCarty: Yes sir. Well, I think it's great and hope she'll continue and get the highest education she can get. Just keep on.

Interviewer: She was a pretty worthy recipient.

McCarty: Yes sir, I think so. As far as I know. The first time I seen Stephanie out there in my front yard, that's the first time I seen her to know her.

Interviewer: What'd you think when you saw her?

McCarty: Oh, I thought that was the greatest thing I had *ever* did in my life.

Interviewer: Y'all have become pretty close too.

McCarty: Yes sir.

Interviewer: And to the rest of her family. Y'all become pretty close.

McCarty: Yes sir. All of them. I didn't know none of them. I knowed some of them but I didn't know them all. I didn't know Miss Hayes and I didn't know Miss Bullock. But I know the Woullards. My mother and the Woullards were very close friends.

Interviewer: Well, Stephanie's wrapping up her freshman year now. She's almost got this first year out of the way. Three more years and she'll graduate. You going to go to her graduation?

McCarty: Yeah, if I'm living I am.

Interviewer: That'd be a real treat to see her graduate.

McCarty: Yes sir.

Interviewer: Knowing that she was the first one.

McCarty: Right. And they adopted me for her grandmother.

Interviewer: That's right.

McCarty: So, that's all right too.

Interviewer: Yeah. Well, the nation's kind of adopted you too, haven't they?

McCarty: Yes sir.

Interviewer: What do you think about all the attention you've been getting?

McCarty: I never have seen nothing to beat it in all the days of my life. But the Lord is in this.

Exercise Service:

- Miss McCarty's generous gift to the university was a great act of service. No matter who we are, we have the potential to serve others in great and unanticipated ways. Do something today you didn't plan. Though it be as small-seeming as helping someone cross the street, the benefits are beyond measure.

- Make a list of things you have done for others that you are proud of. Ask your family members to do the same and talk about your lists together.

- Miss McCarty quit school in the sixth grade, but she wanted other children to be able to get the education she didn't have. Her lack of education inspired her to give education to others. Do aspects of your own life inspire particular kinds of service?

- McCarty's story illustrates profoundly how to make the most of what we have. Are you making the most of your talents and life's work? Give to others and it will bring you great satisfaction and joy.

- When I see the joy on the faces of the many volunteers at the Allen Cathedral who deliver meals to HIV-AIDS victims or feed the homeless twice weekly, it is obvious that they receive as much satisfaction as they serve. Many of the volunteers are retired. Giving service to others is a rewarding way to spend retirement.

Trustworthiness

Blending the qualities of reliability and consistency,
Trustworthiness marks you as a dependable individual,
warranting the confidence of your friends and family.

Black men and women know too well the insulting bite of distrust. We persevere despite suspicious glares cast in our direction, and we endure false accusations leveled at us. Ours is a world in which hatred infects the hearts of many and breaks the hearts of many more. And yet we must trust in our fellow human beings, just as we must always strive to win their trust.

Trustworthiness is the path to security and the ground upon which harmony grows. It is the bond that builds friendships and the glue that holds families together. To be trustworthy is to be dependable, to always follow through on your promises, and to remember your responsibilities. As a Christian, you must ensure that others can count on you for help. To be asked for advice is an honor and to give assistance is a privilege. Strive to be the person others turn to when in need.

The story of Jonathan and David (I Samuel, 20: 1–42)—see

page 376—illustrates that only the trustworthy are afforded the opportunity to do the right thing. When David is in mortal danger, he turns to Jonathan, the friend he trusts most. Jonathan's smart thinking saves David's life, but it is his trustworthiness that places him in the position to set things right.

Even though we may have confidence in our own ability to act virtuously, unless others have faith in us, we'll never get the chance to display the good judgment we know we're capable of. If we do not maintain our reputation as reliable parents, children, and friends, others will think twice before accepting our assistance. Men and women who have been dishonest in the past will have fewer chances to exercise generosity in the present.

To be trustworthy is to be consistent. We all go through times when we are tempted to bend the truth, exaggerate, or leave out a few details. But others will have faith in you only if you adhere to the rules you have set and remain true to your word. Remember that it is far easier to lose someone's trust than to win it. Do not squander the trust you have gained.

You must also recognize that if you expect to be trusted, you must exhibit trust. In her compelling story "The Pocketbook Game," Alice Childress illustrates how demeaning it is to be treated like a criminal. By refusing to trust those closest to us, we can deprive them of their dignity.

Of course, we need to lead cautious lives, but must we always be so skeptical? When people are kind to us, must we always question their "real motives"? Sometimes I wonder when "nice" became a bad word.

As God's children, we should stop focusing on everyone else's flaws and start focusing on their strengths. Instead of mistrusting our friends and family members, we should try to give them the benefit of the doubt. Trust is faith in our fellow human beings, and to be trustworthy is to ensure that others may confidently have faith in you.

E. A. Markham

E. *A. Markham was born in Montserrat in the Caribbean and grew up in London in the 1950s. He is now a professor of creative writing at Sheffield Hallam University. "Mammie's Form at the Post Office" addresses the mistrust and disrespect that results when we do not honor our brothers and sisters.*

Mammie's Form at the Post Office

She remembered it just in time and panicked; but there must be a way of getting the money there today. Her children were heartless, telling her it wasn't necessary: They had no respect for the dead.

At the Post Office, she went to the wrong end of the counter, and felt a fool when they directed her to the right queue, as if she couldn't read; so she tried to explain. There were a lot of openings but most of them said CLOSED, so she had to join a queue. It embarrassed her that all the Post Officers now had bullet-proof glass shutting out the customer: really, it was offensive to treat people like this—she was almost beginning to feel like a criminal. She thought of Teacher Tudy's Post Office at home where people from the village would come and stand in the yard with their back to the Stables (which Tudy had converted to a garage) while their names were read out from the dining room door. Of course, Mammie never had to stand in the yard; she would either send over Sarah or Franco; or if she didn't think of it, Tudy would put the letters aside, and probably bring them over herself the next night. Queuing behind the bullet-proof glass Mammie couldn't help feeling that she'd been reduced to standing with her back to "Teacher Tudy" Stables, waiting for her name to be called out.

When it was at last her turn, she told the boy behind the counter that she wanted to send some money to the West Indies, she wanted to send $100 home. But the boy pretended he didn't understand what she was saying and then asked if she wanted to send money ABROAD. She had to correct him and tell him she was sending her money HOME: That's where she was from. She was indignant that first they treated you like a foreigner, and then they denied you your home. He was just a child, and she wondered why they didn't have anyone bigger who could deal with the customers and understand what they wanted. She wanted to send $100 home.

"D'you want to send dollars?"

"Yes. Yes. A hundred."

"$100. To the West Indies."

"To Murial."

"Yes. Not sure if you can do that, actually. Look, I'll just—"

"And I'm in a hurry."

He was just moving off, apparently to look for something, and stopped. "Look, I've just got to check on this, all right?"

"Yes, go ahead. As long as it gets there in a hurry."

"You'll have to send it by telegraph in that case. Can you . . . just hang on. . . ." He reached under the counter and took out a Form. "I'll just go and check on the rates. If you'll just fill out this meanwhile." He slipped the Form under the bullet-proof glass, and told her to fill out both sides.

Mammie took the Form and started searching for her glasses. And after all that, the Form didn't make sense. It was all to do with people sending money to Bangladesh and Pakistan, and not one word about the West Indies; so the young fellow must have given her the wrong Form.

When he came back—with a big book—Mammie returned the Form and asked for one for the West Indies; and he said it didn't matter: West Indies was the same as Bangladesh. It was the first time in her life she'd ever heard anyone say that the West Indies, where she was born and grew up and where all her family came from and where her mother and the rest of her relations died and were buried, was the same as Bangladesh, which was somewhere in India, where the people were Indian, and she'd never set foot in her life. But she kept all this to herself, and filled out the Form nevertheless.

She put down Murial's name. Murial didn't live in a "Road" or "Street"; she lived in the village (she had a lovely house in the village), so Mammie had to leave out that line and go right on to "Village or Town" and "Country of Destination," having again left out "District, State, or Province." While she was doing this, someone pushed her to one side as if she was a beggar, and took her place; but she wasn't going to argue with any of them.

On the other side of the Form, she had to make a decision. Murial wasn't a "DEPENDENT," so that took care of that. She was tempted to sign her name under "PURPOSE OF PAYMENT," but the money had nothing to do with:

a. for goods imported into the UK up to £50 in value ... subject for the possession of an import license if necessary;
b. of subscription and entrance fees to clubs/societies other than for travel services up to £50 per year per club/society;
c. of maintenance payments under Orders of Court;
d. in settlement of commercial and professional debts up to £50 (see paragraph below).

She was sending the money to repair her uncle's headstone and to weed the family plot. As Murial was kind enough to look after her affairs at home, Mammie thought it might upset her if she sent the money as "PAYMENT," for Murial wasn't someone she employed, Murial was a friend. So in the end, she entered it under "CASH GIFT."

The boy took the Form and said she'd have to send it in Pounds, and they could change it at the other end. That was all right. Then he started filling out another Form, checking with his book, and showing it to the man working next to him, so that the whole world would soon know her business. Then he looked up and smiled at her, and asked if it was urgent.

The boy was a fool, she had already told him it was urgent.

"Then, that'll be . . . £45.50 plus THREE AND SEVEN TWENTY. That would be . . . £55.20. Okay?"

He was crazy. She had £30, which was plenty. He was joking.

"You joking?"

"Sorry . . . ?"

"Last time it cost only £24. Or twenty-three."

Then he said something that she didn't really follow. So she asked him to repeat it, because then he'd surely find out his mistake.

He was treating her like a child now. "That'll be £45.50 for the $100. And there's THREE POUNDS charge for sending it urgently. You want it urgent, don't you . . ."

"Yes. Yes."

". . . and then there's the message, and that's going to cost you another—"

"Cut it out. Cut out the message." The message wasn't important.

The message itself was all right, the message was free. But . . .

Mammie wanted the message out.

He read as he crossed it out, "THIS IS TO WEED THE HEADSTONES."

"Not weed. To weed the graves."

"Yes, well, it don't matter now, I've crossed—"

"It does matter. I'm not illiterate. You can't weed the headstones, you repair them."

"It doesn't cost any more, it's the address that's expensive. Look, do you have to send it . . . It'd be cheaper by telegraph letter."

"Will it get there today?"

His friend, working next to him, made a comment and laughed, but the young lad himself didn't laugh. He came very close to the glass and she didn't like his look.

"It'll get there in a few days. I mean, it's not exactly urgent, is it?"

"All right, all right."

"You'll send it the cheaper way?"

"It's all right, I'll go to another Post Office."

This time he was very rude.

"It didn't cost so much last time." Mammie wasn't going to be defeated. But by then he was dealing with another customer, complaining.

She was too busy to go to the other Post Office now; she had to go home to put on the dinner, in case anyone dropped by; she had to look after the living as well as the dead the quick and the dead: She smiled to herself. The joke pleased her. It occurred to her then that at the Post Office she had just said "dollars" to the young lad; she didn't specify West Indian dollars which were only about four shillings and twopence, which would be less than 25p in the new money (at least, that's what it was in the old days). Last year, it had only cost her £24 to send the money to Murial. At the other Post Office. This year, she was prepared to allow for another £4 for inflation and for telegraphing it.... Unless the boy was talking about some other dollar; but he must know she was West Indian, even though he wasn't qualified to work behind the bullet-proof glass. But what could she do; she was tired: Her mother would have to wait another day, choking in grass.

Exercise Trustworthiness:

- Those of us who are immigrants or who have immigrant parents can relate to Mammie's discomfort in this story. Anyone who has traveled to another country—even on vacation—understands the overwhelming helplessness one can feel in making simple transactions. We can also relate to the hard life that Mammie leads—a life in which she is separated from her people, economically responsible to relatives at home, and a foreigner in a country that depends on her cheap labor. Because of the everyday stresses and indignities that she suffers, she has forgotten that she is a child of God and has put her self-esteem in the hands of people who do not respect her. Psalm 56:4 teaches us that trust in God will eliminate our fear of man: "In God I will praise his word, in God I have put my trust; I will not fear what flesh can do unto me." How might the narrator's interaction with the clerk have been different if she had assumed him to be trustworthy and if she did not fear his prejudice and condescension? Do you think she would have handled the situation differently?

- Have there been times in your life when your mistrust of someone has exacerbated a situation? In contrast, can you remember when you approached someone with a trusting heart, someone who you believed might treat you poorly, and were pleasantly surprised?

Alice Childress

Alice Childress, born in 1920 in Charleston, South Carolina, moved to New York City as a child. In 1940 she joined the American Negro Theater in Harlem, and she became the theater's director the following year. Her first play produced outside of Harlem, Trouble in Mind, won a 1956 Obie award, making Childress the first woman to win an Obie and the first African American woman to have a play produced on Broadway. Childress also wrote the children's book A Hero Ain't Nothing but a Sandwich. Her short story "The Pocketbook Game" explores the mistrust that many white employers have shown toward their black employees. But as we will see, the protagonist teaches her employer a lesson about trust, while maintaining her dignity.

The Pocketbook Game

Marge . . . day's work is an education! Well, I mean workin' in different homes you learn much more than if you was steady in one place. . . . I tell you, it really keeps your mind sharp tryin' to watch for what folks will put over on you.

What? . . . No, Marge, I do not want to help shell no beans, but I'd be more than glad to stay and have supper with you, and I'll wash the dishes after. Is that all right? . . .

Who put anything over on who? . . . Oh yes! It's like this . . . I been working for Mrs. E . . . one day a week for several months and I notice that she has some peculiar ways. Well, there was only one thing that really bothered me and that was her pocketbook habit . . . No, not those little novels . . . I mean her purse—her handbag.

Marge, she's got a big old pocketbook with two long straps on it . . . and whenever I'd go there, she'd be propped up in a chair with her handbag double wrapped tight around her wrist, and from room to room she'd roam with that purse hugged to her bosom . . . Yes, girl! This happens ever time! No, there's nobody there but me and her . . . Marge, I couldn't say nothin' to her! It's her purse, ain't it? She can hold on to it if she wants to!

I held my peace for months, tryin' to figure out how I'd make my point . . . Well, bless Bess! Today was the day! . . . Please, Marge, keep shellin' the beans so we can eat! I know you're listenin', but you listen with your ears, not your hands . . . Well, anyway, I was almost ready to go home when she steps in the room hangin' on to her bag as usual and says, "Mildred, will you ask the super to come up and fix the kitchen faucet?" "Yes, Mrs. E . . . ," I says, "as soon as I leave." "Oh, no," she says, "he may be gone by then. Please go now." "All right," I says, and out the door I went, still wearin' my Hoover apron.

I just went down the hall and stood there a few minutes . . . and then I rushed back to the door and knocked on it as hard and frantic as I could. She flung open the door sayin', "What's the matter? Did you see the super?" ... "No," I says, gaspin' hard for breath, "I was almost downstairs when I remembered ... I left my pocketbook!"

With that I dashed in, grabbed my purse, and then went down to get the super! Later, when I was leavin' she says real timid-like, "Mildred, I hope that you don't think I distrust you because—" I cut her off real quick ... "That's all right, Mrs. E ..., I understand. 'Cause if I paid anybody as little as you pay me, I'd hold my pocketbook too!"

Marge, you fool ... look out! ... You gonna drop the beans on the floor!

Exercise Trustworthiness:

- Hearing Mildred talk about her employer and how she handles the situation, it is difficult not to feel outraged at the conditions she endures under Mrs. E. But there is a deeper message in this story, which reflects the message in Psalm 49:5: "Wherefore should I fear in the days of evil, when the iniquity of my heels shall compass me about?" Read Psalm 49 and consider the ways in which Mildred displays an awareness of the sentiments of the psalm in this particular situation.

- In "The Pocketbook Game," Mrs. E does not think Mildred is trustworthy because of the color of her skin. When Mildred gives her employer a taste of her own medicine by implying that she is not trustworthy either, Mrs. E's shocked reaction—and obvious discomfort with the allegation—reveals that to be thought of as trustworthy is key to building relationships with others. An absence of trust has resulted in warring nations, crumbling marriages, and hatred between religious and racial groups. How might you demonstrate more trustworthiness in your relationships? Choose three people in your life and make a point of proving your trustworthiness to them.

- While standing in front of the United States House of Representatives with Congresswoman Maxine Waters after a very late session, we watched as one cab after another passed us by, only to stop and pick up our white colleagues farther down the block. There we were, representatives of the people, professionally dressed, and having just voted on America's business, but we could not hail a taxi because we were black and mistrusted. Eventually, a fellow member flagged down a cab for us. The next day, we stood on the House floor and shared our experiences with all of the United States by making a public statement to be published in the Congressional Record. We exercised our rights and power to let the entire nation know that even those blacks who represent our country are vulnerable to discrimination. Many African Americans have been singled out in this way, thought to be untrustworthy by cabdrivers, store clerks, and potential employers. I was able to use my position in Congress to bring attention to the taxi problem. But as a nation, we have a long way to go to build trust in one another on this scale. At the same time I am comforted in knowing that I do have the power to earn the trust of the individuals I encounter in my everyday life. You have the same power. Use it.

Therese Folkes Plair

Therese Folkes Plair is a storyteller who has worked extensively in Africa, Europe, and the United States and who recently completed a storytelling mission in west and central Africa for the U.S. State Department. Therese's aunt Flossie Holland is also a member of our congregation at Allen AME Cathedral in Queens. Several years ago Therese was sitting in a garden belonging to Oma, one of the wise women in Takoradi, Ghana, expressing some anxiety about a goal she had set for herself and wondering aloud whether it was possible to achieve. Oma then told Therese this story.

The Clay Pots

Kwame was a good and hardworking cocoa farmer. One evening he was on his way home from the "farm" when he saw two clay pots in the bush. He examined the pots. One was very large and the other a bit smaller. Both were sealed. He couldn't decide which one to take home, so he said to himself, "I'll go and get Afua. She will know which one to choose."

When Kwame arrived home, his wife, Afua, was entertaining a couple who lived nearby. After he exchanged greetings with them, the farmer shared the story of how he'd just found two clay pots in the bush.

"Well, why didn't you bring the pots home with you?" asked the woman.

Kwame replied, "I just didn't know which one to pick, so I decided to fetch my dear Afua to help me."

Then Afua said, "Kwame, let's enjoy our guests and speak about this later."

After a while the guests thanked their hosts and left. On the way home the woman said to her husband, "Foolish man. What does he mean he didn't know which one to pick? Come, we will help him decide."

They went straight to the place Kwame had described, found the pots, and without hesitation picked up the largest pot and carried it home. Once inside, they broke it open. A swarm of bees came flying out, attaching to and stinging the couple. The woman was furious! "So, the man thinks he can make fools of us. Well, I will show him something." She rushed back to the farm, picked up the smaller pot, carried it to Kwame's house, and hurled it through a window. Kwame and Afua heard the sound of broken glass and came running out of their bedroom. There on the living room floor, amid the broken glass and clay shards, was a pile of gold.

Oma immediately followed the story with these words: "Let all that worry and doubt go. Just do your work and trust that whatever is for you will come to you."

Exercise Trustworthiness:

- "Trust that whatever is for you will come to you." In this context, God is the supreme embodiment of trustworthiness. If we accept God's trustworthiness, we can let go of worry.
- Kwame and Afua were not wary of revealing to their guests what Kwame had found on the road. They were trusting *and* trustworthy people, and they were rewarded for their trust. Explore the relationship of trust to trustworthiness. By having trust in others, do we develop a reputation for being trustworthy? Tell this story to members of your family. Ask your children what they would have done in a similar circumstance.
- Kwame and Afua were entertaining this couple as if they knew them. Talk about trustworthiness between friends, acquaintances, and strangers. How do you make yourself trustworthy to someone you have just recently met? How do you measure trustworthiness in others?

Nella Larsen

This is one of the most compelling and unforgettable pieces we've included. Not only does the subject matter directly address trustworthiness, but circumstances surrounding its original publication in 1930 are also linked to the virtue. Nella Larson was accused of plagiarism when this story was published, and although she defended herself in an open letter to Forum *magazine, scholars note that her career never fully recovered from the accusation. She did not write any more novels after* Quicksand *(see page 91 in our chapter on Faith), but is nonetheless considered one of the more important writers of the Harlem Renaissance.*

Sanctuary

On the southern coast, between Merton and Shawboro, there is a strip of desolation some half a mile wide and nearly ten miles long between the sea and old fields of ruined plantations. Skirting the edge of this narrow jungle is a partly grown-over road which still shows traces of furrows made by the wheels of wagons that have long since rotted away or been cut into firewood. This road is little used, now that the state has built its new highway a bit to the west and wagons are less numerous than automobiles.

In the forsaken road a man was walking swiftly. But in spite of his hurry, at every step he set down his feet with infinite care, for the night was windless and the heavy silence intensified each sound; even the breaking of a twig could be plainly heard and the man had need of caution as well as haste.

Before a lonely cottage that shrank timidly back from the road the man hesitated a moment, then struck out across the patch of green in front of it. Stepping behind a clump of bushes close to the house, he looked in through the lighted window at Annie Poole, standing at her kitchen table mixing the supper biscuits.

He was a big, black man with pale brown eyes in which there was an odd mixture of fear and amazement. The light showed streaks of gray soil on his heavy, sweating face and great hands, and on his torn clothes. In his woolly hair clung bits of dried leaves and dead grass.

He made a gesture as if to tap on the window, but turned away to the door instead. Without knocking he opened it and went in.

The woman's brown gaze was immediately on him, though she did not move. She said, "You ain't in no hurry, is you, Jim Hammer?" It wasn't, however, entirely a question.

"Ah's in trubble, Mis' Poole," the man explained, his voice shaking, his fingers twitching.

"W'at you done now?"

"Shot a man, Mis' Poole."

"Trufe?" The woman seemed calm. But the word was spat out.

"Yas'm. Shot 'im." In the man's tone was something of wonder, as if he himself could not quite believe that he had really done this thing which he affirmed.

"Daid?"

"Dunno, Mis' Poole. Dunno."

"White man o' niggah?"

"Cain't say, Mis' Poole. White man, Ah reckons."

Annie Poole looked at him with cold contempt. She was a tiny, withered woman—fifty perhaps—with a wrinkled face the color of old copper, framed by a crinkly mass of white hair. But about her small figure was some quality of hardness that belied her appearance of frailty. At last she spoke, boring her sharp little eyes into those of the anxious creature before her.

"An' w'at am you lookin' foh me to do 'bout et?"

"Jes' lemme stop till dey's gone by. Hide me till dey passes. Reckon dey ain't fur off now." His begging voice changed to a frightened whimper. "Foh de Lawd's sake, Mis' Poole, lemme stop."

And why, the woman inquired caustically, should she run the dangerous risk of hiding him?

"Obadiah, he'd lemme stop ef he was to home," the man whined.

Annie Poole sighed. "Yas," she admitted slowly, reluctantly, "Ah spec' he would. Obadiah, he's too good to you all no 'count trash." Her slight shoulders lifted in a hopeless shrug. "Yas, Ah reckon he'd do et. Emspecial' seein' how he allus set such a heap o' store by you. Cain't see w'at foh, mahse'f. Ah shuah don' see nuffin' in you but a heap o' dirt."

But a look of irony, of cunning, of complicity passed over her face. She went on, "Still, 'siderin' all an' all, how Obadiah's right fon' o' you, an' how white folks is white folks, Ah'm a-gwine hide you dis one time."

Crossing the kitchen, she opened a door leading into a small bedroom, saying, "Git yo'se'f in dat dere feather baid an' Ah'm a-gwine put de clo's on de top. Don' reckon dey'll fin' you ef dey does look foh you in mah house. An Ah don' spec' dey'll go foh to do dat. Not lessen you been keerless an' let 'em smell you out gittin' hyah." She turned on him a withering look. "But you allus been triflin'. Cain't do nuffin' propah. An' Ah'm a-tellin' you ef dey warn's white folks an' you a po' niggah, Ah shuah wouldn't be lettin' you mess up mah feather baid dis ebenin', 'cose Ah jes' plain con' went you hyah. Ah done kep' mahse'f outen bubble all mah life. So's Obadiah."

"Ah's powahful 'bliged to you, Mis' Poole. You shuah am one good 'omen. De Lawd'll mos' suttinly—"

Annie Poole cut him off. "Dis ain't no time foh all dat kin' o' fiddle-de-roll. Ah does mah duty as Ah sees et 'shout no thanks from you. Ef de Lawd had gib you a white face 'stead o' dat dere black one, Ah shuah would turn you out. Now hush yo' mouf an' git yo'se'f in. An' don' git movin' and scrunchin' undah dose covahs and git yo'se'f kotched in mah house."

Without further comment the man did as he was told. After he had laid his soiled body and grimy garments between her snowy sheets, Annie Poole carefully rearranged the covering and placed piles of freshly laundered linen on top. Then she gave a pat here and there, eyed the result, and, finding it satisfactory, went back to her cooking.

Jim Hammer settled down to the racking business of waiting until the approaching danger should have passed him by. Soon savory odors seeped in to him and he realized that he was hungry. He wished that Annie Poole would bring him something to eat. Just one biscuit. But she wouldn't, he knew. Not she. She was a hard one, Obadiah's mother.

By and by he fell into a sleep from which he was dragged back by the rumbling sounds of wheels in the road outside. For a second fear clutched so tightly at him that he almost leaped from the suffocating shelter of the bed in order to make some active attempt to escape the horror that his capture meant. There was a spasm at his heart, a pain so sharp, so slashing, that he had to suppress an impulse to cry out.

He felt himself falling. Down, down, down . . . Everything grew dim and very distant in his memory . . . vanished . . . came rushing back.

Outside there was silence. He strained his ears. Nothing. No foot-steps. No voices. They had gone on then. Gone without even stopping to ask Annie Poole if she had seen him pass that way. A sigh of relief slipped from him. His thick lips curled in an ugly, cunning smile. It had been smart of him to think of coming to Obadiah's mother's to hide. She was an old demon, but he was safe in her house.

He lay a short while longer, listening intently, and, hearing nothing, started to get up. But immediately he stopped, his yellow eyes glowing like pale flames. He had heard the unmistakable sound of men coming toward the house. Swiftly he slid back into the heavy, hot stuffiness of the bed and lay listening fearfully.

The terrifying sounds drew nearer. Slowly. Heavily. Just for a moment he thought they were not coming in—they took so long. But there was a light knock and the noise of a door being opened. His whole body went taut. His feet felt frozen, his hands clammy, his tongue like a weighted, dying thing. His pounding heart made it hard for his straining ears to hear what they were saying out there.

"Evenin', Mistah Lowndes." Annie Poole's voice sounded as it always did, sharp and dry.

There was no answer. Or had he missed it? With slow care he shifted his position, bringing his head nearer the edge of the bed. Still he heard nothing. What were they waiting for? Why didn't they ask about him?

Annie Poole, it seemed, was of the same mind. "Ah don' reckon you all done traipsed way out hyah jes' foh yo' healf," she hinted.

"There's bad news for you, Annie, I'm 'fraid." The sheriff's voice was low and queer.

Jim Hammer visualized him standing out there—a tall, stooped man, his white tobacco-stained mustache drooping limply at the ends, his nose hooked and sharp, his eyes blue and cold. Bill Lowndes was a hard one too. And white.

"W'atall bad news, Mistah Lowndes?" The woman put the question quietly, directly.

"Obadiah——," the sheriff began—hesitated—began again. "Obadiah—ah—er—he's outside, Annie. I'm 'fraid—"

"Shucks! You done missed. Obadiah, he ain't done nuffin', Mistah Lowndes. Obadiah!" she called stridently, "Obadiah! Git hyah an' splain yo'se'f."

But Obadiah didn't answer, didn't come in. Other men came in. Came in with steps that dragged and halted. No one spoke. Not even Annie Poole. Something was laid carefully upon the floor.

"Obadiah, chile," his mother said softly, "Obadiah, chile." Then, with sudden alarm, "He ain't daid, is he? Mistah Lowndes! Obadiah, he ain't daid?"

Jim Hammer didn't catch the answer to that pleading question. A new fear was stealing over him.

"There was a to-do, Annie," Bill Lowndes explained gently, "at the garage back o' the factory. Fellow tryin' to steal tires. Obadiah heerd a noise an' run out with two or three others. Scared the rascal all right. Fired off his gun an' run. We allow et to be Jim Hammer. Picked up his cap back there. Never was no 'count. Thievin' an' sly. But we'll git 'im, Annie. We'll git 'im."

The man huddled in the feather bed prayed silently. "Oh, Lawd! Ah didn't go to do et. Not Obadiah, Lawd. You knows dat. You knows et." And into his frenzied brain came the thought that it would be better for him to get up and go out to them before Annie Poole gave him away. For he was lost now. With all his great strength he tried to get himself out of the bed. But he couldn't.

"Oh, Lawd!" he moaned. "Oh, Lawd!" His thoughts were bitter and they ran through his mind like panic. He knew that it had come to pass as it said somewhere in the Bible about the wicked. The Lord had stretched out his hand and smitten him. He was paralyzed. He couldn't move hand or foot. He moaned again. It was all there was left for him to do. For in the terror of this new calamity that had come upon him he had forgotten the waiting danger which was so near out there in the kitchen.

His hunters, however, didn't hear him. Bill Lowndes was saying, "We been a-lookin' for Jim out along the old road. Figured he'd make tracks for Shawboro. You ain't noticed anybody pass this evenin', Annie?"

The reply came promptly, unwaveringly. "No, Ah ain't sees nobody pass. Not yet."

Jim Hammer caught his breath.

"Well," the sheriff concluded, "we'll be gittin' along. Obadiah was a mighty fine boy. Ef they was all like him—I'm sorry, Annie. Anything I c'n do, let me know."

"Thank you, Mistah Lowndes."

With the sound of the door closing on the departing men, power to move came back to the man in the bedroom. He pushed his dirt-caked feet out from the covers and rose up, but crouched down again. He wasn't cold now, but hot all over and burning. Almost he wished that Bill Lowndes and his men had taken him with them.

Annie Poole had come into the room.

It seemed a long time before Obadiah's mother spoke. When she did there were no tears, no reproaches; but there was a raging fury in her voice as she lashed out, "Git outer mah feather baid, Jim Hammer, an' outen mah house, an' don' nevah stop thankin' yo' Jesus he done gib you dat black face."

Exercise trustworthiness:

- As we say in the Introduction, virtue is colorless. Nowhere else in this book are we made more aware of the colorlessness of virtue—and the colorlessness of trustworthiness—as we are in *Sanctuary*. Talk about the qualities you like to see in a person in whom you place your trust.
- What qualities can you present to others, even to strangers, to make them see trustworthiness in you?

Bible

T he story of Jonathan and his servant, David, retold here from 1 Samuel 20: 1–42, is a beautiful example of the virtue inherent in trustworthiness. When David's life is threatened, David turns to Jonathan for help. What makes this request extraordinary is the fact that David's enemy is Jonathan's father, Saul. Jonathan's innate trustworthiness enables David to believe in the possibility of his rescue. But Jonathan must choose between being trustworthy in the service of good and trustworthy in the eyes of his father. Jonathan's ultimate choice reveals the evil in a lack of trustworthiness, as his own father turns on him, as does David.

Jonathan and David

D avid fled from Naioth at Ramah to see Jonathan. He asked, "What have I done? What is my offense? How have I sinned before your father that he now wishes to take my life?"

Jonathan replied, "God forbid! You shall not die. Behold, my father takes no actions, large or small, without first confiding in me. Why would he conceal this from me? It is not true."

But David pledged, "Your father is aware that I am esteemed in your eyes, and he has said to himself, 'Jonathan must not learn of this, for he shall be grieved.' Yet as truly as the Lord lives and as you live, only one step exists between me and death."

Jonathan told David, "Whatever you wish of me, I shall do for you."

So David answered, "Behold, tomorrow is the festival of the new moon, at which I am supposed to feast with the king, but allow me to go and conceal myself in the field until the night after tomorrow. If your father notices my absence, inform him, 'David earnestly begged my permission to leave for Bethlehem, his native city, for an annual sacrifice for his entire family is to take place.' If he answers, 'All is well,' then I, your servant, am safe. But if he becomes angry, you can be certain that he wishes to harm me. As for you, show kindness toward your servant, for you have brought him into the Lord's covenant with you. If I am guilty, take my life yourself! For why should you bring me before your father?"

Jonathan replied, "If I knew for a fact that my father planned to harm you, would I not inform you?"

David asked of him, "Who will tell me if your father answers you roughly?"

"Come," Jonathan urged, "let's leave for the field." And they went there together.

Jonathan told David, "O Lord, God of Israel, I shall have sounded out my father by this time tomorrow or the day after. If he feels favorably toward you, will I not send word to you and inform you? But if my father desires to hurt you, may the Lord see to me, no matter how harshly, if I fail to let you know and send you safety. May the Lord be with you as he has with my father. But show me enduring kindness like the Lord's for my entire life, so that I may not be killed, and do not block your kindness from my home forever, not even when the Lord has eliminated all of David's adversaries from the face of the earth."

So Jonathan made a covenant with the house of David, declaring, "May the Lord bring forth David's adversaries and require it of them as well." And Jonathan called for David to declare his love for him, for he loved David as he loved his own soul.

Jonathan then told David, "Tomorrow is the festival of the new moon. You shall be missed, for your seat will be empty. After three days, toward nightfall, go to the place you hid when this ordeal began, and wait by the stone Ezel. I shall shoot three arrows to the stone's side, as if it were a target. Then I will send a young boy and tell him, 'Go, fetch the arrows.' If I state, 'Behold, the arrows are to the side of you, bring them to me,' then follow him, for as certainly as the Lord lives, you shall live in peace; there is no peril. But if I tell the boy, 'Behold, the arrows are beyond you,' then flee you must, for the Lord has sent you away. As for the business about which we spoke, do not forget that the Lord shall be between you and me always."

So David concealed himself in the field, and at the festival of the new moon, the king sat down to dine. He sat in his usual seat by the wall, opposite Jonathan; Abner sat next to Saul, but David's seat remained vacant. Nevertheless Saul remained silent that day, for he thought, "Something must have befallen David, he is not clean; surely he is not clean." But the following day, the second day of the new month, David's place was empty once more. Saul asked his son Jonathan, "Why has the son of Jesse not dined with us yesterday nor today?"

Jonathan responded, "David earnestly requested my permission to go to Bethlehem. He said, 'I ask for your consent to go, for my family is having a sacrifice in the city and my brother has commanded me to be present. If I have found approval in your eyes, let me leave to see my family.' That is the reason he is absent from the king's table."

Saul's anger ignited against Jonathan and he declared, "You son of a perverse and rebellious woman, don't I know that you have chosen to ally yourself with the son of Jesse, to your own shame and the shame of the mother who gave birth to you? So long as the son of Jesse lives on this land, neither you nor your kingdom shall be established. Send for and bring David to me, for he must now die."

Jonathan beseeched his father, "Why must he die? What was his crime?" Saul then pitched his javelin at Jonathan to kill him. Jonathan realized that his father planned to take David's life.

Jonathan rose from the table in a fierce rage, and did not eat on that second day of the month, for his father's treatment of David so shamed him.

The next morning, Jonathan went out into the field to find David. With him was a little boy, to whom he said, "Run and find the arrows which I shall shoot." As the boy dashed away, Jonathan shot an arrow beyond him. When the boy reached the place where Jonathan's arrow had landed, Jonathan shouted to him, "Is the arrow not beyond you?" He cried, "Quickly! Make haste! Don't stop!" The boy fetched the arrow and returned it to Jonathan. Of this matter, the boy was ignorant; only Jonathan and David understood. Jonathan handed his weapons to the boy and ordered, "Bring these back to the city."

Once the boy had left, David rose from south of the stone and fell on his knees before Jonathan three times, with his face down. They kissed each other and wept together, and David sobbed the most.

Jonathan told David, "Go in peace, for we have sworn our friendship in the Lord's name, saying, 'The Lord exists between you and me, and between your descendants and mine always." Then David departed, and Jonathan returned to the city.

Exercise Trustworthiness:

• Sometimes proving your trustworthiness to one person means betraying someone else. In this passage, David trusts Jonathan with his life and Jonathan indeed saves him, giving him the message and the time to escape Saul's sword. Jonathan's trustworthiness is rewarded by the knowledge that his beloved friend will not be killed, but now he must face the fact that his own father may never trust him again. Do you think Jonathan's actions were trustworthy or deceitful? Are there certain bonds (such as the trust between a parent and child) that you feel should never be broken?

• Have members of your family make a list of times they demonstrated trustworthiness to other members of the family. Exchange lists and discuss.

• How might you reinforce your trustworthiness with longtime friends? Is it important to do so?

• David is fearful of coming to dinner at Saul's table because he knows that the king's jealousy has reached the point where he wants him dead. Rather than have his own insecurities exposed, Saul falsely asserts that David's failure to appear is due to the fact that he feels unworthy or ashamed to sit at the table of the king. There are always those who will falsely accuse us to cover up their own sins and failures. Discuss how, if we are trustworthy, we will not be tempted to project our own insecurities onto others.

Fanny Jackson

Fanny Jackson was born a slave in Washington, D.C., in 1837. When she was twelve, her aunt, a housekeeper, purchased her freedom. In 1851, Fanny and another aunt moved to Rhode Island, where Fanny lived and worked for George H. Calvert, a descendant of Lord Baltimore, the founder of Maryland. The Calverts, who were childless, took Fanny under their wing and enrolled her in school. In 1860, she entered Oberlin College, where she earned her bachelor's degree. In 1865, she accepted a position at Philadelphia's Institute for Colored Youth; in 1869, she became the first person of color to become a school principal. She retired from the school in 1903, joining her husband, Reverend Levi Jenkins Coppin, a minister in the AME church, in performing missionary work around the world. Jackson died in 1913. In the following letter to Frederick Douglass, Jackson, who had been teaching for ten years, shares her frustrations as a teacher, and realizes that she must trust that her students are learning just as she has learned to trust in the laws of nature.

Letter to Frederick Douglass

Philadelphia, March 30, 1876

Dear Mr. Frederick Douglass:

I cannot tell you how proud and glad I was to get your letter. Many and many a time when you have been to Philadelphia have I wished that I could see and speak with you a little while. I used to wish so much to tell you what I was trying to do here and what purpose has animated me all my life. I feel sometimes like a person to whom in childhood was entrusted some sacred flame: It has burned more dimly sometimes than at others, but it always will burn steadily and persistently, for it will never go out but with my life. I need not tell you, Mr. Douglass, that this is the desire to see my race lifted out of the mire of ignorance, weakness, and degradation: no longer to sit in obscure corners and devour the scraps of knowledge which his superiors fling him. I want to see him crowned with strength and dignity; adorned with the enduring grace of intellectual attainments, and a lover of manly deeds and downright honesty.

I wish you could hear how I speak to the school sometimes. I pour out upon them what my heart is so full of; sometimes I think that it falls upon deaf ears, and then again, I think that it does not. At one time, feeling very much discouraged, I asked them all if there was any one among them who ever thought about what I said to them: that is, my desires for them aside from their merely making fine scholars. Several hands went up, and I—well—I took courage and took up the burden again. I fear, Mr. Douglass, that I have not got over my childhood entirely. If I planted beans and they did not put in, or rather put out, an appearance as soon as I thought they ought to I used to take them up and see if they were all right. Experience has deepened my trust in the laws of nature, but I am ashamed to say that I sometimes feel very much like going among the children, pulling up my intellectual corn and beans, and noting progress. Ah well, I have to teach myself patience. A most worthy man said to me, "Remember, Fanny, that it is seed time now and not harvest." The golden harvest may be reaped in time—who knows? But I must not trespass longer upon your time.

And now, Mr. Douglass, I beg to sign myself—always with gratitude and high esteem.

F. M. Jackson

Exercise Trustworthiness:

• Children, like plants and trees, naturally absorb the nutrients (knowledge, faith, and trust in their abilities) that we feed them. But there are times when we try to force them to grow faster than God intended and we can become impatient with their progress. Jackson realizes that her distrust in her students' growth is rooted in her own need for control, and recalls her childhood exercise in gardening. As difficult as it is for Jackson, a master educator, to accept that her students may not learn at the rate that she would like them to, she acknowledges, "The golden harvest may be reaped in time—who knows?" Do you trust that your children are progressing at the rate that God wants them to progress? Do you find yourself sometimes growing impatient with their rate of growth? How can you let them know you have trust in them?

• Proverbs 3:5 offers a wonderful remedy for those times when we doubt that our children, our lives, our careers, or our spirituality are progressing: "Trust in the Lord with all thine heart; and lean not unto thine own understanding." Think of ways that you can practice trust in God's plan for your life and for your family through the use of this proverb. Trustworthiness in this context may be thought of as the reciprocal virtue of the virtue of faith, meaning that one is given in return for the other. Are you worthy of God's trust?

ACKNOWLEDGMENTS
AND SOURCES

The following people have been hugely instrumental in helping us pull together the many pieces of this volume. We are grateful to each of you for your fresh ideas and enthusiasm, and especially for your diligence and for keeping the faith: Lisa DiMona, Robin Dellabough, and Karen Watts from Lark Productions, along with Siobhan Benet, Bram Alden, and Lauren Kanter; Nikki George, Lakeisha Merrick, Tara Patrick, Christine London, and Gwendolyn Simms Warren from our own Allen African Methodist Episcopal Church; and Charles Harris, Cathy Hemming, Carrie Freimuth, Dawn Davis, and Darah Smith at HarperCollins. Many blessings.

Diligent and reasonable efforts have been made to locate ownership of all copyrighted material included in *Practical Virtues*, and we are grateful for the cooperation and assistance of all the publishers and representatives named below. Any errors that may have occurred are inadvertent and will be corrected in subsequent editions, provided notification is sent to the publisher.

Hank Aaron—From *If I Had a Hammer* by Hank Aaron and Lonnie Wheeler. Copyright © 1991 by Henry Aaron and Lonnie Wheeler. Reprinted by permission of HarperCollins Publishers, Inc.

Roger D. Abrahams—"Salt, Sauce, and Spice, Onion Leaves, Pepper, and Drippings from *African Folktales* by Roger D. Abrahams. Copyright ©

1983 by Roger D. Abrahams. Used by permission of Pantheon Books, a division of Random House, Inc.

Bishop Richard Allen—The prayer is part of the text of Reverend Richard Allen's autobiography, *The Life Experience and Gospel Labors of the Rt. Rev. Richard Allen to Which Is Annexed The Rise and Progress of the African Methodist Episcopal Church in the United States of America. Containing a Narrative of the Yellow Fever in the Year of Our Lord 1793 and the Richard Allen Chronology with an Address to the People of Color in the United States.* Originally published in 1833.

Alma B. Androzzo—"If I Can Help Somebody as I Pass Along." Copyright © 1947 by Lafleur Music Ltd. A Boosey & Hawkes company. Copyright renewed. Reprinted by permission of Boosey & Hawkes, Inc.

Maya Angelou—From *I Know Why the Caged Bird Sings* by Maya Angelou. Copyright © 1969 by Maya Angelou and renewed 1997 by Maya Angelou. Used by permission of Random House, Inc.

Arthur Ashe—From *Days of Grace* by Arthur Ashe and Arnold Rampersad. Copyright © 1993 by Arthur Ashe and Arnold Rampersad. Used by permission of Alfred A. Knopf, a division of Random House, Inc.

Bert B. Babero—from *Taps for a Jim Crow Army: Letters from Black Soldiers in World War II.* Copyright © 1983, 1993 by Phillip McGuire, published by The University Press of Kentucky. Original letter from the National Archives, Modern Military Records Branch.

Cornelia Walker Bailey—"A Make-Do or Do-Without Family" from *God, Dr. Buzzard, and the Bolito Man* by Cornelia Walker Bailey with Christena Bledsoe, Copyright © 2000 by Cornelia Bailey and Christena Bledsoe. Used by permission of Doubleday, a division of Random House, Inc.

Ella Baker—From *Black Women in White America: A Documentary History* by Gerda Lerner, editor. Published by Vintage Books, February 1973. Reprinted by permission of the author.

James Baldwin—"My Dungeon Shook" by James Baldwin was originally published in *The Progressive* in 1962. Copyright renewed. Collected in *The Fire Next Time*, published by Vintage Books. Reprinted by arrangement with the James Baldwin Estate.

Asha Bandele—From *The Prisoner's Wife* by Asha Bandele, reprinted with the permission of Scribner, an imprint of Simon & Schuster Adult Publishing Group. Copyright © 1999 by Asha Bandele.

Melba Patillo Beals—Reprinted with the permission of Simon & Schuster from *Warriors Don't Cry* by Melba Patillo Beals. Copyright © 1995 by Melba Patillo Beals.

Mary McLeod Bethune—From "The Lesson of Tolerance," *Mary McLeod Bethune: Building a Better World—Essays and Selected Documents*, edited by Audrey Thomas McCluskey and Elaine M. Smith. Copyright © 1999 by Indiana University Press. Reprinted by permission.

Arna Bontemps—"A Black Man Talks of Reaping" collected from *Caroling Dusk: An Anthology of Verse by Negro Poets* by Countee Cullen, editor. Reprinted by permission of Harold Ober Associates, Inc. Copyright © 1963 by Arna Bontemps.

Rosemary L. Bray—From *Unafraid of the Dark: A Memoir* by Rosemary Bray. Copyright © 1998 by Rosemary Bray. Used by permission of Random House, Inc.

Linda Brent—From *Incidents in the Life of a Slave Girl, Written By Herself* by Linda Brent. Edited by L. Maria Child. Originally published in 1861.

Gwendolyn Brooks—"We Real Cool" collected from *The Poetry of Black America: Anthology of the 20th Century* by Arnold Adoff, editor. Copyright © 1950, 1959, 1960 by Gwendolyn Brooks. Reprinted by consent of Brooks Permissions.

Sterling A. Brown—"Strong Men" from *The Collected Poems of Sterling A. Brown*, edited by Michael S. Harper. Copyright 1932 Harcourt Brace & Company, renewed 1960 by Sterling Brown. Reprinted by permission of HarperCollins Publishers, Inc. "After the Storm" from *The Crisis Reader: Stories, Poetry, and Essays from the NAACP's Crisis Magazine Excerpts from the Period 1918–1927*. Originally published in *Crisis* in April 1927. The authors wish to thank the Crisis Publishing Co., Inc., publisher of the magazine of the National Association for the Advancement of Colored People, for authorizing use of the *Crisis* material.

Shirley Caesar—From *The Lady, the Melody and the Word* by Shirley Caesar. Reprinted by permission of Thomas Nelson Publishers from the book entitled, *The Lady, the Melody, and the Word*, copyright 1998 by Shirley Caesar.

Dr. Benjamin S. Carson—From *Gifted Hands* by Dr. Benjamin S. Carson. Copyright © 1990 by Review and Herald Publishing Association. Reprinted by permission of Zondervan.

Lorene Cary—From *Black Ice* by Lorene Cary. Copyright © 1991 by Lorene Cary. Used by permission of Alfred A. Knopf, a division of Random House, Inc.

Charles W. Chesnutt—"The Partner," from the Berea College Charles Chesnutt Digital Archive by Dr. Stephanie Browner, editor. Originally published in *Southern Workman* in May 1901. This version reprinted by permission of the Berea College Charles Chesnutt Digital Archives.

Alice Childress—"The Pocketbook Game" from *Like One of the Family: Conversations from a Domestic's Life*. Copyright © 1956. Renewed by Alice Childress 1986. Used by permission of Flora Roberts, Inc.

J. California Cooper—From *In Search of Satisfaction* by J. California Cooper. Copyright © 1994 by J. California Cooper. Used by permission of Doubleday, a division of Random House, Inc.

Fanny Jackson—From the Frederick Douglass Papers Collection of the Library of Congress. A copy of the letter is available via interlibrary loan or for purchase from the Library Photoduplication Service www.loc.gov/preserv/pds. The microfilm collection is also available at Vassar College and the University of Rochester.

Joseph Seamon Cotter, Jr.—"Black Baby" was originally published in *Opportunity Journal*, February 1929. Reprinted by permission of the National Urban League.

Ellen and William Craft—From *Biography of an American Bondman, by His Daughter*, by Josephine Brown. Originally published in 1856.

Ruby Dee—"Aunt Zurletha" from *My One Good Nerve*. Copyright © 1986 by Ruby Dee. All rights reserved. Used by permission of John Wiley & Sons, Inc.

Sarah Louise Delany and Annie Elizabeth Delany—From *Having Our Say* by Sarah Louise Delany, Annie Elizabeth Delany, and Amy Hill Hearth. Copyright © 1993 by Sarah Louise Delany, Annie Elizabeth Delany, and Amy Hill Hearth. Reprinted by permission of Kodansha America, Inc.

Debra Dickerson—From *An American Story* by Debra Dickerson. Copyright © 2000 by Debra J. Dickerson. Used by permission of Pantheon Books, a division of Random House, Inc.

W. E. B. DuBois—From *What the Negro Wants*, by Rayford W. Logan. Copyright © 1944 by the University of North Carolina Press, renewed 1972 by Rayford W. Logan. Used by permission of the publisher.

Alice Moore Dunbar-Nelson—"I Sit and Sew" from *The Dunbar Speaker and Entertainer Containing the Best Prose and Poetic Selections by and About THE NEGRO RACE with Programs arranged for special entertainments.* Edited by Alice Moore Dunbar-Nelson, with an introduction by Leslie Pinckney Hill. J.L. Nichols and Company, 1920. Alice Moore Dunbar-Nelson Papers, University of Delaware Library, Newark, Delaware.

Paul Laurence Dunbar—"The Seedling" originally published in *Lyrics of Lowly Life* in 1896. "Sympathy" originally published in *Lyrics of the Hearthside* in 1899.

Marian Wright Edelman—From *The Measure of Our Success* by Marian Wright Edelman. Copyright © 1992 by Marian Wright Edelman. Reprinted by permission of Beacon Press.

Olaudah Equiano—From *The Interesting Narrative of the Life of Olaudah Equiano, Or Gustavus Vassa, the African, Written by Himself* from the African-American Mosaic Library of Congress Resources Guide.

William J. Faulkner—"How the Slaves Helped Each Other" collected from *The Days When the Animals Talked* by William J. Faulkner. Copyright © 1977 by Follet, Chicago. Republished 1989 by Marie Faulkner Brown. Reproduced with the permission of Africa World Press, Trenton, New Jersey.

Ernest J. Gaines—From *A Lesson Before Dying* by Ernest J. Gaines. Copyright © 1993 by Ernest J. Gaines. Used by permission of Alfred A. Knopf, a division of Random House, Inc.

Patrice Gaines—From *Laughing in the Dark* by Patrice Gaines. Copyright © 1994 by Patrice Gaines. Used by permission of Crown Publishers, a division of Random House, Inc.

Constance Garcia-Barrio—"The Ant Story." Copyright © 1989 by Constance Garcia-Barrio. Reprinted by permission of Constance Garcia-Barrio.

Eloise Greenfield—"Harriet Tubman," collected in *Honey, I Love and Other Love Poems* by Eloise Greenfield. Text copyright © 1978 by Eloise Greenfield. Reprinted by permission of HarperCollins Publishers.

Frances E. W. Harper—"Vashti" and "Go Work in My Vineyard" are reprinted courtesy of the Electronic Text Center, University of Virginia, Charlottesville, Virginia. etext.lib.virginia.edu.

Robert Hayden—"Frederick Douglass," copyright © 1966 by Robert Hayden, and "Those Winter Sundays," copyright © 1966 by Robert Hayden, from *Angle of Ascent: New and Selected Poems by Robert Hayden*. Used by permission of Liveright Publishing Corporation.

Anita Hill—From *Speaking Truth to Power* by Anita Hill. Copyright © 1997 by Anita F. Hill. Reprinted by permission of the author.

Chester Himes—"Mama's Missionary Money" from the book *The Collected Stories of Chester Himes* by Chester Himes. Copyright © 1990 by Lesley Himes. Appears by permission of the publisher, Thunder's Mouth Press.

Langston Hughes—"Mother to Son," from *The Collected Poems of Langston Hughes* by Langston Hughes. Copyright © 1994 by the estate of Langston Hughes. Used by permission of Alfred A. Knopf, a division of Random House, Inc.

Georgia Douglas Johnson—"The Black Runner" was originally published in *Opportunity Journal*, September 1925. Reprinted by permission of the National Urban League.

James Weldon Johnson—From *Along This Way* by James Weldon Johnson. Copyright 1933 by James Weldon Johnson, renewed © 1961 by Grace Nail Johnson. Used by permission of Viking Penguin, a division of Penguin Putnam, Inc.

Nella Larsen—*Quicksand* was first published in 1928 and "Sanctuary" was published in 1930 in *Forum* magazine. Numerous electronic editions of Larsen's work are available. See also *The Complete Fiction of Nella Larsen*, edited and with an introduction by Charles R. Larson, with a foreword by Marita Golden. Anchor Books, 2001.

Andrea Lee—From *Sarah Phillipps* by Andrea Lee. Copyright © 1984 by Andrea Lee. Used by permission of Random House, Inc.

Felicia R. Lee—"Coping: A Letter to a Child in a Difficult Time." Copyright © 2001 by the *New York Times*. Reprinted with permission.

Julius Lester—"People Who Could Fly," from *Black Folktales*. Copyright © 1969 by Julius Lester. Reprinted by permission of the author.

Oseola McCarty—From *An Oral History with Miss Oseola McCarty*, interview by Phil Hearn, 1996, Mississippi Oral History Program, Vol. 657, University of Southern Mississippi, Hattiesburg. Used by permission of the